ADDITIONAL PRAISE
LEAVING LONG BEACH

This is a powerful true crime book written by a courageous author. Mark Jicha and his brother, Jon, were devastated by their sister's murder, but they were unrelenting in seeing the culprits brought to justice. After many long years, three people---including Lynn's miserable husband who masterminded the crime—were convicted and sentenced to life without parole. The Jicha family emerged victorious and stronger than ever. ***Leaving Long Beach*** *is a chronicle of the American justice system and a family's enduring love. It stays with you long after the last page is read.*

Cary Knapp
Librarian, College of Coastal Georgia

A true story depicting the murder of a beautiful woman as her family unites to seek justice for their loved one. Mark Jicha does an outstanding job of telling the story of the murder, his family's sorrow and their plight in following the progress of the Long Beach Police Department's investigation to identify, arrest and prosecute the perpetrators. This is one story you just won't believe!

Jim Daher
Author of RIGHTEOUS KILL and BLOOD MONEY.

Leaving Long Beach

Leaving Long Beach

An Intimate Account of my Sister's Murder

A True Crime Work
by Mark A. Jicha

This book is dedicated to my son Charlie
The hero of this saga and the light of my life.

Pileated Press

Copyright © 2015 by Mark A. Jicha

LEAVING LONG BEACH

Copyright © 2015 by Mark A. Jicha

All rights reserved. No part of this book may be used or reproduced in any manner without written permission except in the case of quotations, articles, or reviews which have been credited to their source.

Printed in the United States of America

Cover design by Jon Jicha
My brother and best friend.

Typeset by Clint Hardin

ISBN-10: 0986146404
ISBN-13: 978-0-9861464-0-4

A True Crime non-fiction book.

www.leavinglongbeach.com

Published by
Pileated Press
www.pileatedpress.net

Our enemy is by tradition our savior,
in preventing us from superficiality.
Joyce Carol Oates

ACKNOWLEDGMENTS

Special thanks to my wife, Susan Shipman, who not only agreed to marry me almost 28 years ago but has also stayed with me through all the trials and tribulations we've faced. She welcomed Charlie into our home and became the mother and adviser to our new son. Without her love and support none of this would have been possible.

I can't begin to list the reasons to thank my brother and his family. The importance of their love, friendship and unconditional support for Charlie and this project cannot be overstated. Thanks to Jon, Libby, Amy and Dylan Jicha.

The same was true for all of Susan's extended family, although both her brother and sister have passed since the beginning of this saga. Bill Shipman and his wife Cyndy Gray were incredibly supportive. The same is true of her sister, Linda, and her husband, David Landgraf, along with their children, Keith and Virginia, whose children are a joy to the world. I can't begin to list the aunts, uncles, cousins in both families who opened their hearts to Charlie, but offer my sincere appreciation.

My gratitude to Jim Daher, author of *Righteous Kill* and *Blood Money*, a good friend and great editor. No thanks could be too much. And to Carey Knapp, and her daughter, Georgia, who helped me find the book in the manuscript.

And thanks, as always, to "Doc" and Gayle, Amanda, Valerie, Bobbi and Jack, and all those others who read the early versions and gave me honest feedback. Special thanks to Kim, for all those therapy sessions that helped me get through the nights.

Blood is thicker than water.

Jon, Lynn and Mark Jicha
circa 1958

PROLOGUE

My sister-in-law once accused me of being "lucky."

I wasn't sure she said that in a good way, but I've been blessed with many good outcomes. I'm pretty sure Libby was speaking of my marriage to Susan, which is an understatement of the highest order; but she could have just as easily cited our comfortable life in a lovely island home, my relationships with family and friends, or any number of fortuitous breaks that fell my way or the bad breaks that didn't. I was in no position to argue her point.

Near the top of that "lucky" list was acquiring a 100-acre tract of south Georgia swamp land we could purchase by selling a rental home which barely broke even after travel and expenses. The house sold for the exact same amount as the property, which I bought the next day. Penholloway Swamp at McMillan Creek became my wetland preserve, a sanctuary formed by tributaries of the Altamaha River and flanked by a long stretch of the Norfolk Southern railroad. The bald cypress, gums and pines had been logged many years before we bought the property, and while that didn't diminish its beauty the lowlands begged for native timber. We started replanting with 200 bald-root cypress seedlings the first year and after a decade had over 10,000 trees in the ground. It was a labor of love. As the nooks and crannies in every creek bend made for a playground shared with wildflowers and wildlife, the landscape became a palette of many colors and textures in the seasons or light. Over the years I've built gardens, food plots, firebreaks and a solar-powered cabin, accumulating a John Deere tractor, a JCB backhoe and what my wife calls "a marble sidewalk to his outhouse." She fails to mention the shower.

I'm proud of the place and drag family and friends to share my dream whenever I can. Back in 2002 my sister brought her young son, Charlie, to see our southern life, the only time she traveled east without her husband. It was a welcome absence. Lynn and I enjoyed fond times, and during that visit, I grabbed the boy for a day at my swamp. Few California experiences could have prepared him for the lush vegetation running wild in semi-tropical humidity, or the free-running black water streams bisecting the forest. He took to the place in a big way, and seemed to favor the idea that his odd uncle could own such an unusual place. He really enjoyed driving the tractor, but who doesn't?

Almost two years later a November sun burned into afterglow just before dark, the autumn light perfectly refracted to highlight maples, oaks, gums and cypress ablaze in fall colors. I'd seen three deer that afternoon - a doe and two yearlings - and passed on the shots, waiting for a trophy buck I'd glimpsed earlier in the season. Even though the 10-pointer remained elusive, I savored a glorious night sky unfolding across my paradise.

My cell phone chirped the moment I returned to the truck, even before I could store the hunting gear and remove my boots. It was Jon, my brother, an artist and avid angler, to whom I would relate the colors and changing light. Chances were good that he, who lives in the foothills of North Carolina's Smoky Mountains, could relate to my experience. Hell, we're Southerners now, and if you don't hunt or fish, you just aren't right.

So I was completely unprepared for his disjointed, even desperate account of what happened to our sister in Long Beach that day, November 8, 2004. Lynn had been stabbed to death at her Bixby Knolls home.

"Was it Schockner?" were my first words.

"No," he said. Police had been at the scene, but couldn't protect her from an intruder's knife, three fatal wounds to her throat, more to her hands and arms. The killer was already in custody.

That was all he knew.

CHAPTER 1

The first dispatch came at 11:03 am earlier that day. "Prowler seen entering backyard in the eleven hundred block of Andrews Drive, Bixby Knolls. Please respond Unit Two." That Monday morning, Long Beach Police Department's Traffic Unit Two was the designation for Officer Efrain Cervantes, who ran his beat around the side streets and avenues of affluent northern Long Beach suburbs, including Bixby Knolls.

The neighborhood is a testament to Baby Boom growth in Long Beach, an era when the rolling hills above the beach drew tens of thousands to a less urban life. Atlantic Avenue's airy width and the futuristic sidewalk architecture exuded a post-war optimism so unabashed that, a half-century later, it seemed to almost embarrass some natives. *These days we often treat it like kitsch.*

The cop snatched the microphone and snapped his reply as he punched the accelerator. "Unit Two responding. Six blocks. ETA five minutes." Whatever the distance, he covered it quickly and received further instructions enroute.

"Neighbor at 1100 Andrews Drive reported suspicious man dressed in black entering backyard next door to his home," the dispatcher reported.

Cervantes's reply was nothing more than an *affirmative* exhaled into the microphone; like most Long Beach cops, he was quiet and unassuming, but serious. He entered Andrews Drive, killed the engine and purposely coasted beyond the house, using the car's momentum to slow the car to a stop at the corner of the block. Lynn's neighbor stepped toward the curb as Cervantes pulled opened his car door. "This is the one."

The neighbor described a prowler dressed in black who entered Lynn's backyard to the cop. He said he spotted the suspect from his rear bathroom, probably the only room in his entire house where he could view the backyard, and called 911.

Moments after Cervantes reached the street, LBPD Officer Donald Radcliff turned his unmarked sedan into the alley behind the house and stepped into position next to his car. The only sound disturbing the quiet Long Beach morning was the jarring, high-pitched barking of Lynn's dog, a snow white dog that greeted every visitor with a furious avalanche of angry yips and howls. Neighbors could hear her barking in the front bay windows beside the door as Cervantes and Rider approached. Weighing twenty-two pounds, "Zoe" was an AKC American Eskimo breed, a little husky with a big heart in a small body. Fearless and ferocious.

After a few moments, Cervantes noticed the drapes pulled open by a slight woman he described as having a "bewildered look" on her face. Two more uniformed police units arrived, bringing Sgt. Curtis Yee and Officer Sean Irving to the front with Cervantes. All three approached the home as my sister opened the door to an infernal racket - the dog at full throttle now, barking a mile a minute.

"What?" she asked through a cracked door. The officer repeated the call. "We had a reported prowler. May we search your backyard? Your neighbor saw a man dressed in black enter your property."

There were many things the police couldn't know at that particular moment; whether the report was accurate or a false alarm, whether a crime had been committed, and if so, whether the prowler was hiding in the yard or had fled the scene. They weren't familiar with this sleepy California housewife, the history of this slender woman with big glasses and wide eyes, shrinking behind a heavy iron and glass security door. They didn't know the true temperament of the noisy white dog or whether the woman was aware of her potential problem.

"What? What?" she repeated before stepping into the front yard, confused by the collection of policemen on her lawn. Regaining her bearings slowly from a late-morning nap, she finally answered. "I've been home all morning - no one's here."

"Mrs. Schockner, we have a report from your neighbor who saw a man entering your backyard." he restated. "May we check?"

• • • •

Cervantes didn't know her sorrows; nor did he care. Aside from the noisy dog, she seemed to be the only occupant. He was there to protect and serve, not advise and console. He couldn't know just how foggy she was, medicated by physicians who passed out prescriptions like breath mints. It took her a few seconds to find a helpful way to answer these determined men. "I can get the key for the gate. I'll be right back."

"Okay, Mrs. Schockner, we'll wait right here." He answered. The glass door swung shut as she turned back toward the family room. This house, by nature and design, didn't welcome visitors or allow inside views of any sort. She went toward the rear family room, separated by sliding glass doors leading to the patio and backyard. The gate key was stashed somewhere in that sprawling, dark home: buried in a drawer or bureau, probably in some box. Shelves contained books and the confusing accumulations of her life. It might have been hanging on a hook in the kitchen, or nowhere to be found.

It would be easiest if I just open the gate and let them in, she probably decided.

The policemen, now three strong, waited in the front yard; but cops on call, by nature, aren't patient. After a little more than a minute the officers agreed something was amiss and entered the house on alert, hands lowered onto their weapons. They were prepared for everything but what they found.

• • • •

I'm sure my sister dismissed their concern: *There's no one here but me, and there's absolutely nothing to worry about - this is silly.*

She stepped through sliding glass door and down the patio steps, the little dog at her side. I wonder if she noticed the sky, a typical southern California morning, another perfect day in paradise. I don't have to wonder about her last steps, the ones that carried her beyond the corner of the porch where she surprised her killer, who used his dagger to stab and slash her more than a half dozen times. She couldn't even scream; there was only time enough for a feeble attempt at self-defense punished by deep cuts on her hands and wrists. She grabbed her throat as she fell, two fatal wounds already torn into the soft flesh on either side of her neck. Desperate to staunch the rush of blood from severed veins and arteries, she lost consciousness as her life poured out on the patio.

It was over in seconds, a minute at most. Police front and back, a small savage white dog at her side, all without effect. Zoe was the only witness to the savagery and sure-handedness of a killer.

• • • •

At 11:15 am that same morning, LBPD Officer Eduardo Saldana, a four-year veteran of the force, answered a call for backup behind the Schockner house. When he arrived, he found the two units already in back alley position: Radcliff and LBPD Officer Leticia Carranza, guns drawn with a suspect in their crossfire, prone on the pavement. Saldana pulled his pistol and assumed a back-up position behind Radcliff. Carranza holstered her weapon and bent to handcuff the muscular suspect with her knee in the small of his back, hoping for compliance but ready for anything.

Radcliff had been there for almost ten minutes, logging on scene at 11:06 am. Carranza reached the address a few minutes later, and within a minute, Radcliff saw a man dressed in black vault over the fence. Surprised by the police presence, the suspect ducked into an alcove in the alley just as Carranza slammed to a stop and emerged with her weapon drawn, covering Radcliff while he barked commands at the suspect.

"Down! Get down! Do it now!" he shouted, demanding compliance from the imposing man dressed entirely in black. Carranza shouted her own warning. Both hectored him to surrender. The suspect measured the distance across the alley, compared it to their crossfire, and didn't like his odds. He emerged from a narrow recess carved into the alley wall before dropping to in the pavement. If there had only been one gun, he might have taken his chances (he later admitted); had Radcliff and Carranza been just a little less prompt, a little slow on the draw, the man would have cleared the block and disappeared into the suburban maze; but LBPD's actions were well within any definition of a *reasonable response*, and he surrendered.

As they placed him into custody, their radios blared dispatches and confusing reports from other cops on the scene. Then they realized their radios weren't necessary to hear the panic – Radcliff and Carranza could hear shouts and shocked calls from fellow officers on the other side of the privacy fence, so close to the alley but completely hidden from the back porch.

As the suspect reluctantly complied with their commands, Carranza twisted his right arm into his back and then forced him to the pavement. Seeing her testify three years later at trial, I saw her as a woman who had taken her share of crap from the world and wasn't especially ready to take much more; tough and muscular, she looked like the kind of partner you wouldn't mind having at your side. Pinning him in the alley, she pulled the suspect's right arm but he refused to reach back with his left hand, which he used to stuff his black cap into his front pocket. Harvey probably didn't realize Carranza had pulled her Taser and picked a target at the base of his neck. When he resisted again, she nailed him with 50,000 volts to help him comply. She retrieved his wallet and examined his driver's license.

Nick Harvey was under arrest.

• • • •

Minutes earlier, Cervantes and Yee entered the front of the house cautiously, stopping every few steps. They didn't want to intrude on the private life of this slight woman, but their suspicions left them no choice. Glancing left to the dining room, they found nothing amiss with the massive breakfront and table, family furniture carefully treasured all these years. Ornate tables held massive carved mastodon tusks and other ivory treasures; intricate oriental figures and landscapes carefully incised the length of each ancient ivory six-foot trophy tusk.

On their immediate right the police officers peered into the subdued light of a stilted, formal living room, austere and oddly empty despite two lighted glass showcases filled with scores of heirloom-quality ivory Japanese netsuke matched, incongruously, with Lalique polished crystal animistic carvings. Lions and tigers, dungeons and dragons. Despite a wide bay window, the room remained dim behind drapes and the corners were dark. The officers continued through the living room to where the kitchen angled to the left, and were joined by a pair of young patrolmen at the expansive sunken family room and sliding doors leading to the patio and pool. A long couch and recliner faced a huge Sony plasma screen on the near wall, and an extravagant antique carved Chinese dragon guarded the coffee table while more netsuke cases lined the walls.

Halfway into the sprawling residence, the young pair shifted their search right toward Charlie's bedroom in the front corner of the house while the other cops inched into the cavernous master bedroom in the back, glancing toward different sets of ivory ornaments displayed on the wall. Closer scrutiny of the carvings revealed pornographic details, men and women coupling with each other and copulating with farm animals and beasts - a collection even more strange and disturbing than the mastodon tusks up front.

A stingy single window allowed little illumination of the bedroom, and even the brown shag carpet seemed to suck up the light. Bed covers were thrown over rumpled sheets. The officers found a pair of large dresser drawers slung randomly in the back of the room, the floor littered with sweaters, socks and clothes - something clearly amiss in the house. The bedroom led into a deep walk-in closet behind the wall, where they found the drawers of a four-foot jewelry cabinet dumped at their feet. There were hundreds of gaudy costume pieces strewn across the floor like glitter.

At 11:20 am Cervantes and Yee went back to the family room and turned their attentions to the sliding glass door leading to the back yard. They found blood on the handle, a red smear on the glass. Their radios announced the impending arrest: *Suspect seen in alley - backup in place.*

• • • •

The streetside officers opened the front door while Nick Harvey, the suspect, was being subdued beyond the back fence in the alley. Cervantes and Yee walked out onto a terraced patio overflowing with dozens of cacti, succulents and flowering shrubs, potted plants crowding all corners of the porch. A kidney-shaped pool, deep enough for a diving board, nestled nicely in a warm landscape of lush grass and trees.

Out on the patio, Cervantes and Yee found my sister lying on her back, eyes open and empty, her torso awash in a halo of fresh blood. Unknown to the trio, Saldana, Radcliff and Carranza had the suspect in custody in the alley.

Nick Harvey wasn't going anywhere but jail.

CHAPTER 2

Long Beach: *Gateway to the Pacific.*

The moniker was chosen by an advisory committee of community representatives, eight city council members, a senior advisor to the mayor and representatives of the business community. More than 700 entries were submitted in an effort to upgrade the city's existing slogan - *The International City.* Other slogans that didn't make the grade included *Port of Dreams* and *Ya Gotta Love It!*

This was the sort of abstract knowledge I accumulated on many visits to the city someone also wanted to call *Sun, Fun and More!* I wouldn't know about that - Long Beach doesn't kindle many fond memories, even though I've had a few with great friends who call this pacific place their home; but the city holds a piece of my heart, the empty part my sister once occupied, and always will. It is a place I always look forward to leaving.

Long Beach is a massive port and transportation hub founded upon historic petroleum reserves, an economic behemoth connected by a network of interstate highways and rail, a startling contrast to bucolic life at the beach. Glittering twin towers in the downtown district pierce a skyline backlit by the *Queen Mary II* and the Aquarium of the Pacific. Beaches are lined with panoramas of progress and prosperity cooled by a Pacific breeze; a place where sandals and shorts are standard, boys and girls of all ages keep surf boards ready for a curling wave or to steer tiger-tailed fighting kites in the sand. Just south of town, radio-controlled model buffs weave little aircraft through winds that funnel up onto Belmont Shore. Drivers and follow Pine Avenue north to The Pike at Rainbow Harbor. There one finds an eighteen-screen Cinemaplex flanked by a Ferris wheel, an incongruous throwback to simpler times. Attractions extend across the street at Shoreline Village, home to bayside restaurants and a boardwalk around the city's large marina.

But when you leave the beach and follow the Los Angeles River north toward the San Gabriel Mountains, the city shows its inner self. Long Beach is an accumulation of many layers: neighborhoods spilling into each other over time, some eroding into poverty while others flourish. The well-mannered shoreline gives way to bail bondsmen and vacant lots, pioneer suburbanites long gone. Within a few blocks of Broadway the urban environment evaporates, and is replaced by sure signs of despair. Depression-era bungalows, begging for renovation, blend into barrios and bodegas; transition neighborhoods, clustered around strip malls, restaurants and oil wells.

Travel far enough inland, still well inside the city limits, and the boulevards branch into suburbs: larger lots, lush landscaping, parks and country clubs, scrubbed stucco and tile roofs. In some ways Long Beach ceases to exist, and gives way to well-maintained enclaves: Vista Del Mar, Douglas Junction, Sherer Park, and dozens more. The transformation is unique in each block and area, but the effect is mesmerizing and the landscape remains almost the same. Anyone unfamiliar with the intricate highway network can get turned around in a few blocks, as I have done many times.

The city that starts near the sea stretches more than 30 miles inland. Concrete and asphalt have consumed almost every geographic feature, save the few acres sacrificed to scrubby oil wells and public parks. Los Angeles County boasts eighty-eight municipalities, including Long Beach and LA; with ten million residents in four thousand square miles, it is America's largest metropolitan area.

The Long Beach neighborhood of Bixby Knolls is flanked by California Heights and the Virginia Country Club, tucked in between East Carson Street and Del Amo Boulevard. It is an orderly network of established streets and alleys, tended lawns and shrubs, all but a few backyards hidden by privacy fences. Thefts and burglaries are not uncommon, but violent crimes are rare, and almost all domestic.

My sister's home sits between Tehachapi and East Amelia Drive. I come back to this particular house every time I return to southern California – usually my first stop from LAX – hoping to find something that would explain the terrors hidden behind locked doors and drawn curtains. When Lynn was killed in 2004, I hated the house enough to set it afire. I didn't burn it down, but I did sell it to a stranger a couple of years later, glad to be rid of Lynn's killing ground.

It's been more than ten years since then, her bloody murder muted by time and distance, but on sleepless nights I suddenly recall the shocking forensic photographs taken at the crime scene – grisly images forever etched into my mind's eye. I learned more about my sister's domestic life than I ever wanted to know, much of it so sordid I would have gladly remained uninformed; but my blackest thoughts begin and end in this three-sided ranch home with pool and hot tub modestly ensconced in the backyard, all of it tucked behind a stained, six-foot redwood fence.

This bright and prosperous facade disguised a dark interior, ruled by her husband, Manfred Schockner. It was the stage for many indignities: emotional abuse, physical traumas and marital rape. This was where my sister struggled a quarter century to keep a safe home and raise a happy boy. Her house was deceptively large, over three thousand square feet, one of the largest on the block. White bay windows pushed out into the neat front yard. It was a structure that could pass for a hundred others within a ten-block radius.

Lynn's marriage to Manfred Schockner was just like Long Beach - not just an edifice but also an accumulation of layers, bitter memories sandwiched in between salad days. Her happiness was leavened with sorrow, heartaches applied with a hard hand. In the same way I learned the boulevards and byways of Long Beach and Los Angeles County, I began to understand the quiet desperation of my sister, a woman battered and abused in domestic opulence. Her's was the fate of a woman damaged by undisclosed sexual abuse as a child, a neighbor's grandfather. Those insecurities multiplied over the years, culminating in the cruel joys of a sadistic husband who lived to deprive his family of any amusements but his own.

• • • •

Like most people, we believed *real* crimes didn't happen in our family; but domestic violence was only a prelude to the main event. It began when Lynn separated from "Fred" in May and filed for divorce three months later. She predicted his retaliatory nature but even she couldn't appreciate the lengths he would go to protect his fortune.

It all began at 1125 Andrews Drive in picturesque Bixby Knolls in a cavernous collection of dark rooms sprawled across a half-acre lot. The place held the prize of my life – a nephew who would become my son – and a mission to see justice served and brutalities avenged.

CHAPTER 3

LBPD has a policy dictating case assignments for serious crimes: the department rotates five homicide teams through weeklong "on-call" duties while one pair remains available around the clock. Detectives Richard Birdsall and Chris Cardoza caught the call Monday but traveled separately to the Schockner home. Birdsall arrived from headquarters in less than an hour, and his partner got there in two.

The block had been cordoned off moments after the murder. The detectives interviewed the neighbor who alerted police, but their most startling discovery was that six LBPD officers were on scene during the killing. They also learned their suspect was apprehended on site and was now isolated in a holding cell at headquarters. After the detectives developed their first impressions of the property and learned the sequence of events, they interviewed officers Curtis, Yee, Cervantes and Radcliff. The crime had all the trappings of a home invasion gone terribly wrong, but even then, the detectives sensed something inconsistent about the Schockner home; the master bedroom had been ravaged, but, aside from blood on the family room door, everything else remained untouched.

"At first it seemed like we had a burglary gone bad," Birdsall would later recall, "but there was something strange about the home: there were hundreds of valuable ivories in easy reach, but the thief tossed the bedroom and took cheap costume jewelry.

There was another drawer filled with gold and real jewels within reach, open but untouched. That just didn't make any sense."

• • • •

Birdsall was a second-generation cop. Both he and his brother followed their father into law enforcement, partially because he was still something of a legend in the department, a fallen hero. Robert "Birdie" Birdsall was caught in a midnight ambush in the oil fields of Signal Hill, killed by a rape suspect after he and his partner separated to search a rocky tract filled with oil derricks. Hidden behind an embankment that surrounded a pump, Fred Harvey (unrelated to Nick Harvey) fired a single shot into Birdsall's chest from close range. He was pronounced dead at St. Mary's Hospital. The thirteen-year veteran was just 40 years old when he was killed, leaving his sons to live up to his legend and still become their own men.

Imbued with their father's dedication to police work, the boys earned their stripes with the LA County Sheriff's Department. As capital crime victims themselves, they carried a special understanding – Richard was just nineteen when his dad was killed. He became a deputy sheriff in 1980 and spent eight years on that force, and then moved his family to western Colorado for a stint with the Rio Blanco County Sheriff's Department near his uncle's ranch east of Meeker. He lived about 100 miles from his wife's folks in Steamboat Springs, and he looked forward to more of a family life. One of America's largest counties, Rio Blanco shares its western border with Utah and was home to only about six thousand people, a handful by California standards.

"Two years, three months and a couple of days later I turned in my badge," Birdsall said with a shrug, "but who's counting?" His days with the department were numbered the moment he opened his locker to find DUI evidence against the son of a prominent rancher removed on orders from the chief. He resigned within the week when he realized some wealthy families were entitled to their own brand of law enforcement. "There was no going back after that order to stand down," and he quit.

He considered returning to LA County, but also inquired at the Long Beach PD, where he was welcomed with open arms. "Long Beach took me on like family. I tested out first on my entrance exam, and after six months I was assigned to investigations – burglary and then robbery." Six years later, he made homicide, and still remembers his first week with the gold shield in 1996. "I was handed a triple murder followed by two officer-involved shootings. I couldn't believe what I had gotten myself into. They even changed the rules (after those assignments) so that you could call 'no joy' after receiving three homicide cases in a week."

Birdsall and his partner almost made it through that first week in November 2004 without a new case before the call came out: the Schockner murder joined a list of eighteen open homicides they were working by the end of the year.

• • • •

Chris Cardoza was different from his partner in almost every way, except for a skeptical intelligence refined by years of experience behind a badge. Birdsall stands a strapping 6-foot-3 with long, rangy arms, and still carries 235 pounds with a spring in his step. Think outside linebacker, some time ago. Cardoza was both shorter and lighter, but trim and athletic in his own way. An easy conversationalist, his quiet curiosity could engage even the most reluctant witness into unguarded admissions. More than that, however, both were skilled listeners, men who could spot an incongruous suggestion or a trip of a tongue, sensing miscues with disarming nonchalance. And both kept their cards close to the vest.

Cardoza joined the LBPD in 1987 and made detective two years later. During a stint with the department's Career Criminal Apprehension Team, he worked with seasoned veterans like Det. Kris Nelson, a founding CCAT member who would figure prominently in the Schockner case, as would Birdsall's connections with the LA Sheriff's Department, who would house Harvey in their jail.

• • • •

The Bixby Knolls crime scene was still chaotic when the detectives arrived.

"There were at least a dozen emergency vehicles around the house and alley, and there was a lot of commotion everywhere," Cardoza said. "Richard was already on the scene, and as I approached I saw an officer crying in a patrol car. He was really upset, crying, I could tell. I said to myself: 'What the hell happened here?'"

"We went around back and saw the victim – that poor lady – she never stood a chance," he said. "Someone said they found him [Harvey] with some cheap jewelry. We went back into the house and looked into the master bedroom. The bottom dresser drawers were pulled out – underwear, pajamas and other clothes were scattered all around the floor; but the top drawers remained in place. In my experience, burglars always go for items that are easy to pawn, and most people keep their valuables in the top dresser drawers. That didn't make sense."

"Then we walked into the closet. I saw this big chest of jewelry, all cheap costume stuff, strewn across the floor," he continued. "Then there was this small jewelry stand, a very nice piece of furniture, but it wasn't disturbed. I opened the top drawer – I saw real gems and gold, valuable stuff. I also knew our suspect had nothing but inexpensive jewelry when he was caught. That bothered me more."

Like many detective teams, they had a bit of "Mutt & Jeff" personality as a pair, and they made it work. Their instincts for clues and contradictions suggested something other than a simple burglary. There was no doubt Nick Harvey was the killer, but inconsistencies in the crime left any number of unanswered questions.

"We went into the living room, where there were all these cases with valuable ivory carvings – small ones, easy to carry – and I'm thinking: *What's going on here? Why aren't these gone?*" Cardoza said. "Something just wasn't right – that just didn't fit the profile of a thief; and in all my years on the job, I'd never seen a true 'burglary gone bad.' You hear the phrase, but you rarely see that crime. Burglars just aren't violent sorts. This wasn't a robbery, and it wasn't a takeover; something just wasn't right."

Their investigation had been underway for an hour before an officer found Fred Schockner's cell phone number on a yellow note near the phone. Cardoza dialed the number, dreading the call. Lynn's husband answered at his gym – the LA Fitness Center in Long Beach. Cardoza said he was calling from Schockner's home and there was an urgent matter that needed his attention: "Could you please come here?"

"I'll always remember his first words," Cardoza recalled. "Schockner said he'd be home in an hour." The detective reiterated the urgency of his call, but Schockner insisted he would be at least an hour, maybe more. "There's a very serious matter here, sir. I think you should come here as soon as you can," Cardoza repeated. He didn't want to reveal details over the phone. The detective told him officers had already called counselors who had excused his son from his classes. "Charlie will be okay, Mr.

Schockner," the detective said, even though Schockner never asked. "Please just come here right now."

Schockner ignored the detective's demands.

He insisted he would pick up Charlie at school, a freshman at Beach Polytechnic High School about five miles from the house. "No, Mr. Schockner, that won't be necessary. We've already got officers enroute to the Charlie's school," Cardoza reiterated. "We'll pick him up." Schockner once again rejected the arrangement, insisting he would pick up his boy and then they would meet the detectives at the house. Then he demanded an explanation for the call.

"I had to tell him his wife was dead," Cardoza said. "I told him exactly what happened. He got quiet for a second and then said it would be at least another hour before he could get to the house. That seemed just *wrong*. If it had been me, I would have left without delay; but Schockner said he would pick up Charlie and be there as soon as he could. We didn't know when he'd arrive."

Even though the detectives worked the crime scene late into the November afternoon, they didn't interview Manfred Schockner until the next day. He finally arrived after they'd left for headquarters to begin documenting their case: processing evidence, preparing warrants and reports while developing strategies that would become their investigation. The interview with Lynn's husband would have to wait for the next day.

• • • •

When Manfred arrived home with Charlie late that afternoon, after Birdsall and Cardoza returned to HQ, the house was still a bizarre scene; rooms filled with strangers speaking in hushed tones, a crowd between Lynn's corpse and her beloved son, who already knew she was dead.

"I was in my math class when someone came in and took me down to the principal's office, and that's where they told me my mother had died," Charlie recalled. "They told me she had been murdered and then sent me to the care center." Even more than ten years later, his brow wrinkles as he drifts into a hard memory of that despair, eyes misting with his mother's ravaged body in mind. "Then Manfred arrived from the health center with a guy driving his Cadillac. He spoke to me briefly, gave the guy directions to my house and kept quiet all the way home.

"When we got there, everyone was standing around, and the house was surrounded in yellow tape. I tried to pull myself together and called Uncle Jon to tell him the news, but when he got on the line I couldn't say what happened. All I could say was: 'Lynn had…; or Lynn is…;' Lynn's gone.' Then I dropped the phone," Charlie said. "Fred didn't even say anything, nothing at all, until the police were gone."

When Charlie and his father arrived, the house was alive with investigators and technicians, and it would be hours before they were finished with the scene. An officer asked Schockner if there was somewhere they could go, perhaps for the night. Everyone assumed he would want to take his son away from the blood-stained porch, but they were surprised; he insisted they would spend the night at the house, citing "unnecessary costs of getting a motel." Despite their advice to the contrary, he finally agreed they would wait at a local coffee shop and would return when police were finished cleaning the scene, requesting a quick job. "I hope we can return in a few hours," he said. Officers on hand wondered why Schockner would subject himself and his son to the savage scene, but they let them cross the lines and retrieve a change of clothes. Detectives said they would call when they completed their tasks.

Father and son returned to the house less than three hours later. After a quick inspection of the premises, Manfred asked everyone to leave. He wanted to mourn with his son, he said. As soon as everyone was gone, Manfred ordered his son to clean up the chaos in Lynn's closet, Charlie remembered. "Fred made me pick up the jewelry in the back bedroom. He said he didn't want anything lying around and made me pick up all Lynn's stuff and put it back in the drawers. I was crying and sobbing, but he made me finish the job.

"That was when I truly realized Lynn was dead, that she was gone," he said. "I thought about killing myself and even went up on the roof. When I was up there, I thought I saw a shadow out in the backyard...in my mind it was the killer. I don't remember much more than that."

• • • •

A veteran investigator with more than 150 cases under his belt, Birdsall called Lynn's murder "the biggest case of my career. Hell, it was one of the biggest cases in the whole city's history. Having the murder happen when there were all these cops on the scene was a huge black eye for the department, and the media were having a field day."

The prima fascia case could not have been more clear. An eyewitness saw the suspect arrive, called 911 and six police officers were on scene when the murder was committed. The suspect, splattered with his victim's blood, was apprehended within a minute of his crime, bloody jewelry and his dagger in hand. It seemed like a slam-dunk. But the truth ran much deeper than anyone, even the police, could possibly suspect. Even though neither detective realized it at the time, their lives would irrevocably change as they retraced the killer's steps, chased down false leads before finding a well-rehearsed plan to kill my sister. Time raced by as they battled a court-ordered appearance. They had forty-eight hours before Nick Harvey

would be charged in court. Police had to file charges within that deadline, and for all intents and purposes, they only had two days to solve the *real* crime.
At the same time, Birdsall's marriage was unraveling and Cardoza faced his own family problems at home.

• • • •

"I've heard it said that if you want to be good in homicide, *really do the job*, then you've got to dedicate yourself," Birdsall said. "You forfeit a lot of your humanity just to deal with these kinds of scumbags; but mostly, you give up your time, a lot of your time, and that includes family time. My wife and I decided we just couldn't work things out."

With divorce in the works, Birdsall lived for his job. He logged long hours on active cases, often working alone while Cardoza followed other leads and struggled to find time for his own wife and children. Eighteen-hour days became routine as the detectives interrogated all six police officers on scene when the killing occurred, sifted through forensic evidence gathered from the scene and studied the premises and property. They paid special attention to the wounds inflicted on Lynn's corpse and the evidence found in the killer's pockets. After completing their preliminary investigation at the house, the detectives returned to headquarters Monday afternoon where Harvey was isolated in a holding cell. The suspect waived his right to counsel and said he was willing talk about his crime.

"It was a burglary gone bad," Harvey confessed. "I was there to rob the place and she surprised me. I didn't want to kill her." He described himself as a novice thief who chose the neighborhood because it appeared affluent, all the back yards were hidden from view and the alleys offered easy access. Harvey admitted being driven to the scene by an accomplice but refused to name the driver or identify his car. He portrayed himself as a "tough guy," looking for an easy score, and didn't expect anyone to be home.

"This house had everything a burglar wants," Birdsall stipulated in a press release prepared by the department's public affairs officer. "A place to hide from view in the alley, bushes to hide from view while looking at the house. Even though he had no training and no experience, this was the best house (for a burglary) because he could do it without being seen." Despite their statement, both detectives believed Harvey was holding something back, certainly his driver. That pursuit took almost another day, precious hours they hoped to continue pressing Havey for leads. When they finally spoke, he said he panicked and never intended to kill her. Still he carried a Taser device and push dagger, and was dressed entirely in black, seemingly prepared for more than just a simple burglary.

The detectives carefully considered every item Harvey carried when he was apprehended: the unusual knife – a push dagger – as well as a stun gun, bloody gloves, all stuffed into a black knit cap with a few pieces of costume jewelry. But the killer's cell phone would clue them to other suspects, and provided probable cause to search the records everyone he called leading up to the crime.

"As soon as we got the phone logs, we found a connection," Cardoza said. Nick Harvey's cell phone and Manfred Schockner's cell phone showed recorded calls to a third phone – one used by Frank Jaramillo. "What are the odds the killer and the victim's husband called the same person on the same day? It was just inconceivable. Right then we had a good idea what was up."

Birdsall enlisted a former partner, LBPD Det. Richard Conant, to trace the cell phone records, one of the many leads they farmed out to other detectives in the department. Then he called the LA County jail, hoping to trace Harvey's contacts and calls. They suspected a conspiracy before the sun went down, and they didn't know where it would lead. Their first interview with Schockner would be a critical step in their investigation.

• • • •

The detectives returned to the Schockner house the next morning, mindful of the family's trauma. Manfred seemed composed as he provided a melancholy greeting and ushered them into the front room. Charlie was receiving grief counseling at school. The detectives answered as many of Fred's questions as they could, providing bits of Harvey's confession while withholding their suspicions. They asked Schockner to describe his recent activities and his relationship with his wife.

"We wanted to lock him in a story," Cardoza recalled. "It's what we do with everyone connected to the crime." Like many detective teams, each followed different threads during the interview, paying special attention to every response. "If I asked a question, Richard would listen quietly, and vice versa. I could be taking him down a road Richard didn't know about, or he could be doing the same thing; but we were both trying to catch the suspect in a lie.

"After we covered the basics, we asked him to tell us everything he had done and the calls he received that day," he said. The detectives casually shifted their questions, dropping one line of questioning to pursue another. Finally, they provided other details from their investigation. "Our game plan was to make him our friend, to make him rely on us for information so we would have more opportunities to come at him again."

During a convenient break, Charlie returned from school. A classmate's mother drove him home with her daughter, with whom he shared tearful partings. Not long after she left, the detectives heard alarming details about Schockner's relationship with his wife and their divorce, Cardoza said.

"As soon as Charlie walked through the door, I knew something weird was going on between them," Cardoza said. "When Charlie joined us in the living room I asked if he would answer some questions for us. Manfred immediately volunteered to remain in the room with his son, but Charlie looked right over at his father and said: 'No thanks, I'll be fine without you.'"

Cardoza led Schockner out to the back porch while Birdsall and the boy walked out of the front door to the curb. Charlie immediately began to question his father's account of the killing. He refuted his father's claim that his relationship with his wife was *great*, he described his mother's anxious divorce and the ways Schockner manipulated his money to control their lives, Birdsall recalled.

"When I told Charlie his father described his relationship with Lynn as 'peachy keen,' he became angry," the cop said. "Charlie said that was a lie. He told Birdsall about Lynn's desperate efforts to leave her abusive husband and recounted injuries she had sustained during their long marriage. He also told Birdsall his mother found forged documents proving Schockner was hiding more than $1.2 million from their divorce settlement through a bogus loan to Schockner's college roommate, Marty Chernoff.

The soft-spoken detective also asked Charlie about access to the home alarm code because instructions had been found on a business card in the burglar's wallet. Lynn changed the alarm codes for her security service in the past month, the boy advised, after Schockner moved out of the home in August; even so, she had provided that code to her estranged husband in the event of a "family emergency," at his insistence.

"You've got to remember, we didn't know all the other connections right then," Cardoza said. "This is just the initial contact with the husband, and already we're seeing red flags everywhere. We knew this wasn't going to be a slam dunk.

"Charlie also told us his dad was very secretive, very evasive," the detective added. "It wasn't until later on we figured out what kind of a man he really was."

• • • •

Before they could resume their interrogation with Harvey, the department demanded another arrest, if for no other reason than to mute mounting public outrage over the crime. The detectives were ordered to drop everything to apprehend the second suspect from the scene – the driver – Jason Curren.

"We were under the gun to solve the case from the moment we arrived, but we got derailed when we learned about Curren," Birdsall said about the driver had turned himself into custody in Port Heueneme the next morning, admitting his role in the staged burglary. The detectives left Long Beach for the arduous drive north, at least another hour north of Six Flags, and then more than three hours to take him back into LBPD custody. "We didn't know if he was part of the crime or just a driver; but we knew headquarters wanted something done for the press and the public."

When they got there, he was gone. The local cops released him after he gave them his statement, evidently because he earned a form of exoneration when he cooperated so eagerly with police. When they arrived at the PH police department, Curren was gone. Birdsall and Cardoza were screwed.

Curren immediately became the subject of a massive manhunt spanning the seventy or so miles between Bixby Knolls and Ventura County. He admitted driving Harvey to the house but didn't know dozens of cops were on his tail just a few hours after the crime. He returned Harvey's sedan to the Park & Ride off the Ventura Highway in Oxnard and drove his own car back home to Port Hueneme. He said he didn't learn about the killing until a friend called the next morning to tell him about the gruesome murder that headlined the news.

Curren surrendered Tuesday morning to the local police, but they logged his statement and sent him home with his personal promise not to leave town. At the same time the LBPD detectives traveled seventy miles north to take him into custody, only to find he had been released. After the detectives returned to Long Beach he voluntarily re-appeared at the Port Hueneme police station, where he was arrested and transported to Long Beach, but he was allowed to post bail. An LBPD operations commander discovered the mistake and issued yet another warrant for his arrest. He returned to Long Beach, where he was arrested for the second time that day by city officials. Curren's final arrest, spurred by public outrage over his release, not only eliminated his usefulness as potential source of information, but delayed the detectives yet again.

"Yeah, I saw all the cops there at the house," Curren told the arresting officers, "but I didn't know what Nick was gonna do."

The detectives figured he had time to spin his story. "I don't know if he had talked to an attorney, but by the time we caught up with him, he knew what to say," Birdsall said. "He said: *I gave the guy a ride down there. He told to drop me off in the alley and return when he called. Hey, I didn't know what he was gonna do.*"

Subsequent testimony confirmed Harvey hired Curren to drive him to and from the Schockner residence. In fact, Birdsall questioned Curren about all sorts of details leading up to the crime. After dropping Harvey off in the alley behind the house, the Oxnard bouncer drove Harvey's Nissan around Bixby Knolls, wasting time until he received a call to pick him up. After steering off Atlantic Avenue to make another circuit around the neighborhood, he found the streets swarming with police and turned quickly back into traffic. Curren was off and running, fairly certain his companion had been apprehended at the house. The driver was a big, twenty-three year-old oaf who pumped weights to intimidate bar patrons, just like Harvey. Not abundantly bright, Curren probably didn't learn about his partner's crime until the next day.

The detectives spent more than an hour trying to crack Curren's story while insisting his assistance might save him from a murder charge. Despite the consequences, his story never varied.

"He had been out of work and the prospect of some 'easy money' was too much to pass up." Birdsall said. According to Curren, Harvey promised him $1,000 if he would drive him down to Long Beach, at least twice. The burglar had been vague about his plans, inferring he was going to break into a house or brace a guy who owed him some money, Curren said. "We finally figured he really didn't *know* what Harvey had in mind. Curren was the driver, nothing more."

When the homicide team interrogated Harvey again that same evening, the killer corroborated Curren's statement and reiterated his unpremeditated version of the Lynn's death: *she surprised me in the backyard – I didn't come there to kill anyone.*

Eventually cleared of all criminal suspicion, Curren was released by Long Beach later that night. He cooperated fully with every detective, distancing himself from willful participation in the crime. He gave officials just enough room to clear him of criminal charges, but at the time, his release from custody flew in the face of reason. Long Beach residents were still shocked by the gruesome murder and incensed by LBPD's inability to protect this helpless housewife. When the media reported police had released the killer's apparent accomplice in a two-man job, Long Beach officials faced unbridled derision.

Curren, the detectives learned, had driven Harvey's sedan to the crime scene not just that day, but on two previous occasions a week before the crime. Harvey promised him the money to drive him to inspect the house and plan the crime. With so much of the case now hinging on cell phone contact between suspects, they cut him loose. The detectives hoped he would believe he had allayed their suspicions, unaware they were monitoring his calls.

Even though the driver was eventually exonerated, most of the cops still couldn't believe the killer could find someone so stupid or greedy; but even Harvey readily owned up to the deal: "You're gonna pay him a grand just to drive you to our city so you can break into a house?" Birdsall asked Harvey. "And he had no problem with that?"

"No," the killer replied. "Why? Is that too much or too little?"

CHAPTER 4

May you live in interesting times is the English translation of an ancient Chinese proverb, the first of three curses. The second invites that person to earn the attention of those in authority, and the third hopes he finds what he seeks. I hit all three.

Our family assembled from different directions: I flew out of Jacksonville, Florida on Tuesday morning, the day after the murder. My wife, Susan Shipman, left a meeting in New Hampshire and followed me out to LAX, where we connected with my brother and his wife, Libby, and their teenage children, Amy and Dylan, who had arrived from North Carolina. Our first stop was the Schockner home, which had been cleared as a crime scene after being thoroughly cleaned by considerate officials. True to form, satellite vans circled the block when we arrived.

We shouldered our luggage through a small crowd of hopeful reporters and made our way into the house. I dropped my bags when Charlie leapt into my arms. We hugged for all we were worth, and squeezed out a few more tears before extricating ourselves from a lengthy embrace. Stepping toward Manfred, I paused to swallow years of animosity, and then shook his hand sadly before hugging his shoulder.

Never a family favorite, this was my sister's husband, father of their only child. Our history was more than strained, and then deteriorated to a point where he was no longer welcome in my home, hence my sister's earlier solo visit. I wouldn't visit her house and we hadn't seen each other for almost ten years. Grief is a great leveler and I shared his apparent sadness, oblivious to the real story. He endured a few minutes of random but routine questions, mumbling responses, and then thrust me Tuesday morning's *Long Beach Press-Telegram* with the story spread across the front page:

Best in the West: Boys' hoops

Jon Brockman

LBSU's Crosby top AL rookie

SPORTS / B1

Press-Telegram

www.presstelegram.com

Long Beach, California ★ TUESDAY, NOVEMBER 9, 2004 25¢ (plus tax)

Police at door, woman killed in yard

Crime: Bixby Knolls mom found dead after telling officers she'd get keys.

By Tracy Manzer
Staff writer

LONG BEACH – A Bixby Knolls mother was stabbed to death in her back yard as police officers stood at her front door following a report of a possible prowler Monday.

Neighbors and police were staggered by the brutal knifing, which instantly killed Lynn Schockner, 50.

"She was just the most wonderful, giving person," said her husband, Manfred.

"She was very unselfish," added her 14-year-old son Charlie. "She always put the needs of others first.

Police were called to Schockner's home, which sits in the 1100 block of Andrews Drive, at 11:04 a.m. after a neighbor noticed a man dropped off in the alley behind Schockner's home was peering over her backyard fence, said Sgt. David Cannan, a Long Beach Police Department spokesman.

Officers were on the scene within three minutes, and when they knocked on the front door they were greeted by a calm and cooperative Schockner.

"The officers explained that a neighbor saw a man who was acting suspicious behind her property and asked if they could check the yard," Cannan said. "She said that was no problem, that she just needed to get her keys and would be right back."

Schockner's American Eskimo, a fluffy white dog, was barking furiously at the officers, prompting the woman to close

PLEASE SEE **YARD / A7**

Lynn Schockner, 50, enjoys a trip to San Francisco earlier this year with her husband Manfred and son Charlie. The Long Beach mother was stabbed to death after she told police she would get her keys to let them into the back yard.

Family photo

Police at Door, Woman Killed in Yard
Crime: Bixby Knolls mom found dead after telling officers she'd get keys.

LONG BEACH – A Bixby Knolls mother was stabbed to death in her back yard as police officers stood at her front door following a report of a possible prowler Monday. Neighbors and police were staggered by the brutal knifing, which instantly killed Lynn Schockner, 50.

"She was just the most wonderful, giving person," said her husband, Manfred. "She was very unselfish," added her 14-year-old son Charlie. "She always put the needs of others first."

Police were called to Schockner's home at 11:04 a.m. after a neighbor noticed a man dropped off in the alley behind Schockner's home was peering over her backyard fence," said Sgt. David Cannan, a LBPD spokesman.

Officers were on the scene within three minutes when they knocked on the front door and they were greeted by a calm and cooperative (Mrs. Schockner).

"The officers explained that a neighbor saw a man who was acting suspicious behind her property and asked if they could check the yard," Cannan said. "She said that was no problem, that she just needed to get her keys and would be right back."

Schockner's dog was barking furiously at the officers, prompting the woman to close her front door to keep the dog away from police, Cannan said.

She would never come back.

As the seconds ticked by, the officers on Schockner's front porch began to call out to her. At the same time, an officer in a black and white that had pulled into the alley behind her home saw a man bound over the fence.

Nicholas Harvey, 22, of Port Hueneme was immediately arrested, and allegedly found with a knife and jewelry taken from Schockner's home. He was booked on a charge of murder, and held without bail at the Long Beach City Jail Monday night, Cannan said.

When the officer in the rear of the property radioed in that he had caught Harvey, the officer at the front door immediately went through the house and found Schockner in a pool of blood in her back

> yard, right next to her back door. Police said she had been stabbed in the upper torso, and appeared to have died instantly.
>
> A chaplain was dispatched to help comfort Schockner's son, a Poly High student. Grief counselors were called in immediately for the officers, who weren't identified.
>
> Schockner and her husband had just started pursuing a legal separation, Manfred said, though he still carries his favorite photo of his wife in his wallet. They had been married for almost 25 years, he said. Monday night. [He provided that 2003 photo to the newspaper, depicting a smiling Manfred between Lynn and Charlie at San Francisco's Fisherman's Wharf.]
>
> "The more you tell me, the worse I feel," Manfred said, before covering his face with his hand and shaking with tears. "I would rather she have had everything than to have this happen to her."
>
> Lynn Schockner was a longtime volunteer nurse with the Long Beach school district who spent most of her time at Hughes Middle School, though she also volunteered at Poly, Charlie said. "She was my best friend."

• • • •

The huge flat screen TV filled the family room with news about Lynn's killing. It seemed every LA television station, radio and newspaper covered this bloody tale of savagery and bizarre circumstance. The story even reached the national media. *Nightline* called, but I declined comment. Schockner aside, our family wasn't going to grieve for the cameras. As a former journalist, I knew the drill, and realized it's never too early to consider pre-trial publicity regarding the criminal proceedings. Even though Lynn's murder remained atop the network news cycle for only a day or two, the story only found traction with the local newspaper – the *Long Beach Press-Telegram*. Veteran beat reporter Wendy Thomas Russell inherited the story a few days after the crime and ran three years with the saga, following Lynn's murder investigation through three trials and final verdicts. She earned our trust, over time, learning to rely on her accurate, even-handed coverage. Later on, we provided her background details about Lynn's marriage and insight about the state's case. Over those years Wendy prepared dozens of stories about the proceedings, and then the newspaper's editorial staff endorsed and expanded upon the court's findings. Almost every story on the "Schockner murder" led the news budget and was printed on the front page. In America's sixth-largest city, where murders occur every day, this prominence is something of a story itself.

But the coverage also verified Warhol's iconic, cynical prediction. Lynn's moment of fame happened just after she died – not fifteen minutes but three days – mostly because it was a murder at a *good address*. The media coverage blossomed into open criticism of the LBPD as many residents questioned the competence of their local police. An article in the *Press-Telegram* published the day after the crime reported the outrage:

> As neighbors stood clustered near a line of police tape Monday, they were stunned to hear of the stabbing. Several said they have had cars or garages broken into in the past, but nothing that even came close to the shocking crime.
>
> A few wondered why police did not insist on going with Mrs. Schockner to get her keys. Sgt.

> Cannan also said that if there had been evidence that pointed to anyone being in her home or in the yard, they would never have allowed her to go back inside. "Because of her demeanor and the dog, which was very alert, they thought they only needed to check the yard," Cannan said.
>
> Another alarming thought for neighbors was the matter of Harvey's accomplice. Witnesses told police that the man was driving a dark, mid-size car, possibly a Ford Taurus. Anyone with information about the slaying is asked to call LBPD Homicide Detectives Richard Birdsall or Chris Cardoza.

• • • •

Sudden death strikes every family differently; some mourners demand attention, others demure. We preferred to suffer Lynn's loss on a personal level, keeping our sorrows inside the house, which was still surrounded by media. Most of the coverage emphasized a sleepy Long Beach neighborhood slammed into the limelight by a brutal and bizarre sequence of events. While denying interviews, we still watched it unfold with a morbid fascination that was undeniable.

Months later, after we had become close friends, Birdsall described the shattering experience he shared with so many victims, sad episodes from his career as a cop. "The veil of grief" was the way he described the phenomenon: a week or two of mental anguish combined a general malaise, followed by the inevitable instinct to reset lives and return to familiar surroundings. As a fellow victim of a violent family trauma, the detective could relate to criminal killing on a personal level; he couldn't ease our pain, but he did provide his personal understanding of the loss.

We stumbled around those first few days, stunned and shaken by a seemingly random act of brutality, unaware of the larger conspiracy. Everyone fought depression, and to this day, almost no one remembers much about that first week beyond the foul mood that enveloped the house as we prepared her funeral. After the initial shock, my brother and I were determined to find a coherent explanation of the killing, but everything we learned came from the newspapers, which included Schockner's mournful statement: "I just want my wife back."

The *Press-Telegram* provided painful reading, but it was nothing like watching Charlie's torments. He was lost and frightened, but never lost composure. Unfailingly polite, he suffered in silence before vanishing into the house like a ghost. I recognized his disappearing act for the defense mechanism it was, a carefully choreographed way to avoid interaction with his father. He also possessed the disarming ability to appear at a moment's notice, ready with answers or to offer assistance, any accommodation, only to melt out of sight when he was done. Schockner seemed oblivious to his son, preoccupied with moving back into the house and "getting on with his life." He complained bitterly of his own problems or shuffled off to examine the contents of every drawer and dresser on the premises, which he searched obsessively. We never minded his absences.

"They won't tell me anything," Schockner complained about the police. "I don't know more than what has been reported on the news. I'm devastated. I just wish I could have done something to prevent this awful crime. What about me, my loss? How will I ever find the strength to overcome my grief?"

Less than twenty-four hours after we arrived in Long Beach my brother and I arrived at police headquarters for a Wednesday morning appointment with the detectives assigned to the Schockner killing. We met Birdsall and Cardoza in the drab

LBPD lobby on Beach Boulevard where they offered sincere condolences. Their gravity was real, but kept a neutral distance. No one else was present. They deflected questions about the crime, and revealed little beyond what had been reported. "It seems to be a burglary gone bad," they reiterated, "but we're still investigating a bunch of leads." Both promised to apprise us of any developments in the case and, after an exchange of business cards and cell phone numbers, we said our goodbyes. It was over in ten minutes or less.

The detectives withheld their suspicions about the killing or the scope of their investigation, which had expanded to include other detectives, including veteran Bryan McMahon, who called Cardoza the night after the murder. "Bryan took time off his vacation and came in the next day," he said. "He'd seen Schockner interviewed on television and called me that night: '*That's not a real cry*. Something is up with this guy,' Bryan said to me."

McMahon played a key role in the investigation, as did many other detectives and forensic specialists who added their own brand of skills to the mix, but no one could anticipate the critical admission that would be extracted on Wednesday, just hours before Harvey was arraigned in Superior Court. From that moment on, the detectives side-stepped our questions with disarming ease, while concealing their criminal investigation with telephone wiretaps and surveillance on our sister's home.

Without revealing the full truth about Manfred Schockner almost a month, Birdsall and Cardoza juggled an ever-expanding investigation with almost a dozen detectives. They maneuvered Charlie away from the house, used my brother and me as willing, yet unwitting, allies in their effort to isolate Schockner and expose the true criminal behind the crime.

When we left LBPD headquarters, we walked north on Beach Boulevard to the ARCO Plaza's twin 222-foot towers

Manfred Schockner and Lynn Jicha were married in 1979 by a boat captain in Long Beach Harbor. The skipper, pictured at left, was never named by my sister and is unknown to me. Charles David, cavorting in the bathtub with his father below, was born August 18, 1990 in Long Beach.

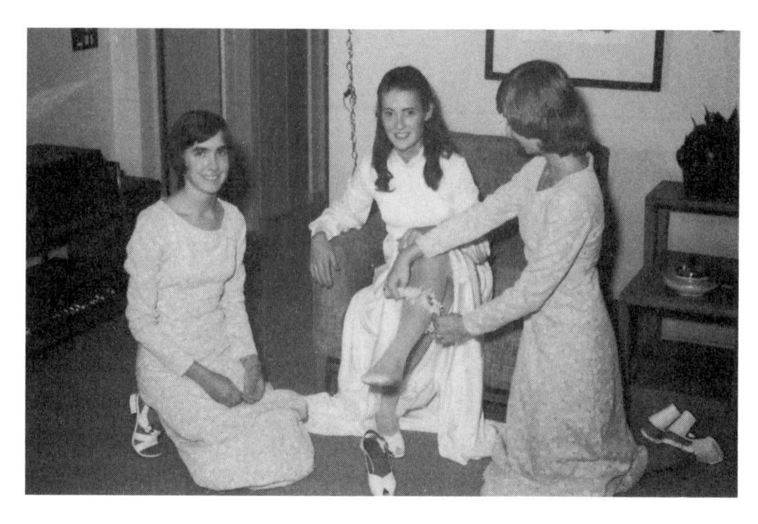

Lynn makes last-minute preparations with her bridesmaids before marrying her first husband, Dan, in a small ceremony at our family's Methodist church in northern Ohio in 1974. Below, my brother and I finish preparing her car for their post-nuptial journey. She met Dan in southern California on a summer vacation in 1972 their with our mother. After settling in Ohio after their marriage, the young couple returned to California the next year, divorcing amicably shortly thereafter.

Manfred Schockner married for the first time in the early 1970s, although he would never confirm the date or even speak about his ex-wife, who he hated. The bride's parents are seated while Schockner's brother, Ronnie, is pictured at right.

Manfred Schockner is caught in a candid moment a few years before Lynn's death. This admittedly unflattering photograph accurately portrays his personality and behavior. At right, an inadvertent "selfie" Lynn took of herself captures the uncertainty which framed most of her married life.

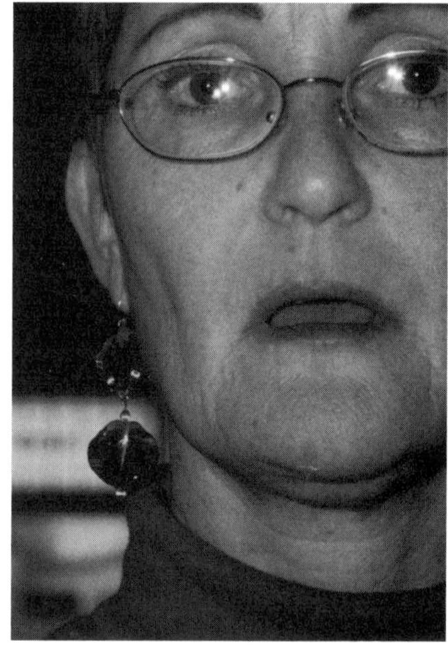

at Oceangate to meet Lynn's divorce attorney, Lisa Brandon. The buildings are striking: the two fluid towers joined by a glass atrium lobby and surrounded by terraced gardens. Their roofline undulates in the skyline, quite unlike any other building in the city; their "unusual shape and orientation are dictated by the sun, the location, and desired views of Long Beach Harbor," promotional literature boasts. "The ARCO Plaza towers reflect California's attitudes toward fashion and informality, as well as the rolling blue Pacific."

We rode the elevator up to the fifteenth floor of the East Tower and found Lisa's lobby, which offered a striking view of the city and harbor. She welcomed us into her office, extended her condolences and explained her history with the couple and offered any assistance with our family's affairs.

Brandon met Manfred at her office on August 24, less than three months before Lynn's killing. Even though my sister warned her about Schockner's temper, the attorney was stunned by his rude outbursts and relentless self-pity. Domination over his household was second only to his money, and no amount of money would ever be enough. Much later, after Schockner's trial, Brandon portrayed his nature to a tee: "Manfred's soul has been rotten for decades."

Schockner didn't contest the divorce; in fact, he didn't care if Lynn wanted to end their marriage. He just wasn't going to give up any money, and only planned to use their son as a pawn to gain leverage in the negotiations. He did, however, stonewall her filings, physically threatened Lynn and her attorney, and disregarded a civil court summons to forestall the settlement. He was able to bully my little sister with his wild rages, but Brandon, a seasoned divorce lawyer, was a different story. She ignored his bluster and wouldn't bend to any insult or outrage. She also understood why he was so fearful of an equitable divorce - he stood to give up more than a million dollars from joint holdings, not to mention his share of the house and their expensive furnishings. Then there was child support to consider. Manfred was more than contentious; he was an "unadulterated ass," and refused to participate in California's unequivocal no fault process, she said.

He insisted Lynn "keep the divorce simple and fair, and leave the blood-sucking lawyers out of their business," my sister said. He refused to negotiate with her attorney, delaying any discussion about their divorce. In the past, Lynn had always buckled before his temper; but twenty five years was enough. She would fight her husband, probably as much for herself as her son, but was terrified of the consequences. Brandon filed for Lynn's separation in June, and had the divorce ready by Labor Day. Say what you will about the California legal system, their no-fault divorce concept was created with men like Schockner in mind.

A 1983 graduate of California State University, Brandon obtained her law degree from Southwestern University School of Law in 1987 and practiced nothing but family law, one of the most respected lawyers in her field. Brandon's office commanded a stunning view of the city and the immense port complex, but the gleaming towers seemed a long way from the Schockner home in Bixby Knolls. Still, she would become one of our most trusted allies in just a few weeks, a crucial link to the complicated web of litigation we would inevitably file.

When I asked her to represent me as Charlie's godfather she welcomed the opportunity without missing a beat. That was a huge relief. Regardless of what happened with the cops and criminal court, my brother and I intended to protect Charlie from his father as best we could. Brandon shared our concerns for his welfare, as she had with our sister, because she was uniquely aware of the kind of marriage Lynn had endured. Everyone in the family strongly supported her decision to divorce Manfred those few months before her murder, but her nerves were tested to the limit. Lynn was more tense and nervous than ever, alternately tearful or giddy, clearly perched on a narrow ledge. Schockner had been married once before, in the early 1970s, and lost six figures after that woman managed to flee. In quiet moments Lynn told me his promise to kill her before letting her share his fortune, and with that prior knowledge, none of us trusted Schockner to share Lynn's estate with anyone, including his own son.

I had a long history with Schockner, little of it pleasant, beginning when we met in 1980, a flashback I couldn't help but remember. This was the first of very few social outings with my brother-in-law, a miserable companion on his best day and truly beyond the pale when we made the short drive to a Redondo Beach restaurant.

"Get the fuck off the road if you can't drive," Schockner screamed at an elderly woman driving the car beside us. I was sitting in the passenger seat. He rolled down the right window when we stopped, yelling across my chest, leaning into my left shoulder.. "You are a menace, you filthy bitch."

I tried to shrink back into my seat as he berated the woman. She had pulled into the left lane, in front of Manfred's Cadillac, to skirt a city bus. Once clear of the bus, she returned safely to the right lane without delaying traffic one bit, but he pulled even with her car.

"You cunt - you don't deserve a driver's license," he snapped.

Lynn reached over from the back seat and patted his shoulder. "That's okay, Honey," she pleaded. "It's no big deal."

He seethed in rage, gripping the steering wheel with a white-knuckled temper. I kept my eyes glued to the road, hoping for a gap in traffic and some sort of calm. Lynn and Manfred had been married for about a year, and he was proving unlikable as a brother-in-law.

He relaxed quickly after his outburst, his psychotic anger assuaged, cruising confidently through the side streets of Redondo Beach. He even hummed a little tune and made happy. As we approached the restaurant parking lot he accelerated into a handicapped space in front of the door.

"Here, lemme get this," he said, reaching to the glove box to remove a handicapped sign he clipped to the rearview mirror. "That'll do," he smiled.

"The food is fantastic!" Lynn gushed. "And they have the best burritos in town." Like most Mexican fare, the food was adequate and ample. Both the burritos and the chilies were tasty. My sister was eager to enjoy an outing with her new husband and brother, and I was pleased to see her so happy after many difficult years. Toward the end of the meal, Lynn tried to pass a tamale onto my plate, but I groaned in mock protest, my appetite always too big for my belt.

"Stop it, Lynn!" he whispered harshly, fixing her with a hard stare. "Your brother already told you he didn't want your food."

"It's okay," I offered. "Yeah, Lynn, give me a bite."

"Dammit, I said NO!" he snapped. Lynn bowed her head. Manfred forced out a muted apology and changed topics quickly, a changeling between moods. "Everything is just fine," he crooned. "I love your sister so much."

As the check arrived, Schockner made a show of grabbing the bill. "I'll get this one - you're our guest." The tab was just shy of twenty bucks – I promised to pay for our next meal on the town. He peeled a sawbuck from a roll of bills and laid it with a flourish on the tray.

I considered the tip a little light and added a five to the total, then excused myself to the restroom. When I returned, Lynn and Manfred got up and made for the door. Before we left the restaurant, Schockner said he also needed to use the john and walked to the back. We chatted comfortably as we walked out the door and I glanced back through the plate glass window to see if he was on his way to the car. As he passed the table, I watched his hand snatch the five and stash it into his pocket without breaking stride.

CHAPTER 5

Police discovered many interesting items on Nick Harvey when he was arrested, none more than his two weapons, an electronic taser and his knife, a "push dagger." This unusual blade, a double-edged dagger that became popular with gamblers and riverboat sharps back in the 19th Century, is now favored by martial artists who train to use lethal force. This pattern is exclusively designed for close-quarter fighting. Detectives also collected his cell phone, loose papers in his pocket, and a thin wallet. Tucked among four one-dollar-bills was Manfred Schockner's business card, complete with family names and a numerical alarm code noted on the back. They withheld this key piece of evidence from our family and the media, and used it effectively in the trial. While television stations still headlined the sensational aspects of the crime, the local newspaper, *The Press Telegram* reported the details of the story.

Alleged Slasher Says He Panicked

Wednesday, Nov. 10, 2004

LONG BEACH - A first-time burglary suspect with no known criminal history told police he panicked when he was startled by a homeowner and slashed her throat to keep her quiet, authorities said. Nicholas Harvey, 22, of Port Hueneme was arrested within minutes of Monday's slaying, which instantly killed Lynn Schockner in the back yard of her Bixby Knolls home while police waited on her porch. Because Harvey allegedly slit Schockner's throat, her death was quick and she never had a chance to scream, LBPD officers said.

"Harvey, who is unemployed, allegedly confessed to the murder Monday night and told detectives he chose Long Beach because he had been there before and didn't want to commit the crime near his Ventura County home and be recognized, LBPD Homicide Detective Richard Birdsall said.

"This house had everything they look for: a place to hide from view in the alley, bushes to hide from view while looking at the house. He just knew this was the best house because he could do it without being seen," Birdsall said.

"Manfred and Charlie Schockner said they planned on speaking with a therapist and described Monday's events as 'surreal.' Charlie, a 14-year-old freshman at Long Beach Polytechnic High School, was the first to learn of his mother's death when he was called into the principal's office and found a counselor and two police officers.

"She had a lot of illnesses but she never let that stop her," he said. "She was the most unselfish person I've ever known and my best friend."

• • • •

Unknown to few outside the sixth-floor detective division at LBPD headquarters, the full homicide investigation began with Harvey's cell phone. Detectives focused on dozens of calls from

Harvey to Frank Jaramillo, a California native who (falsely) claimed Cuban-American heritage in Miami. "Francisco Fidel Jaramillo VII' boasted of family connections to Castro and offshore ventures in other Caribbean islands, and his Long Beach apartment was a shrine to his fabricated lineage and his athletic achievements, playing upon his waning status as a local sports hero.

"Jaramillo was a pretty good athlete at San Diego State University, and played on the football team with (former NFL star) Marshall Faulk. His dad was some kind of big baseball guy, and he had all kinds of sports memorabilia in his apartment – signed footballs and baseballs and gloves – stuff like that," a detective said. "But Frank lived in a something of a fabricated world. I mean, he had Rolex and Cartier watches, played golf with some the big-name sports broadcasters, but he lived way beyond his means. He came off as some sort of hot-shot facilitator, and tried to insert himself into different promotions and deals for a cut of the action. He might have been good at what he was doing, but I know he regretted doing his arrangement with Schockner."

Jaramillo brokered luxury cars and expensive watches for "friends" while employed as a manager who rotated through different LA Fitness franchises: one in Port Hueneme, another on the Miracle Mile in west LA, and a third in Long Beach, near the intersection of Cherry Street & Carson Avenue, less than two miles from the Schockner home in Bixby Knolls. A simple "burglary gone bad" seemed less likely with each new revelation, especially when detectives learned the estranged husband had placed five calls to Jaramillo on the day of the crime. We wouldn't learn these findings for weeks.

• • • •

Birdsall and Cardoza braced Harvey with cell phone records during their third interview of the suspect, Wednesday morning, a few hours before his formal charges were filed. "I'll never forget this for as long as I live," Cardoza recalled with pride. "I've got the phone records in my hand, and I leaned over to him and said: 'You need to tell us the truth and get it all out. Face the facts - you've been set up – how else do you think the cops got there so quick? We're not geniuses, you know.'"

"I let him see the cell phone records," the detective said. "He smiled and gave it up on the spot: 'Damn, you guys are good. You got me. I might as well break it down for you guys. I was hired to hit the house.'"

Testifying at his 2007 trial, Harvey explained how he was chosen for the task. "Not to sound macho, but I'm one of the local bad-asses in Port Hueneme. No one really fucked with me," he said. He worked nights as a bouncer at local nightclubs, and had been hired as a fitness attendant at the LA Fitness Center in Ventura in 2003, then managed by Frank Jamarillo. He remembered hinting with Frank about becoming a contract killer one afternoon at the gym. "We were joking about it," he testified. "It was in jest, like, 'I'd do it if someone paid me enough.'

"But when he asked me direct, I said I'd do it. No shit," Harvey confessed.

When Jaramillo, who Harvey nicknamed "El Cubano," offered $5,000 for a contract killing in the summer of 2004, the twenty-two year old bouncer snapped up the chance. "Yeah, no problem," he said. They met at the El Torito restaurant in the San Fernando Valley where Jamarillo paid him $2,500 in advance, pledging the balance upon completion of the job. He also gave the killer Schockner's business card, with an alarm code inscribed on the back. "They wanted the burglary staged," Harvey said. "I was convinced I could do it. That's easy. But from the time I got to the house, I began to question whether I could actually do the job."

Harvey admitted hiring Curren to drive him to and from the location, explaining he "just didn't like to drive." Even after repeated interrogations, Harvey insisted he never told the driver any details beyond his plans for a suburban robbery. He said Curren drove him down to Long Beach twice to case the house, but he still delayed his move, but then Jaramillo finally called Harvey a half dozen times on November 8, demanding he fulfill the contract.

Harvey complied and enlisted Curren to drive him again that day, arriving a little before 11 am. He jumped the fence and ran to the corner of the house, but said he was caught off guard when, just a few moments later, Lynn walked out onto the patio and surprised him in the back yard. "That's not what I was going to do," he told the detectives. "I didn't plan for it to happen in the backyard. I was sitting at the door, wondering if I could even do this, and that's when she came out. I tackled her and she fought a little bit, and what happened happened. I felt my blade hit her neck, and from that point, it was like, well fuck. I finished it"

Still unaware the police were on scene, Harvey told detectives how he moved around her body and entered the back bedroom to stage his crime scene. He overturned a couple of dresser drawers and grabbed a handful of jewelry before hearing anxious voices at the front door. A moment later he heard another officer shout a police warning from the side of the property. He dashed from the house at a dead run and cleared the back fence into the alley where Radcliff and Carranza confronted him with guns drawn. The entire event lasted less than three minutes. He even asked officers on how they had arrived so quickly, and wondered if he had been sold out.

"That's the very first thing that popped into my head when I came over that wall and saw the cops," Harvey said, remembering Carranza twist the handcuffs in place. "Why didn't you just confess to the contract killing?" Birdsall asked during their third and final interrogation. His answer surprised the detectives: "I figured I might be able to plead to Murder Two," Harvey admitted, anticipating parole in ten or fifteen years. "I was going to find Schockner when I got out of jail and waste his ass; but there are just too many connections, especially with all these goddam cell phones."

• • • •

Two hours after his confession, Harvey appeared in Long Beach Superior Court. He was charged with murder, first-degree burglary and second-degree robbery. Judge Bradford Andrews ordered that Harvey be appointed an attorney and set an arraignment date for November 29, the Monday after Thanksgiving.

When Harvey appeared in Long Beach Superior Court that day he was wearing a Long Beach Marathon tee shirt and jeans provided by police. My brother and I still believed the crime began and ended with this single young man, never suspecting a conspiracy. Police wouldn't reveal their findings for nearly a month and it would be three years before we understood the full extent of the crimes. We attended Harvey's court date to lay eyes on our sister's killer and try to discover what brought him to Lynn's back door.

Finding the Long Beach Superior Court building and the third floor courtroom was a lot easier than finding a parking space downtown. After settling on a vacant bench in the crowded hall, we found ourselves within earshot of the killer's family and friends. A dozen or more men and women lamented young Harvey's plight and predicament. His mother and young wife were in tears, their friends sympathizing with their confusion and loss. I made an intentional insult in their direction, making sure my voice carried to the group. When one fellow locked eyes with me I strode across the hall and pushed my forehead into his face and demanded: "Did you have a hand in raising this piece of shit?" My brother pulled me back to our bench and a deputy posted himself near our seats, and by the time the court convened, the moment had passed. After the public defender entered a "not guilty" plea on Harvey's behalf, the judge denied bail and he was marched out of court. That was it.

• • • •

Back at the Bixby Knolls house, Schockner, who didn't join us at court, remained engrossed in Lynn's account statements and financial records. At regular intervals he would emerge from his private office to commiserate briefly with the family, professing sadness and profound grief, adopting a self-deprecating air in admission of his small failures. He claimed his shortcomings were far out-weighed by his love for Lynn, and to paraphrase Andy Rooney, "he was even a little proud of these small mistakes, because it provided the appearance he hadn't made any big ones."

Each of us mourned Lynn at our own pace, but Schockner seemed quick to put the sordid event out of mind, repeatedly suggesting he and his son needed to express their sadness and "get on with our lives." It almost seemed he was putting the bum's rush on our sister's funeral, which still hadn't been planned. Once we finished those obligations and returned home to Georgia and the Carolinas, we realized Charlie was going to be alone with his father, without Lynn, a protective mother of uncommon devotion. She and her son shared a complex bond, a web of deception and common interests allied against a common foe, and now the boy faced the daunting prospect of life without his mother in a household dominated by a cruel and unforgiving father.

Like most families, we had history, and tried to be tolerant around in-laws who got under our skin. My brother and I have been close since birth, and both of us were lucky we found Southern women to wed. We all doted on the children, but we didn't have a whole lot of history with Charlie, although Lynn's boy and I had forged a pretty strong bond during my visit the previous month, early in October 2004. Without children of our own, my wife and I spread affections among our nieces and nephews, and their successes made for many happy times. Charlie was no different, but we were worlds apart. Susan and I lived on the south Georgia coast, a sleepy place where swampy forests and saltwater marshes that still stretch for miles; my brother raised his family in western North Carolina, perched near the trout streams of the Smokey Mountains. In truth, we shared little with Charlie's suburban life in California. For entertainment, we sought woods and waters, not a day at Disneyland or a season pass at Six Flags. However, more than the different lifestyles or the time zones between us, our distance had more to do with Manfred than all of the miles combined. This would never change.

• • • •

Grief is an irrepressible emotion. Our family went through the typical rituals obeyed when a loved one passes, consoling each other in quiet conversation. We took to the sidewalks in family groups, led around the neighborhood by Charlie's little white dog. We met Lynn's pastor, Rev. Jan White, of the Bixby Knolls Methodist Church, who offered calm solace and helped us absorb the loss. She asked for recollections of our sister as she prepared notes for the funeral service on Saturday.

In the interim, we took to the endless highways that can drive one to distraction, often getting so turned around we would have to retrace our steps to find our way back through the suburban maze to Bixby Knolls. No matter how we filled those hours, everyone kept an eye on Charlie, trying to gauge his ability to process this loss. Just beneath his calm surface, it was easy to see him drift off into a thousand-yard stare, trying to find a way through this loss. Luckily, due to the pending divorce, both Charlie and Manfred had been involved with a family therapist whose office was just minutes from the house. She had already contacted the family and arranged for whatever guidance or assistance she could provide. Both my brother and I were keenly aware of the emotional trauma caused by the death of a beloved parent - our father died suddenly of a massive heart attack in 1970 just before I graduated from high school. We were also aware of the damage family members can inflict upon each after such a transforming event, and hoped the therapist could provide Charlie the kind of advice we could not.

But we also learned more about Lynn's recent situation. The Schockners began family therapy in late May, just before their separation, but the sessions didn't help the boy overcome his fears or resolve their marriage difficulties. "I started seeing stuff when I turned my head," Charlie said. "I would see a black figure – like a shadow – where I had been looking. It happened all the time, about every thirty minutes. It started in June, but then it really got bad the next month." Charlie began his weekly hour-long appointment alone with therapist, who would eventually admit Lynn and Manfred. "Every appointment was the same," Charlie said. "First I met with the doctor. She liked to sit there and wait for me to say something. Sometimes we'd just sit there for a long while, not saying anything. I guess she wanted me to talk. "Then Lynn and Fred would join us, but by the end of the session, Fred was always yelling at someone – or everyone.

the therapist would have to tell him to 'calm down.' Finally we would leave." All summer long Charlie regularly experienced his recurrent demons. She referred Charlie to a psychiatrist who prescribed two medications: Effexor and Seroquel. "They made me woozy, and sleepy," he said.

I wasn't particularly impressed with results of these therapy sessions, and while I believe too many modern families apply counseling over common sense, I appreciated her concern. My sister had been undergoing some sort of medical or psychiatric treatment for most of her adult life, regularly consulting different physicians all around southern California; her therapists offered a soft shoulder and her doctors enabled her to wrap a pharmaceutical cocoon around her pains and problems, but they couldn't do a damn thing about her husband.

• • • •

Francois De La Rochefoucauld identified the reluctance of men to believe their worst fears when he noted: *Those incapable of committing great crimes do not readily suspect them in others.* In coming weeks, we would find our innocence undone; now we struggled for equilibrium, recovering in fits and starts, but later I would be ashamed of my willingness to block out so many obvious clues.

Despite being married 25 years to our sister, none of us really knew Lynn's husband in any meaningful way. She often bragged about his financial smarts and business acumen, and spoke glowingly of his family fortune. Before his semi-retirement, he held a mid-level management position at Garrett AirResearch when Lynn joined the workforce as a service representative in 1978. Beyond his substantial salary at the firm, Schockner managed a family fortune of almost $6 million dollars.

Over the years, we all arrived at our respective opinions

from increasingly unpleasant holiday visits, deliberately brief. Lynn regularly reported new bouts of depression and pain, but defended her husband and claimed he had "promised to change." They were married in 1979, and three years later Lynn proudly shared photographs of the home they bought in Bixby Knolls. After so many years, our feelings were universally the same – we couldn't stand him - but our sister stood by her man.

Given the twelve-year difference in their age, there's no doubt his money entered into their proposition. Both my brother and I remember all the ravages of our father's death, not the least of which was instant poverty. Without any investments aside from our childhood home, our mother became the bread-winner on her salary as a part-time elementary school librarian. The three of us – Jon, Lynn and I – learned frugality along the way. Lynn was just sixteen when our dad died, and since that day, none of us were cavalier about emotional or financial security.

Manfred could be uncommonly generous, she said, showering her with impressive jewels or expensive vacations, but he could also be very mean. He admitted his faults, regretted his tempers and apologized profusely, but the anger always returned. Over the years, he convinced my sister she was too sick to work. He found physicians who would document acute fibromialgia, carpal tunnel syndrome and other maladies to secure her disability. He filed for medical benefits through company insurance and Social Security, even obtaining food stamps and public assistance. He permitted Lynn to have her Social Security check for an allowance but handled all her other finances from a trust that measured in the millions, parsing out a measured pittance when he felt particularly generous.

My wife and I were married on April 4, 1987, but a week before that happy occasion, my sister had a complete nervous breakdown. She was hospitalized for depression, and couldn't attend our wedding. Schockner called to pass along their regrets, bemoaning that his wife had been admitted to a psychiatric ward for an undetermined stay, alternately catatonic and then suddenly hysterical. He claimed she had "discovered she had been abused as a child" during a particularly long-running session of hypnotherapy. Lynn recovered slowly, alternating brief, euphoric moments with depression and despair. She finally admitted she had been molested by a playmate's grandfather, a closet pederast who had haunted her ever since early childhood. At the same time she maintained love for her husband, and said Manfred, failings aside, was her greatest strength. We saw him as her tormentor, but Lynn was determined to make a success of their marriage while he manipulated her like a marionette.

In 1990 they proudly announced the birth of their son, Charles David. Charlie became her life, and she feasted vicariously on his gymnastic successes, his artist's eye, and a well-groomed dramatic flair. He auditioned for a couple of high-profile Hollywood roles, even reading for the part of Draco Malfloy in the first *Harry Potter* film. He tested for appearances in Disney's *Even Stevens*, and modeled for a swimsuit photo published in the *O'Neill* catalog, an upscale Santa Barbara surf shop.

The Schockners came across country to visit in 1996, but that was the last time Manfred was welcome in my home. He proclaimed his love for my sister when we gathered together, but behind closed doors he badgered and berated her every chance he got. As he intended, he drove a wedge between Lynn and those who loved her, and my wife and I couldn't wait for them to leave.

Other than one memorable cross-country trek when Lynn brought Charlie to Georgia and North Carolina in 2002, the only times we actually saw her and her son were during infrequent visits to our mother's home outside San Diego. Those were brief, almost furtive encounters, sans Manfred. Lynn was

Working as the editor and publisher of The Southeast Georgian newspaper, I was able to invite Lynn, Charlie and Manfred to join me for a tour of Kings Bay Naval Submarine Base, and actually tour an Ohio-class Trident nuclear submarine. At top, Charlie and I pose for the camera while below, Lynn handles the controls of the impressive vessel while Manfred and Charlie look on.

Jon, Lynn, Mark and Charlie pose in the backyard of my mother's home in Lake San Marcos near San Diego in the late 1990s.

always under pressure to return to their home, and despite an ongoing battle to improve her self-esteem, her health, both physical and mental, invariably seemed to be on the wane.

Our mother died at eighty-six later that year, living her last thirteen years in southern California if for no other reason than to keep in touch with her daughter and grandson. A demanding but devoted mother, she had rebuilt her own life after our father's death thirty-four years earlier. Remarrying three times, she finally settled in picturesque Lake San Marcos, about 150 miles south of Long Beach.

Lynn and mom had a bond both miserable and magnificent; a love-hate relationship, not unlike that between so many mothers and daughters, depending on their mood. Both were intelligent, and their connection undeniable, but our mother's will and determination were second to none. She was harsh and opinionated, always much stronger than my sister, and they battled without end. Mom claimed Manfred not only poisoned their relationship, but also caused most of her daughter's health problems. She detested her son-in-law, and was right; but that criticism just widened the rift between mother and daughter. The more Lynn asserted her independence from maternal bonds Manfred increased his manipulative control and marital abuse. Sadly, mom's insistence seemed to make my sister strive that much harder to make her marriage succeed, as if she would die trying to prove her affections weren't wasted on the marriage and her man.

After mom passed, Lynn began to realize she had traded more than her body to Schockner for a secure family life, and no longer had her mother to blame. It was a bad bargain, she finally admitted, but one she had to keep for Charlie's sake. Our family visits stopped. We all did our best to avoid the Schockner home and saw little of Lynn or Charlie. Prolonged absences and infrequent visits drove more distance between us, and just as mom had warned, Schockner blamed Lynn for our caustic opinions of him and their relationship. I was proud to remain his adversary, but never fathomed Manfred's true brutality or his determination to control his domestic domain. He isolated his wife and son by design and used any means to keep them from leaving him on anything but his own terms.

But Lynn was tougher than he figured. She demanded a separation in June 2004 to evict Schockner from their house, and just before Labor Day she filed for a no-fault divorce. Having finally extricated herself from Manfred, she insisted I visit her Long Beach home. I was quick to comply and proud of her resolve. That visit was both fortuitous and fateful, a beautiful October weekend with Charlie and Lynn, a few weeks before her death. It was a happy reunion with my sister and a chance to learn more about my nephew without Schockner to spoil the mood. In the quirky and complex ways fate guides the course of our lives, Lynn's impending divorce allowed me to settle back into the role of doting uncle. It was a role I really wanted, and our connection clicked almost overnight. Charlie and I hit it off and never looked back. I gave him an acoustic guitar, brought Georgia white shrimp fresh from the Atlantic, and regaled them with stories from my stretch of swamp and invited them east for Christmas. I even rode the Riddler rollercoaster at Magic Mountain in Valencia with my nephew, but lost my cookies after the wild ride. Charlie was amused by my nausea and green pallor, and ran off to another coaster to continue his day at Six Flags. I reveled in his happiness.

Charlie was a freshman at Long Beach Poly. He was a real showman at school, very strong in drama and the performing arts, adept at foreign languages, and had an artistic flair that we attributed to his grandfather, Charlie's namesake. Dad was a talented artist who rose to become advertising director at D'Arcy Advertising Agency in the 1960s where he created graphic print and billboard advertising layouts for many national brands at the international firm. His work could be found in billboards alongside highways and inside *Life, Look* and the *Saturday Evening Post.*

Charlie was an exceptional and gifted child, but he and Lynn also had a special bond, a friendship that defined them beyond the parental connection. They were partners allied against a common foe, their relationship almost telepathic, synchronized to vacate the house when Manfred arrived and before he could begin another tirade. Manfred cursed his wife at least a half dozen times a day, often extending his diatribe long into the night, Charlie said.

My sister engineered daily escapes from home by volunteering at Charlie's school as a nurse, an instructional assistant, and finally as a librarian, just like our mother. She took positions that would allow her to stay near her son, who sometimes seemed more like a baby brother than her child. He was a precocious child, his manners impeccable but often contrived to be another line of defense.

• • • •

Lynn and Charlie traveled South only once without Manfred, two-and-a-half years before her death, staying at our Georgia home for nearly week. The signs of Schockner's malicious treatment were apparent. Lynn was permanently scarred, a shell of her former self. Charlie also showed the signs of verbal and emotional abuse, cowering in fear of my loud voice, which rises in volume commensurate with my impatience. He hovered around Lynn, always quick to hug her side in a protective way, and deflected criticism deftly with sharp, intuitive skills. He reminded me of a soldier back from combat, at ease on a short leave but living with haunting realities from the front where he would inevitably return.

I couldn't understand why she stayed with this miserable man, and finally raised my voice in frustration. I had never been angrier with my sister than at that moment, furious at her cowardice and willingness to accept his abuse. Charlie clutched his mother close, petting her hand and arm to allay her fears. I reduced her to tears in a matter of moments and felt the same self-loathing I experienced each time I won an argument with my helpless sister, still a girl in so many ways; but I pressed my case, insisting on some sort of resolution. Just before ending their July 2002 visit to our home on St. Simons Island, I gave my sister a letter to the boy's father and dared her to hand-deliver this message to her husband. She did leave.

> *Fred,*
>
> *It is painful to watch your son, a wonderful, bright boy, recoil in fear when he makes the simplest mistake. I know that is because he has conditioned himself for tirades from his father. The marks of abuse are obvious, and I can't really tell you how much I despise you for bullying him during his younger years, as you have been doing to my sister all the time you have been married.*
>
> *Shame on you.*
>
> *I don't want to hear from you and I don't care what you do with yourself; but I very much care what happens to Lynn, and especially Charlie, who still has a chance to become something completely wonderful. You can give him the way to enjoy life, but that primarily means a life free from abuse. You owe him what's left of his childhood.*
>
> *I don't have any desire to discuss anything with you. Fuck you. The years of your abuse have taken their toll on Lynn and Charlie. The next time I visit*

Charlie, I'll KNOW whether you have stopped being an abusive parent, and until then, I have no respect for you whatsoever.

Signed, Mark

• • • •

Three days after her death, I'm ashamed to say, I made amends with Lynn's husband, trying to put aside my misgivings for the sake of their son. In one of the most bizarre episodes in our strange history, Manfred, who had been living outside the house for almost six months, leapt to his feet and rushed into the bedroom where he located this letter. He presented it to me with a flourish, and asked me to renounce it. We were all stunned into silence, no one more than I. My own copy was tucked away in my home office, but it would have taken me some time to lay my hands on the document. Manfred had performed the same feat in a few seconds, in a home he had vacated some six months earlier. I accepted the letter from his hands, and with all the ceremony I could muster, I tore it to shreds.

CHAPTER 6

Three days after the murder, when Birdsall and Cardoza stopped by the house to "clear up some details" with Schockner, my brother and I retreated to the back yard to provide them some privacy. Less than ten minutes later, the detectives emerged from the house to share a cursory update on their investigation, without Schockner. Their manner was courteous but non-committal: A *burglary gone bad,* they reiterated. Years later, Chris Cardoza described this uncomfortable encounter with us at the house.

"We had a lot of questions for Manfred, but we also wanted to learn more about what Charlie knew," he recalled. "We asked them if they had any idea who might have wanted this done, but neither really had anything to offer. We briefed them on some of the details of our investigation, mostly what had been reported in the newspapers, and then answered a few questions.

"But then Charlie asked his father if he could ask a question, insisting he wanted to do so in private, he said. "That was very odd, to say the least," Cardoza said. Manfred protested, but Charlie neatly deflected his father's suspicion by claiming he wanted to know about a specific piece of Lynn's clothing – her shirt sleeve - which he had found on the porch Monday night, the detective said.

"I basically asked him if my dad was involved," Charlie remembered some years later, retreating to that quiet moment after he and Cardoza moved out to the sidewalk. "Cardoza told me he didn't think so. *We checked him out and you should have nothing to worry about.* I only talked to him for a minute, and now I realize he didn't want to say anything to me that could hurt their investigation. He did promise to tell me if they learned anything new about Lynn's death."

They returned to the family room where Birdsall directed Schockner's attention to the back of the house, asking about his extensive ivory collection, including hundreds of antique netsukes displayed throughout the house, providing the proud collector a chance to boast on his trophies.

Netsuke is a form of miniature sculpture, both functional and aesthetic, developed in Japan for traditional kimonos that had no pockets. Affluent Japanese men suspended tobacco pouches, pipes, purses or other personal items on a silk cord from the kimono sash. To prevent the cord from slipping through the sash, a small toggle was attached. That toggle is called a netsuke. The entire ensemble was then worn, at the waist, and functioned as a sort of removable hip pocket. *Netsuke* literally means "root for fastening" (*ne tsuke*). Far beyond their practical use, their owners considered them a status symbol. Soon netsuke developed from a simple practical object to an impressive piece of art of high standard, and have become coveted as collector's items.

"Manfred relished his ivory collection. The Japanese carvings were 'expensive, one-of-a-kind' art objects," Charlie said, and that he had purchased about two hundred in San Francisco the year before. The two detectives couldn't help but wonder why the burglar hadn't bothered with any of these valuable antique miniatures. Each piece was insured for hundreds of dollars, some more than a grand, and a dozen could easily fit in a deep pocket.

At Cardoza's request, Charlie described home security measures Lynn had taken after her divorce was filed, and he told them about her recent changes alarm code and new door locks. The detective noted his remarks, and Charlie retired to his bedroom, and my brother and I left the house for a walk around the block.

When Charlie was gone, Cardoza lobbed a quiet question Manfred's way: *Who had he seen the day of the killing, and who had he called that day?* Manfred dismissed his dealings with a sorrowful wave, claiming his grief clouded his memory, but the detective persisted. "There is one phone number we don't understand," the detective asked, advising Schockner of the killer's phone records. "There's a guy named Frankie Jamarillo. Nick Harvey called Jaramillo on Monday, and we found the same number on your cell phone. Did you call him that day? We can't figure out where he fits in this scenario, and we don't know if he had a role in what happened."

The somber husband suddenly turned into an accommodating host, glad to help the detectives understand the reason for his contact with Jaramillo that day. "I met him at my health club," he explained. "He managed the place and I got to know him. We've even done some business – I lent him some money."

Bingo, Richard Birdsall thought. *He's our guy.*

Cardoza continued: "I asked him how much money."

"Oh, about $50,000." Schockner said.

Do you have something in writing – a promissory note or something that would validate the loan?" Cardoza asked. "No, I trust him; it was something we just kind of worked out.'"

"I just looked at him and asked: *You're gonna tell me you lent a guy fifty grand and you don't have anything written up on the debt?* I trust my partner a lot, but if I lent Richard fifty grand, you can be sure I'd get something in writing."

Manfred couldn't come up with an answer. He shrugged his shoulders. "The next question was obvious: *Did Jaramillo ever pay you back?*' Cardoza asked. "Schockner told us he bought him a car. I said: 'Good, so you have paperwork on that, right?' And then he said: 'Not really,' that Jaramillo was in the process of buying his car or something. His whole explanation was getting kind of thin. 'What the Hell, what is it? Did you buy a car or didn't you?' I was really banging on him at this time, and he was going on about this and that, avoiding a straight answer on anything; but I didn't want to press him too much about the car until we knew more about his dealings with Jaramillo, so I just backed off.

"That's when we switched gears," Cardoza said. "Richard asked him when he had talked to Jaramillo most recently, but Manfred said it had been a while because Frank was out of the country. That was crap, and we knew it from their phone records, but Manfred insisted he hadn't been able to contact him for almost a month. I leaned over to him and said: 'What if I told you he wasn't out of the country?'"

"Well, that's what he told me," Schockner said.

The detectives ended the interview abruptly and left the house, promising more details about the case; but they already had enough circumstantial evidence to charge both Frank Jaramillo and Manfred Schockner in the killing. At the very least, both had lied to police, but their investigation was just getting underway. That's when the LBPD really expanded the inquest, directing manpower, resources and overtime to the investigation. As different inquiries revealed new leads, the detectives realized the three-way conspiracy but couldn't reveal a single detail to our grieving family. Successful prosecutions depended on admissible evidence, and they still had nothing on Schockner.

• • • •

As we prepared Lynn's funeral, the detectives respected our sorrow from a discreet distance while keeping tabs on their lead suspect. We never sensed the surveillance teams in place. Whenever we spoke, they advised my brother and me to take Charlie from his home with us when we returned to the South. "Charlie needs to get away from here – as soon as he can," Birdsall suggested. "It would be great if he could be with you for Thanksgiving."

We figured Manfred would balk at the plan, looking for leverage within the family; but even before the funeral on Saturday, Schockner agreed his son could travel to my St. Simons Island home just after the holiday, little more than two weeks hence. Then he added an ominous rejoinder: "I can't stay in this house with my memories," he sobbed. "I just can't stop thinking of Lynn and how much I loved her. Everything here reminds me of her. Maybe I'll find a place out by you in Georgia. I have a friend in Atlanta."

Birdsall raised an eyebrow when he heard Schockner's impromptu plan, but both he and Cardoza refused to elaborate on any part of their investigation and were reluctant to share additional details about their inquiries or information about the killer. We wouldn't learn the truth for almost a month, and didn't understand the complete picture until three criminal trials took place in 2007.

While the detectives advised patience, the press was having a field day with city officials. Just to make matters worse, Manfred promised a civil suit against the department's "gross incompetence," and even his civic indignation prompted the politicians to lamblast the police.

No one outside the immediate circle of investigators knew the facts of the case, but few secrets are safe in any large organization, even behind a thin blue line. Almost every detective in the felony bureau had been assigned some facet of the investigation and the department also deployed undercover cops and patrol officers for surveillance. They obtained wiretap warrants and ran "soft" stakeout posts on the suspects from discreet distances, always mindful of their presence. The Schockner killing soon became one of the most intensive (and expensive) criminal investigations in the city's history.

Already threatening legal action, Birdsall and Cardoza worried Schockner would stop talking to them, even hire a lawyer. He had already suggested a move to the East Coast, but he could also take his passport and disappear with his fortune. They would approach him in a non-threatening manner, probing gently with as few new questions as possible while apologizing for intruding upon his grief. The last thing they wanted was for him to invoke his rights and cut off their direct contact.

• • • •

My brother and I followed a different trail entirely. Lawyer Brandon shared divorce documents implicating Manfred in a multi-million dollar fraud, and we conducted our own inquiries within the home. Jon found the forged promissory note after I led Manfred out the door to the Methodist Church, ostensibly to finish the funeral arrangements, but really to allow my brother a chance to search the house.

"Manfred went with you to the church when Jon and I found that document proving he had hidden a lot of his money from the divorce," Charlie recalled of the post-dated $1.2 million note. "We couldn't take the original because we figured Fred would realize it was gone, so we took digital pictures for the police. We also sent a file to Lisa Brandon." This would be an important factor in my subsequent litigation.

California's "no-fault" divorce law stipulates a simple formula for splitting property: everything accumulated during the marriage is split equally, but both parties are allowed to keep assets each possessed before the marriage. During divorce negotiations, Manfred claimed a $1.2 million "loan" to a former business partner who had been his college roommate in Denver, CO. Jon found the agreement, dated before their marriage, proving her husband had forged the notes to defraud Lynn in family court.

But we still didn't really know how far Manfred would go to fight for *his* money.

• • • •

Four days into their inquest, Birdsall and Cardoza had a solid confession from Harvey, but little else; they had almost no evidence to convict their two yet-unnamed suspects, Jaramillo and Schockner, neither with a criminal record. The "primary," as Manfred would be known, was a millionaire with a wife still unburied, someone without any direct ties to the killer, already singing a victim's lament. While the detectives plowed every moment into an intense investigation, many Bixby Knolls residents expressed their low opinion of police tactics in the press and across the airwaves. Given the brutality of the killing with a half dozen officers at the scene, public sentiment continued to sour. Even Lynn's next-door neighbor, who had spotted the killer as he entered her back yard and met the cops on the street, wondered how the police could have apprehended and then released the driver. He claimed fear for his life, and the media ate it up, but police still couldn't reveal what had been discovered without compromising their ongoing case. LBPD brass and city officials were anxious to find a solution to the gruesome crime, but more anxious to get the reporters off their backs.

A week later, Birdsall and Cardoza bucked pressure and refused to arrest Schockner and Jaramillo, a move that silenced few LBPD critics but also pissed off key officers in the chain of command. The two detectives almost became pariahs in their own division, a homicide team facing all sorts of conflicted reasons *not* to close one of department's most embarrassing chapters, crossing swords with superiors up the chain. They earned life-long enemies along the way; even allies and former partners who remained faithful had to be circumspect in their support. Everyone seemed to watch their progress, no one more than the budget officials who tracked mounting expenditures and watched with horror as the costs soared.

Before their investigation was complete, Birdsall would commit the ultimate indiscretion: early one morning outside headquarters, he waited for his Police Chief Anthony Batts to arrive in his parking slot where he confronted the boss in the lot. He explained the intricacies of the case, how little "hard" evidence they had on the two remaining suspects, and why their inquiries should continue. Batts agreed with Birdsall's assessment and allowed the detectives to follow the crime from murder to conspiracy, a complex web among three perpetrators, and gave them free reign to find enough admissible evidence to convict all three for their role in the killing.

Even though they got a green light from the chief, the damage was done. There are few sins in police departments as grievous as skirting the command structure. With nothing left to lose, the detectives decided this case would be their ultimate achievement in the homicide department, because it would probably be their last.

• • • •

The weapon Nick Harvey chose to fill his contract was a reputable Cold Steel brand. It was a push dagger, ironically called the "Safe Maker" from their inventory of well-made knives. This type of dagger features a handle designed to be held inside one's fist, the blade protruding between the index and middle fingers.

It is a weapon equally suited for stabbing or slashing, three or so inches of hammer-forged steel known for edge retention. Knife-fighting experts describe the push or punch dagger as "one very nasty edged weapon. No better 'thrusting' edged weapon has ever been devised - as good as it gets for the given blade length. Push daggers are strong, being a fixed blade, and highly concealable. They thrust well, they slash and hack and are almost impossible to defeat."

When they cornered him in the alley, LBPD Officers Carranza and Radcliff found the knife and small pile of costume jewelry in Harvey's black cap, everything covered in blood. It took a while for the six officers on the scene to make sense of the sudden violence, but even veteran cops recoiled in shock from the brutality of the crime, sharing the small consolation that the killer was apprehended within minutes of his deed. "Everyone there took it hard," one cop said. "No one was prepared for what happened, especially all the blood. They couldn't be." More police arrived and began compiling crime scene evidence, confirming statements while photographers and forensic experts cataloged anything that might serve as evidence. Sooner or later, most of the cops took a long, hard look at the knife.

The killer was a robust young man who poured his lifetime of strength into one forceful rush at the defenseless woman, our sister. When she was down, he went in for the kill. So much for my little sister's chances in a house she called her own. Believing herself rid of Schockner's fearsome presence, she had underestimated his reach, as had I. Her sudden, fearsome pain was followed by swift exsanguinations. Lynn's life poured out without a sound.

Death highlights strange coincidences that penetrate the veil of loss. Some notions seem prescient, almost clairvoyant, and Lynn's death was no different. Everyone in our family found ironies and coincidences about her end, the alignment of random events that seemed to have relevance to the horrible deed. Yet when we each learned the bitter truth of this horrific killing and settled our minds to the hurt that had been done, we all discovered connections that would even make a cynic blush.

• • • •

Mine were knives.

I developed an appreciation of cutler's steel at an early age, studying iron and its alloys, blade symmetry and edge design. It was a hobby that became a part-time profession I pursued after college, but it all began with lessons learned at my father's side. He honed my interest and encouraged my simple skills to experiment with steel, brass, antler and exotic hardwoods. I learned how carbides align in the tight formations to provide superior cutting properties, and I learned how to make a knife handle fit the function.

Nick Harvey probably didn't know much about the metallurgy involved in his dagger, but he had trained in the killing arts. His knife was new, purchased specifically for the job, and the blade was factory sharp, the receipt among his possessions when he was caught, purchased for this purpose. The cuts that killed Lynn were horrific, and the hate I would find for Harvey was immense.

But I still have my knife collection today.

A few years back I renewed an interest in European knives, buying up fine old high-carbon German steels and Scandinavian laminates. Back when I lived in the mountains of Idaho, I picked up a Ruana knife in an old junk shop, a utility-grade skinner the old master hammered out in his backyard. I also found a stylized Rod Chappell 440-C creation in Spokane and a British Columbia creation with a differentially-tempered carbon blade. All remain solid and serviceable tools.

As we learned nearly a month later, Nicholas Harvey was something of a tool in his own right, claiming his martial arts studies made the weapons an "extension of his body." He also believed he was some sort of mystic who understood the temper of a well-trained warrior, and named his own daughter *Katana*, which "is Japanese for knife." Harvey made an informed decision to use a push dagger for his prey. The stainless steel blade was virtually unbreakable and finished to a precise bevel, then honed to a keen edge. The knife was sharp enough to kill anyone, especially a helpless woman.

• • • •

Two and a half years later, in February 2007, even after Harvey's public defender had exhausted his supply of Superior Court Judge Gary Ferrari's patience, there were postponements and last-minute exceptions. Finally, when the court date seemed "set in stone," another untimely continuance came about after jury selection was complete. Scrambling for anything to mitigate the client's blame, Harvey's defense attorney discovered an "expert" to lay the foundations for a *steroid-induced rage reaction* theory, setting an examination date in the jail. Unfortunately, the defendant had been cast adrift in the vast LA County Detention Center, a jail housing up to a thousand new prisoners every night. When Dr. Ronald Siegel arrived for his interview, his subject was nowhere to be found, and Ferrari reluctantly granted a last minute delay to the defense.

My brother and I had been in Long Beach for 96 hours and now had a five-day weekend to kill. We invited Birdsall to dinner. Over a second glass of wine at PF Chang's, I told the detective about my life-long fascination with knives and the extent of my collection, one my wife considers "astounding," and not in a good way.

I described one of my prized blades, a five dollar garage sale purchase from the estate of a French Canadian who had retired to St. Simons Island. I purchased a small acetylene torch set, shovels, rakes, picks and even an antique adze, but the real prize was a pre-WWII Collins & Co. machete, a twenty-eight inch blade that narrows to a sharp tip. It is a "Legitimus No. 872," a model proudly carrying *MADE IN U.S.* forged into the company's crown logo. I kept it sharp.

I tried to tell all this to Birdsall, my friend, over a tasty spread of pan-fried noodles, sizzling Szechwan chicken and sautéed sea bass; I described my history with knives and appreciation for steel, and I remembered my sister's murder. *He hurled you to your end, and now you are gone,* I thought. *I would butcher him in an unfair fight, and toss his corpse to the great unknown. Just give me a few minutes with Harvey and my machete, that's all that I ask.* I never got there, but I got as close as I could.

CHAPTER 7

Four days after Lynn's murder Birdsall & Cardoza finished their separate interviews with Manfred and Charlie and drove the fifteen minutes from Bixby Knolls to LBPD headquarters downtown to prepare their list of warrant requests for the district attorney. The Los Angeles County DA has offices in twenty-five districts throughout the sprawling metropolitan area and lists almost 200 different departments, everything from Accounting and Insurance Fraud to Bad Check Restitution and the Child Abduction Unit. In Long Beach, the prosecutor's criminal division shares the block with the police department, an easy walk to Chief Deputy District Attorney Mike Tranburger's office on the third floor of the Long Beach Superior Court on Ocean Blvd. Most LBPD officers, including Birdsall and Cardoza, enjoyed a close working relationship with Tranburger and the dozen or so attorneys on his staff. For this case, however, they had a specific prosecutor in mind - Cyndi Barnes – a young attorney with whom they shared history. The dynamic DDA coupled a superior intelligence with the will to prosecute capital cases with absolute resolve. A beautiful honey-streaked brunette, she turned heads in every room. Both detectives boasted about the cases they worked with Barnes, and admired her for more than her looks: the tough prosecutor who wasn't shy about getting her way. "She's a good person with a good heart, and tough. We knew she'd do the right thing," Birdsall said. Their confidence was well founded.

• • • •

By the end of that first week we had planned funeral details, contacted friends and acquaintenances, trying our best to insure Lynn's memorial would be both personal and appropriate. Outside of close ties at Charlie's schools where she volunteered, the Schockner family had few very friends, only one in the entire neighborhood. I hadn't realized how isolated she had become as Manfred's wife, a reclusive man who didn't like to share anything in his life. He distanced himself from the funeral arrangements, and seemed relieved to let family members handle the job. We didn't argue. My sister's pastor, Methodist minister Jan White, was a steady source of compassion and practicality, taking charge whenever we faltered. She assured us her ceremony would be all the Bixby Knolls United Methodist Church and congregation could provide.

Our wives, Susan and Libby, handled most of the plans, and my wife still recalls the peculiarities of the event: "The night before, Jan came over to share the service and the script for her memorial. She described how the ceremony would precede, what to expect and the details of the service," she recalled. "Charlie's friends and their parents came by the house to express their condolences – everyone had good words for Lynn although many hadn't even met her husband. One restaurant owner dropped by with a huge delivery of food: meatloaf and chicken, rice and potatoes, vegetables and dessert, everything we could possibly eat. He obviously held Lynn in high regard – he kept saying '*she was nice lady, a very nice lady.*'"

"But their dog almost drove me crazy, barking all the time," Susan continued, "and there was Manfred, moping around the house, hiding in shadows, acting sorrowful and aggrieved. He remains the most melodramatic, self-absorbed man I've ever known, and a bad actor in the bargain."

While these matters progressed, largely thanks to our spouses, Jon and I continued to update Lisa Brandon with details that could be helpful in family court. The more we learned, the more we worried about Charlie's long-term prospects, especially since our sister died without a current will. Her 1999 testament was prepared by her husband and his friend and attorney, Neil Ivan. It was the most deceptively simple testament anyone could imagine - upon the demise of either party, Lynn or Manfred, the proceeds of the estate reverted to the Schockner Trust. It should come as no surprise that Manfred Schockner was Trustee, with survivorship passing to Lynn; it demonstrated his complete confidence that if only one spouse survived, it would surely be him.

I was Charlie's godfather, but I was surprised to learn I was named "successor trustee" in their will, a provision my sister inserted in case both parents pre-deceased their son.

But what was most surprising, even stunning, was that were no provisions for Charlie, who was born in 1990, and no mention of the boy in any section of the Trust, except as beneficiary of his grandfather's $50,000 scholarship fund, which would be available when he went to college. Pouring through her journals and letters, we couldn't find any other testament declaring her half of the estate for her son.

We had already found Schockner's post-dated loan agreement with Marty Chernoff, his college roommate, the document Lynn had discovered during their divorce. Having that proof of his forgery, Lynn believed she had the linchpin that would salvage her share of the estate, something Manfred promised to prevent. Hiding these assets wasn't a problem for Schockner – he handled all the financial dealings for the entire family; his difficulties would arise after he signed an affidavit certifying his complete assets for their divorce. Once the perjury was proven, the proceedings would shift to an independent mediator, who could (and probably would) enforce an equitable division of their property. Lynn was confident her husband wasn't aware she held this key document, but despite our most stringent warnings, she included her husband's lawyer, Neil Ivan, as her main confidant and friend.

Ivan introduced Lynn and Fred at an LA Dodgers baseball game in 1979, and remained a fixture in their lives. At the time of her death, he was a non-practicing attorney, having dodged professional complaints by letting his bar license lapse. He was the family's best friend and regular guest. When we finally met, I saw a slovenly, obese figure, filled with contentious opinions.

He cultivated a close relationship with my sister while tethered to Schockner with financial ties, also served as Manfred's de facto attorney, a scribe to draft all sorts of legal filings: everything from their will and promissory notes to civil complaints, disability and insurance claims. In turn, Ivan was the only person Schockner eventually allowed to be Lynn's "friend." Damn her innocence and steadfast heart, she never believed he would reveal her deepest secrets, but, of course, he did. Thanks to this cozy relationship, Schockner knew Lynn's hopes and fears most of their married life. He used this private information to crush the former and nourish the later at her weakest moments, which were many, keeping her subdued half her life. Ivan betrayed her time and time again, right to the very end; and although police couldn't determine any legal culpability for his crimes, he made Schockner's control possible. I'll never pardon his treachery, and I can't forgive my sister for her unfounded faith in this sleazy man. Then again, I never could quite understand the fear and profound loneliness of her married life until it was too late.

Aside from half of the $1 million Bixby Knolls house, Lynn didn't accumulate any assets from the 25-year union; Manfred managed all the money, including his brother's trust and Lynn's money from our mother – more than $100,000. When they split their joint account, it held a few hundred dollars. Manfred controlled every valuable item in the estate, with deposits of more than $5 million, and other assets in the house, including the ivory, jewelry and art. Charlie was never mentioned.

Schockner wanted to settle family affairs before the funeral, providing a promissory note for our share of mom's estate, drafted by Ivan, with a financial release attached to the note. This was the man we had come to expect, someone only concerned with money; we later realized he was quick to settle family affairs because he was anxious to see us leave.

• • • •

"Manfred finally enlisted the Boy Scouts to take care of food and refreshments at the reception following the funeral," my wife recalled. "He agreed they should bring sandwiches and soft drinks, but when our wives decided additional supplies were required, he drew the line. "He was so damn cheap he refused to pay for the food, so I just paid for it myself."

Both Southern ladies, our wives subscribe to fairly rigorous standards of etiquette and decorum, and despite his boorishness they wouldn't ignore formalities or forget manners. After the ceremony they bought cards for the close friends who attended the funeral and then asked Fred and Charlie to provide names and addresses, but both drew blanks. They were able to find most of the names from the church and prepared the notes for the mail, but Manfred demanded that Charlie hand-deliver every card in the large neighborhood.

"To this day, I really don't know if he didn't know addresses, or if Manfred just didn't want to pay the postage," she said.

• • • •

Most of what happened at my sister's funeral service remains blurred. Memories from the ceremony that Saturday afternoon are vague, a black day despite the California sun. The pastor delivered a suitably somber yet buoyant eulogy, illustrating Lynn's generous and caring nature in the community, and her consuming love for her son. There was a formula to all these formalities, much of her script built around the family memories we had shared. She voiced our sorrows, and expressed confidence that Lynn had been stalwart in her faith. It was a sincere ceremony, but there were undercurrents through the wake, familiar trepidations that could not be allayed.

Charlie refused to accompany his father on the short drive to the church. Manfred seemed surprised by his son's insistence, but he didn't press the point. After we loaded into our rental cars, he declined a ride, opting to walk the eight blocks to the church alone. There was another perplexing move on Manfred's part: everyone but Fred arrived at the church and took seats on the front row. He arrived a few minutes later, walked to our row in the front. He ignored an opening we had allowed for him, glanced around, and then took a seat in the row behind us, alone. We had to urge him to join us, which he finally did.

The Reverend opened the memorial service with readings from the Bible, and then described her relationship with Lynn, a member of her congregation. After an obligatory musical interlude and just before concluding the service, she passed a portable microphone to the congregation and asked mourners to stand and share personal experiences of the deceased. Of the hundred or so who attended the service, only a handful eulogized my sister. The microphone passed through the pews and worked its way back to the front row filled by our family. I sat at the very outside of the aisle, just crying. I couldn't say a thing. My brother poured out a few phrases before breaking down in tears, unable to finish his thoughts.

When the microphone reached the end of the pew, Schockner whispered something that stunned us all: "Lynn was an angel, a wonderful sweet girl, but she also had something of the devil in her, and I had to live with that," he said.

I shook with tearful tremors, unable to react. It was both sinister and bizarre, but very much in keeping with what we would later learn about Lynn's husband. Charlie kept his head bowed. His cousins, Amy and Dylan, cast sidelong glances at Schockner. The entire congregation sat in stunned silence, now anxious to see the ceremony end. This was my final memory of her legacy, his last insult.

• • • •

I recalled a family outing in late 1950s, a time when Lynn was four or five years old, Jon and I each a couple of years older, a happy family visiting a friend's rural Ohio home with our folks. As usual, Jon and I dashed off to the pond, fishing poles and bait bucket in hand. Our sister raced to keep up with our pace, wobbly on toddler legs. We played around those waters, catching panfish, frogs, turtles and even a garter snake. After the afternoon romp, our dad led us back to the house and prepared for the drive home, filling our 1958 Chevrolet Biscayne wagon with coolers and the remains of our picnic lunch. That car, later known as the "Nomad," was the first and only new car my father ever owned.

I chased my little sister around the shiny car and into the yard. She squealed with delight, dashing toward the house, and then slammed her head into a huge hornet's nest papered into a low tree limb. A swarm poured from the silver globe; dozens of angry insects emptied from their lair, unleashing their attack on her unprotected face, shoulders and arms. Her smile crumbled in agony, eyes brimmed and then overflowed with tears as the toxins took hold. Huge ugly welts rose from more than a dozen stings, and even though my dad swooped in within seconds to rescue his little girl, she was already badly stung. Her anguished screams and cries, echoing time and time again, still appear like newsreels in my mind's eye.

For some reason I remembered that horror during her funeral.

She recovered in a couple of days, no worse for the wear. Kids, even sweet little girls, are tough critters at heart. Lynn was no exception. When we played tag a few days later, the welts had subsided and her face blossomed into a wide-eyed grin. Lynn had a beautifully round Slavic face with high cheek bones, only a few sharp edges where crow's feet gather, her smile sunny and bright. I think she even felt a little guilty for letting herself get stung, even though I chased her into that nasty swarm. Her recovery restored my sense of rightness in the world because I not only loved my sister, I liked her.

• • • •

Chief Anthony Batts represented the Long Beach Police Department at my sister's funeral, introducing himself after the service. A tall, solid black man with a stately bearing, he faced our grieving family without flinching, even though we remained confused by complaints directed at his department. LBPD boasts a well-deserved reputation for having some of the nation's top cops, and despite their credentials and the department's professionalism, they found their competence called into question. The funeral gave the media another free shot at the department, and they obliged by repeating questions about the police presence at the scene of the crime. Chief Batts came forward to offer condolences coupled with a solemn promise that *all* suspects would be brought to justice.

One late mourner, a hold-over from the obligatory reception, stands out from that foggy gathering of our family and her friends. Like so many aspects of the Schockner marriage, his connection was money, their financial advisor. He brokered the $6 million Schockner Family Trust in a dozen Wachovia investment accounts naming Lynn, Charlie, his brother's adopted son, their elderly mother, and even his now-deceased father, Herbert, all listing Manfred primary trustee of the entire fortune.

He approached my brother and I near the punch bowl during the reception, and offered his card with his condolences. "Lynn was a nice lady," he said. "I was hoping you could give me a call next week – I think there are matters you need to know about. Lynn claimed Manfred had withdrawn a lot of money from the trust during their separation, and your sister told me she had proof Manfred was falsifying financial records to defraud her in their divorce."

Furtively glancing toward Schockner who was sitting alone, across the room, he whispered: "Please call me - there was something going on," and then beat a hasty exit.

• • • •

When we returned to the house for our last night in Long Beach, the tables were still heavy with food. My wife and I planned to stay at our motel and return home on the first flight from LAX the next morning. I had my own business to run, and my wife had pressing duties with the Georgia Department of Natural Resources. My brother and his family, who were staying at the Schockner home, were set to leave the next day for their home in the mountains of western North Carolina where

Jon teaches at Western Carolina and Libby is employed as an intervention counselor in the local school system. Their kids had their own semesters to complete.

Even after Susan and I left for the motel, the events of that night held even more surprises. After we left, Ivan remained around the house long into the night. The kids were already in bed and their parents hoped to join them soon, but the obese man refused to budge until well after midnight, when he finally left.

"Libby was relieved when she could finally go to bed, the kids were asleep," Jon said. "I was still wide-awake - I couldn't figure out anything that was going on between Charlie and his old man. So many pieces just didn't fit: the police investigation, Schockner's behavior, and then the broker's warning. We still had so many unanswered questions, but after the funeral, it felt like the entire event was ending almost before it began."

Sitting in the family room with Manfred, Jon remembered his complaints about his insomnia which morphed into a sudden confrontation with his son.

"Out of the blue he yells for Charlie to come to the master bedroom. I was surprised no one woke up," Jon said. "When Charlie walked through the family room I could tell he dreaded the encounter. He shuffled into the back bedroom, and even though Manfred closed the door, I walked close to the door so I could hear what he was saying."

This is over right now, Fred shouted. *You have to forget about all this.* Charlie marched out of the master bedroom and straight into his room.

"I knew that Charlie was afraid, and I knew what it was about," my brother said of the affidavit Charlie had signed attesting to his father's forged loan document. "I realized I had to do something about the situation."

He claimed insomnia until Schockner slept, and then woke

Charlie and Dylan and told them he would call the police the next morning from the church. Long before Schockner rose, not long after first light, they met the Reverend at the church and called Birdsall on his cell phone. He arrived within 30 minutes. Jon reported Schockner's strange outburst the previous night, and then advised the detective he would remain in Long Beach while police continued their investigation.

"I told Richard something was wrong with Schockner, and that Charlie might be in jeopardy. I told him I would stay in California until I was sure Charlie would be safe."

Birdsall enthusiastically endorsed his plan. "When I got back to the house later that Sunday morning I informed Schockner: 'I think you and Charlie need me – why don't I stay another week?' He seemed puzzled, even a little annoyed. He tried to talk me out of staying, but Charlie was obviously relieved."

Despite Schockner's reticence, my brother would not be dissuaded. My wife and I were already back in Georgia when my brother called to explain his change of plans. He stood with Charlie in his greatest crisis and protected him from his cruel father, and I was on the other side of the world. My brother's presence that following week was crucial for our eventual emergence as a complete family.

Later that night, Jon dropped his family at LAX, returned his rental car, and hitched a ride back to Bixby Knolls in Schockner's aging Cadillac. Jon asked Manfred to join him on an errand the next morning. While they were gone, Charlie found important papers tucked in his mother's bureau, hidden among his old yearbooks and texts. Following Birdsall's advice, Jon dropped Charlie at the school to visit counselors at Long Beach Poly, and then left to meet Lisa Brandon at her office. Jon provided Charlie's affidavit for her file, discussed her progress, and then returned to the school. He and Charlie took a long lunch, walked Marina Village and then ended their day visiting the boy's childhood haunts. They traded observations and ideas about the police investigation, memories of Lynn and our progress with Brandon before returning for an early dinner with Manfred. Claiming exhaustion, both Jon and Charlie retired soon after the meal. The next morning all three left early together. They dropped Charlie at his school, and drove to the crematorium where Lynn's body awaited final dispatch, and a last insult.

"Manfred called earlier and the staff expected our arrival," Jon said. "The assistant manager welcomed us into her office to discuss the cremation, and she asked if we would mind if a new employee joined us for the consultation. Manfred immediately said he would agree, but only if he would get a discount for their services for the 'training session.' Then he started laughing." Both the woman and the girl blanched and sat in stoney silence for a moment, regained their composure and continued without reply.

"I was stunned. He couldn't have been more offensive," Jon said. Watching him haggling over Lynn's remains was bad enough, but Schockner found it hilarious. "He laughed and giggled for a few minutes."

The meeting grew even more bizarre when Manfred suddenly pulled a cheap urn from a package he had carried into the crematorium, providing his own receptacle for the cremains obtained by his brother from a foreclosure sale. "I only paid $20 for this," he boasted while signing the contract, indicating he would pay the $500 when he returned later that week to retrieve the package. When asked if he wanted to view his wife's body before leaving, he begged off: "I just want to live with her memory. I want to remember her when she was alive," Jon recalled.

That was the last moment for our sister and Charlie's mom, a sweet woman now just dust and ashes, her body slashed and gone.

• • • •

After collecting Charlie from school, only a few minutes after they had returned home for lunch, Manfred got a surprise visit from Birdsall and Cardoza, who arrived unannounced just before they ate. They murmured their apologies but claimed they were ordered to interview Schockner again, if nothing else but to assuage the brass. They asked a few innocuous questions and then promised to keep the family appraised of any developments. There was almost nothing to their visit, hardly an interview. My brother followed the detectives to their car and asked pointed question, which they dodged with practiced nonchalance. Without comment, Birdsall pulled him aside. "We'd like you to take Charlie in the morning. Leave the house for a few hours tomorrow, and don't come back until lunch," he said. The detectives hoped for a three-hour window when they could brace Manfred alone at the family home the next day, and they left.

Jon woke Charlie woke early Tuesday morning and immediately left the house for an breakfast and school, but Schockner was having a fit when they arrived home at noon.

"He said the killer (Nick Harvey) called him from jail while we were out," Jon said. "Schockner was really upset. '*I don't know what's going on! How can he call me? I don't even know him.*' He was shrieking and shaking his head, flapping his hands above his head, using all those helpless gestures he perfected. Fred was going nuts, but I could tell he was really rattled. This was beyond anything I'd ever seen."

Jon offered to question the detectives, if for no other reason than to reassure his brother-in-law their investigation was proceeding without delay. "I called Birdsall to ask him about the phone call," he said. "He told me he was in Ventura County, and he would get there as soon as he could, probably an hour"

• • • •

What none of us knew was that the detectives had already created a number of "legends" to penetrate Schockner's criminal conspiracy, including the call placed by Det. Kris Nelson, who we would befriend three years down the road. Since they couldn't find a link between Schockner and the killer, they didn't have to worry he would recognize Harvey's voice. He placed the call and demanded money.

That was just one role played by Nelson, who also assumed the roughneck role "Uncle John" from San Francisco, a close friend of the Harvey family. In upcoming weeks he would repeatedly called Schockner trying to collect the killer's promised payment upon completion – another $2,500 – so Nick could afford his own lawyer.

Nelson was a grizzled veteran who had mentored Cardoza during his early days in the department, and a founding member of the Career Criminal Apprehension Team (CCAT). He would play a key role as the undercover officer who cozied his way into the conspiracy and placed that phone call to the Schockner residence, stunning Manfred while the veteran cop performed the role of Nick Harvey.

A few days later – in character as Uncle John - Nelson confronted the middleman, Frank Jaramillo, demanding he pay Harvey. The suspect promised to pass his worries along to Manfred; he did, as in their recorded conversations.

Birdsall and Cardoza continued to approach Schockner from oblique angles, usually arriving unannounced at the home once or twice a day. They would ask Manfred a few questions, mostly in private, and then leave with apologies and promise to keep the family appraised of developments in their case. That became their throwaway line.

Thursday afternoon, November 18, ten days after the murder, my brother finished his extended stay in Long Beach and planned to return home to North Carolina. We still didn't know anything more about the crime than when I'd left – the police still called it a "burglary gone bad" – and we had all sorts of unanswered questions about our sister's estate. Most of all, we worried about Charlie, who faced the prospect of living alone with his father. Jon walked the detectives to their car that afternoon; Manfred remained inside the house and Charlie was off on an errand. He implored the two veteran cops to provide some sort of reassurance he wasn't leaving the boy at risk.

"Cardoza looked directly in my eyes, and said: '*You will know something as soon as we find out, and we hope that's real soon.*'" Jon said. "Something gave me a sense there was more going on than what we had been told. I remember Chris didn't even blink. It was like he wanted me to know something was happening, something he couldn't convey. I made a light remark to break the tension, but Chris just reiterated his statement: 'You'll know something soon.'"

The time my brother spent with Manfred and Charlie in that large suburban home became a confused mix of emotions. Strange days and scary nights. The detectives were fully involved in their investigation, attentive and sympathetic, but revealed nothing beyond their initial assessment. Back in Georgia, we kept close contact with my brother and our lawyer, preparing for some sort of action after Charlie came east after Thanksgiving. California law allows for a limited adult majority at age fourteen; that, coupled with my legal status as both Charlie's godfather and "successor trustee" to the Schockner estate in family court, I could still advocate for my dead sister and offer an alternate home for her son.

CHAPTER 8

Just as they began to *really* understand the conspiracy within the crime, the detectives faced mounting pressures to conduct interviews and draft warrants, the mechanics of their case; at the same time, they caught media requests and residents' complaints which also pulled them away from their priorities. Everyone wanted an explanation why six cops couldn't prevent the crime. When the widowed husband, Manfred, raised liability issues in the media, the urgency jumped another notch. With the department taking a beating in the press, Birdsall & Cardoza tracked Judge Larry Paul Fidler, presiding judge of Los Angeles County, to his home. They waited there until he returned from the relatively sacred grounds of his regular Saturday morning round of golf at the country club, getting him to sign-off on wiretaps for land and mobile lines of both Frank Jaramillo and Manfred Schockner. That was the same day Chief Batts paid his respects to my sister at her funeral, and didn't display the frantic pressures police faced while laying the groundwork for an intricate investigation. We knew nothing of the eight detectives assigned to the case or Detective Nelson's role in undercover and his career filled with high-risk assignments. The twenty-year veteran would infiltrate the trio for the evidence that would tie the two other men to the crime.

• • • •

A native of Fallbrook, just inland from Oceanside in north San Diego County, the 5-foot-11 Nelson weighed in at 175 pounds in high school. A self-confessed "gym rat," he played defensive end for the Warrior football team and graduated in 1975. His twin brother and football teammate, Kurt, joined him in law enforcement after college. Kurt partnered with Chris Cardoza when that detective joined Nelson on Long Beach's CCAT unit in the early 1990s. Their father, Harold "Hal" Nelson, was the fire chief at the Naval Weapons Station at Camp Pendleton. Despite a BA in business management from Long Beach State University in 1980, he could easily pass himself off as a crusty square-jawed ex-Marine with bulky biceps and a burr haircut.

But he knew he didn't want to *sit behind a desk all day*, and began taking fire science courses in an effort to get a job as a Long Beach firefighter. During off hours he attended night school finally, but he learned of police openings with the LBPD and enrolled in the academy October 1984. He pulled the obligatory years with patrol before he was named to a Metro Squad, where he advanced to become a sniper/observer with the SWAT Team detailed with the unit. Three years later the city reorganized the department. Nelson moved back to patrol and then joined the burglary squad, but in 1990 he became an SOB.

"There's a funny story behind that name," he said of the familiar figure of speech that doubled as an LBPD acronym. "It was created as the Suppression of Burglary (SOB) squad, but even back then, we called ourselves the *SOBs*." The team specialized in undercover surveillance, and in 1990 made a headline arrest of Cedric Scott, a suspect later convicted of kidnapping and torture. The story made headlines all around the region and was featured in an episode of "America's Most Wanted" television show.

"LBPD Detective Bryan McMahon, one of my partners at the time, arrested Scott one night in July," Nelson said. "Before he reached his holding cell at headquarters he knew we had him dead to rights, and mugged for the cameras during his perp walk to the station. With television cameras rolling, he confessed: 'I was caught by the best SOBs out there.' The story got plenty of airtime, but our chief at the time didn't appreciate the humor in the nickname. Within a week, they changed the name to the Career Criminal Apprehension Team (CCAT), and it has been known that way ever since."

His career in law enforcement reached a watershed when he played a pivotal role in one of the most notorious shootouts in LBPD history – the May 2000 ambush of two members of the department's Gang Suppression Unit: Det. Daryl "Big" Black and his partner, Det. Rich Delphine, close friends of both Kris Nelson and Chris Cardoza.

"It's been called the 'Daryl Black shooting' because Daryl died that day," Nelson said. "Rick was critically wounded. Both were great guys and really good cops – guys you could depend on. During a routine patrol, they found a car double-parked in the middle of the street. When they slowed to check out a pedestrian walking away from the car, gunfire erupted from the other side of the street.

"The shooters were gang bangers from *Bario Pobre*, Nelson recalled. "Four of them were there to rip up a house where a rival gang lived when Daryl and Rick stumbled upon the crew. When they saw the unmarked patrol car pull up behind them, the gang just opened up. Daryl, in the passenger seat, noticed one guy carrying a handgun across the street, but he didn't see the other who popped up between two parked cars with an AR-15 and emptied his 30-round clip into the passenger compartment of their unit.

Nelson was up at Mammoth Mountain with his wife when he heard the story on the news. "We were scheduled to vacation there a couple more days, but I looked at her and said, 'We gotta go,' because I knew our unit would be involved in the manhunt. Two days later we caught up with one of the killers - Juan Camacho. He was known as 'Pipas' a guy with a reputation for violence. We found him and two other guys who were wanted in a separate murder of an LA County deputy up in Compton. I chased Juan down and shot him about five times, but, of course, he didn't die," Nelson said with a wry chuckle. "The other two guys went into a house but eventually surrendered, and all three were convicted for murder."

• • • •

It is true irony that public condemnation of the police conduct in the murder accelerated soon after the department committed huge funds and added this experienced undercover operative to the team, kicking the second phase of the investigation into high gear. Nelson went into character – first as the killer calling Schockner from the LA County jail, and then connecting with the middleman by posing as a close friend of the Harvey's family. "Uncle John" became the surname for this fictional character, a conduit for the police to stimulate the suspects into reckless acts or admissions. He initiated contact with Schockner as Harvey to complain that he faced capital murder charges with only a public defender at his side.

"I actually had to drive to the county jail in LA," Nelson said, "because we wanted the switchboard to deliver the appropriate recorded warning: *You are receiving a call from a California penal institution, are you willing to accept the call?* The first time Schockner said 'no.' I called him right back, and during the recording I thought maybe he could hear me and I said: 'Fred, don't hang up,' and he didn't."

That was ten days after the murder.

"I'm not calling to threaten you – I just want to talk," Nelson said as he pretended to be Nick Harvey. "And then Schockner said, 'Well, do you realize this phone call could be recorded?' And I said that's why you and I are only going to talk in terms we can understand. Do you know who this is? He said, 'I think I do.' I said, 'Well this is the guy who did that work at your house for you.' He said, 'Okay.' I said, 'It's kind of strange. I went down to your house four times and looked at the job to see what I would need, and I never ran into anybody.

"You can imagine my surprise, when I come out this time, and there are cops all over the place," Nelson relayed his conversation as the killer.

"I don't know anything about that," Schockner replied.

"Well I'm not saying I was set up or anything, but I said I need my other half," Nelson described. "He goes, 'Well, you already got it.' I said 'No, I haven't. And then he said, 'Well, you need to talk to Frank.'

"Of course, I already knew who Frank was," Nelson said of the middleman. "I said, '*Well, okay, can you get a hold of him for me?*' Schockner said he'd try to do something for him. I said I would need some help, and I let it go at that.

"Once he gave me Frank, I knew I was in the mix! I didn't want to threaten him – I just wanted him to need me," Nelson said. "My plan was simple: I'm the golden uncle that can control Harvey – I'm the one who can keep the lid on this problem. And my price was getting Nick a better attorney.

"But I also wanted to gauge his reaction to my call," he said. "Schockner didn't say: '*Hey, you motherfucker, you killed my wife!*' Why would a grieving husband even take that call, once he knew who the caller was? There was no outrage or anger from him – nothing a grieving husband would say or do."

Nelson outlined the critical components the case would require for court. "Any kind of conspiracy requires three acts of furtherance," he said. "The phone call would be one, any payoffs would be another, and then additional phone calls would be more acts to the crime. That was our triple play."

• • • •

While some – including a few police officers - still consider the initial police response a botched job, Nelson answered critics from his own perspective: "Everyone likes to 'Monday-morning quarterback' a big case, and this one was no exception." But right from the start, the LBPD spared few expenses, investing countless overtime hours in everything from forensics to surveillance to see the case solved. By then, the television cameras were almost gone, but the *Press-Telegram* dutifully filed updates and stayed with the story.

> **Bixby Knolls Homicide**
> **Prompts Tense Residents' Forum**
> Thursday, Nov. 18, 2004
> LONG BEACH - Emotions ran high in the wake of the death of a Bixby Knolls woman who had her throat slit in her back yard by a burglar as officers stood at her front door. Residents peppered North Division Cmdr. Frank McCoy with questions about policy regarding such calls, with some demanding to know why the officers allowed Lynn Schockner to go back inside her home after making contact with her. One woman accused the police of allowing the woman to be killed right under their noses.

Two weeks after the murder, as Birdsall and Cardoza bucked pressure to reduce expenses and close the case as soon as they could, mistakes were made. One officer almost revealed the wiretap on Schockner's line by inadvertently placing a call to the suspect's home. The detectives were determined to keep pulling strings and plug leaks from the department. Twice the investigators were ordered to shut down the wiretaps that were chewing up so many overtime hours, but Birdsall refused a direct order both times and kept the lines running.

"It seemed like right from the start we were up to our asses in alligators," Birdsall recalled. "We were fighting for this case, trying to do the right thing with our investigation; we wanted to get the best facts and the best case. We already had the dumb ass that did the deed, and we knew we had Jaramillo, a pathological liar who was involved for the money. But we didn't have any hard connections with the guy who set the whole thing up. We wanted to get Manfred most of all, and all the time he thought he was slipping away."

But when a newspaper reporter backed Birdsall into a corner and asked him to confirm details about key evidence found in Nick Harvey's car, he came close to losing his temper. Important details were leaking from any number of cops looking for a little ink or, better yet, face time on TV for those who angled for on-air gigs with the local stations. "The reporter asked me if we had recovered Schockner's business card from Harvey's car. She also knew the amount of money Nick Harvey was supposed to receive for killing Lynn," Birdsall said. "I provided a daily status report with every pertinent aspect for our case, but we never told those details to anyone but our immediate supervisors. Now they were out on the street.

"At this point I said to the reporter: 'I know you have your job to do, but you've got to keep those details out of your paper, at least for now,'" he recounted, successfully plugging the leak. He promised the reporter an exclusive interview when and if more arrests were made, and later provided timely details that allowed her to break the story.

"Up until that point we told everyone in the agency what we

were doing, because I've always believed more eyes looking for information would produce more results. But now things were leaking from the department and we had to be careful with our information; we almost felt like we were looking for a mole in our own ranks, someone who could spill something – accidentally or on purpose – that would close down our investigation.

"I went into my commander's office, closed the door, and told him about the problem. I told him the case could blow up because our office is a sieve for information. We both know that would be just *wrong*. Word went up the chain and the leaks stopped, but even so, the story stayed in the headlines weeks after the killing and the detectives were pressured daily to make a high-profile arrest before Thanksgiving.

Nelson corroborated the tension between cops with different career tracks in mind, and considered it common to most large police departments. There were unending complaints between "streets cops" and "desk jockeys" which invariably involved *resources*, a code for *money*. It always comes back to the bottom line.

"To have so many men monitoring so many phones around the clock means overtime, and that means money, a lot of it," Nelson said. "Typically, some upper management type who's been 'out of the game' for a while gets the problem cases like this one. Their job is to see the case closed. These guys think they know they know the drill from back in the day, but they don't, because they don't know how these matters play out in court today. They see the budget as their primary responsibility, not the case. We have to make sure the DA has enough to get the job done, not just solve the case."

Despite their departmental skirmishes, the chief backed the homicide detectives in the quest for convictions, allowing Birdsall and Cardoza great latitude in the last week of their investigation. Two weeks after the killing, on Monday, November 22, Nelson, posing as "Uncle John," called Jaramillo and began a dialogue that would ultimately reveal the entire plot.

Nelson could pass himself off as a longshoreman on the street or the telephone, and his gruff, rough-and-ready demeanor belied a keen insight into the criminal mind. The transcript doesn't do justice to the tone of their conversations – the recordings revealed Nelson's talent for the role. "Uncle John" badgered Jaramillo with uncomfortable questions, alternately entreating him on behalf of the young killer as his family friend, then squeezing the middleman into other revelations about his arrangement with Schockner. An innocent man would have denounced the payoff, at the very least, and probably called a lawyer. Not Frank Jamarillo. He wasn't aware his cell phone had been bugged since the murder, and he had already placed dozens of calls to the killer as well as Schockner.

John (Nelson): Hey, Frank, my name's John. And, hey I just got off the phone with Nick.

FJ: Okay.

John: He told me to get a hold of you or some guy named Fred…

FJ: Okay

John: He needs some money, I guess for an attorney. Apparently he's really fucked up. I know a little bit about what happened. He seems to think you or Fred will help him out – he doesn't want a public defender. He says you know him.

FJ: I know Nick. I know him.

John: He admits he fucked up, but he doesn't want to face this thing with a public defender. He doesn't have any money. I put a little money on his books, but he needs a lot more, and he said to reach out to you first. He said he really didn't know Fred.

FJ: Yeah, Nick used to work for me.

John: Oh yeah, that's what he said, at the gym. I came down to see him when this shit happened but he said somebody owed him some money. Do you or Fred owe him some money?

FJ: I don't owe him any money.

John: Why would he think that?

FJ: I couldn't tell you.

John: Maybe he's talking about Fred?

FJ: I don't know. If I could help him in any way, I would, but I can't.

John: Well, he seemed to think, that if somebody didn't reach out to him he was going to talk to the cops. He told me to tell Fred. Somebody needs to reach out to him or I think he will talk.

FJ: I'll try my very best but I can't make any promises. I mean, there's very little I can do. I can try to get a hold of Fred, but that's all.

John: He thinks you could reach out to the old man. Nickie seemed to be more upset with him than you. How long would it take for you to get a hold of Fred? I can call back.

FJ: I can try to get a hold of him tomorrow. Let me see if I can find him.

John: All right, I'll call you tomorrow – I know this shit takes some time. Do you have Fred's cell? I guess that's his name? Maybe I can call him if you can't get a hold of him?

FJ: Give me a call tomorrow and I'll see what I can do.

The detective played Jaramillo, feeding him lines and then demanding something in return, pressing the suspect at every turn. Jaramillo bragged he built his reputation as a "go-to guy," someone who could handle all sorts of requests and fix deals, anything from a private massage at the fitness center, a deal on a used car or an expensive watch, even the elimination of a bothersome wife and the expense of a no-fault divorce.

• • • •

While Birdsall and Cardoza managed a steady flow of information forthcoming from fellow detectives, other investigators combed phone records between the trio. Comparing financial records with official statements they were able to reconstruct the financial relationship between Harvey, Jamarillo and Schockner – the money trail. A few days earlier Cardoza received copies of Schockner's bank records and called him November 15 to explain his payments to Jaramillo.

CC: This is Cardoza.

FS: Hello officer, this is Fred Schockner.

CC: Hey, Mr. Schockner, how are you doing?

FS: Ah, there, there has never been anything as bad as this in my life.

CC: Oh, right, right.

FS: But you asked me a couple of questions and I wanted to give you some information. The check that I wrote to Frank was cashed on October 29th. I put it in the account. It was cashed by my bank. Due to the size it probably took a while to get through the system.

CC: Right. So is that the check Frank paid you back with?

FS: No, that's the check that you asked me about, the check that I wrote to Frank.

CC: Correct. And he cashed it on the 29th. Was that one for $100,000?

FS: No, that was for $25,000.

CC: $25,000? For the BMW?

FS: Yes.

CC: Perfect, I'm trying to get this straight. And then the other one you said for $100,000, was that wired into his account?

FS: It was miscellaneous, bits and pieces. Some here, some there. Five, ten, that sort of thing over a period of about a year.

CC: So that would have started at the end of this year?

FS: It started in 2003.

CC: Okay. And they were just miscellaneous checks?

FS: Yeah.

CC: Okay, that was for your businesses and his financial problems.

FS: Yeah, and now you've got me thinking I've been played as a sucker.

CC: Well, you know, he (Jamarillo) said you're a nice guy and maybe there's nothing wrong. It may all check out.

FS: I called him today and asked him about the status of the car on the voicemail.

CC: Okay. You didn't happen to ask him if he was back in the country yet, did you?

FS: No, I just left a voicemail.

CC: Okay, I just wanted to see if we could have a little chat with him. He can call us or whatever he wants to do.

FS: Yeah.

CC: I'm sure he'll be meeting you again.

FS: I'm sure. I'm not worried.

CC: Any other questions you have for us at this time?

FS: Happy fishing. Why is it going so long? Is it because the fishing isn't good right now?

CC: I told you from the beginning; it's a pretty simple case.

FS: You're just trying to determine what's going on?

CC: Yeah, you know, our biggest concern is why they chose you, and to make sure you and your son are okay. Our biggest concern is why this kid (Harvey) came all the way down from Port Hueneme and picked your home.

FS: The kid from Port Hueneme may have been someone that was associated with the lock change (when Lynn re-keyed locks). He may have been associated with someone she met and tried to help. I have no idea.

CC: That's what makes our job kind of tough. We may never know.

FS: Yeah. I have consoled myself because I know you got the man. I'm not concerned about anything any more.

CC: Unfortunately our responsibility is to look at the entire picture and that's what we're doing right now. You know, what could have been the motive for this guy is not telling us his reason. Our job is to look at all avenues.

FS: Harvey probably doesn't even know why he did what he did.

CC: He probably doesn't. We may talk to him again and find out the real deal, but he may not want to talk to us any more. Like I said, that's our biggest concern at this point is your safety.

FS: He's got an attorney now.

CC: Excuse me?

FS: Harvey has an attorney now.

CC: You know what? I believe he does. He's already been arraigned.

FS: My brother told me he has a court-appointed attorney.

CC: Yeah?

FS: But I don't know if he went out and got his own attorney.

CC: A lot of times during the arraignment, it's a court-appointed lawyer, and then he might decide to get his own. At this point we may be fishing, but we'd like to walk away confident that you and Charles are going to be safe.

FS: I know I'm going to be safe because I'm already thinking of moving.

The week before Thanksgiving both cops were relieved to have Lynn's brothers and their families out of their way, and were even more pleased that Charlie would fly to Georgia before the end of the month, but that could be a couple of weeks away. Both Jon and I called Schockner daily to confirm Charlie's plans, but we also pressed him for details about the investigation. He was especially evasive about the phone call he had received from Harvey, and claimed he had received no more. There was nothing from the police, and he remained "paralyzed with grief" over Lynn's killing.

CHAPTER 9

Schockner probably resented his wife's new found resolve when she mentioned a trial separation early in 2004, but he envisioned the end of his marriage soon after she did. He had no intention of sharing the estate with his wife or his son, and began formulating his plan almost a year before the murder. He set the wheels in motion when she filed for divorce at the end of August, moving quietly, enlisting the services of Jaramillo to broker the contract and distance himself from the killer, and the police never found a single direct connect between Schockner and Nick Harvey. As the investigation entered its third week, Jaramillo wanted to extricate himself from their arrangement as soon as possible, looking to close the deal in another telephone conversation with "Uncle John" on November 22. He didn't realize he was digging himself even deeper.

John: Hey, Frank, did you get a hold of Fred?

FJ: No, but between you and me, I don't mind taking care of Nick.

John: You don't mind taking care of him?

FJ: Yeah. I'll take care of him.

John: That's probably a good idea. I went back and saw him and he told me what happened. I know Freddy had his old lady killed.

FJ: Uh huh.

John: I figured you brokered the deal. I told him: 'hey, they need to shut you up.' There's no use in Nick spilling that. It doesn't do him any good at all. Nick just wants what's coming to him.

FJ: Okay. Can you give me about a week to get it together? The police are looking at me right now. I can get it to you within a week.

John: Okay, how much you think?

FJ: Um, I can probably give you like two, if that's okay.

John: Well, that's a start...

FJ: And I'll do my best to get you more and more and more gradually, but you know what I mean.

John: So we're starting at two grand?

FJ: Yeah. Two grand. Two thousand dollars.

John: Alright. That works. I'll put some more money on his books (Harvey's jail account) and told him to shut up until after the holidays.

FJ: Between me and you, I'll just work with you personally and that's off the record.

John: Yeah, cool. You want to meet next week?

FJ: Call me next week and we'll meet wherever you want.

For another ten days, Nelson pressed Jaramillo on Harvey's behalf and forced him to call Schockner for the money. Meanwhile, Birdsall and Cardoza came at the grieving husband from different angles almost every day, never revealing much of anything. Despite their progress with the investigation, and Jaramillo's problem finding funds, the homicide detectives were told wiretaps would be shut down the day before Thanksgiving, and that the warrants would not be renewed because funds were exhausted. Both detectives were stunned, but Birdie wasn't willing to give up any ground, refusing their order at full volume in the crowded squad room.

"We're not going to do that. If we have to go straight eight-hour days, we'll do that, but we're not gonna let money dictate when we're gonna make an arrest," Cardoza said of the tense stand-off after Birdsall's tirade. "They just didn't know what to even say. They were stunned and just left the room; but then they came back a little while later and said they *found* more money. The warrants were extended and the wires stayed up through the holiday weekend."

While the lead detectives fought to keep investigative avenues open, Nelson introduced yet another character into the mix. He claimed Harvey's brother – another fictitious character - was ready to confront Schockner directly if the money didn't come through, and demanded another meeting with Jaramillo on November 29.

As much as he hoped "Uncle John" would just pack up and return to San Francisco, Jaramillo finally knew he would have to come to him with some cash. Police recorded his phone calls to friends for short-term loans, even offering to pay exorbitant street rates, but his credit was gone. Nelson was back on the line, calling to confirm their meeting near the Macy's department store in the Thousand Oaks Shopping Mall. Nelson arrived early to scope the location and insure the suspect would arrive alone, calling him just ahead of schedule. A few minutes later, Jaramillo drove a Lexus LS470 to their meeting. Detective Nelson was wearing a wire to record their conversation, and even on tape in the courtroom three years later, it was obvious the detective had the suspect's complete confidence.

Uncle John: Frank?

FJ: Yeah, that's me.

John: Nice car. Now I know what you spent your money on.

FJ: I gotta get going. I got a grand for you right now because the detectives are still monitoring my accounts.

John: Are they looking at you?

FJ: Yeah.

John: I knew they were sketchy on Fred 'cause I went down there with Nick's mother. She talked to the detectives, and they seemed to think something was up with Fred or with you.

FJ: Fred brought up my name. That's why they keep questioning things, but I don't mind taking care of anything I can.

John: How did this thing get so messed up? Did Nick just screw it up that bad?

FJ: I couldn't tell you. I don't know what happened.

John: I knew he wasn't the sharpest knife in the drawer, but this is bad. I couldn't talk to him a lot, but he seemed to think somebody owed him half. Now, I don't know what that is.

FJ: I owe him $2500 bucks.

John: That's what you owe him?

FJ: Yes. And what I'll do. I'll even give him a little bit more on top of that.

John: Yeah, you better, because he seems to think he should have it. And I don't like being in the middle of this fucking thing either.

FJ: I talked to the girl at the bank. She said that the police have a 30-day monitor on my account. When the 30-day monitoring gets off on the 8th (of December) I can come through.

But Jaramillo had bigger problems than the money he owed the killer or "the big ugly guy with a moustache." Every day for almost a full week, Birdsall and Cardoza came back with more questions for Jaramillo, demanding he explain his financial relationship with Schockner. They braced Schockner with the same regularity, downplaying their suspicions during interviews with either suspect, never suggesting any sort of complicity in the crime while insisting they were simply wrapping up loose ends in their investigation. Nelson documented Jaramillo's admissions, and the homicide detectives used that information to take down their primary suspect.

FJ: The detectives were over at my house. They asked me everything. I told them: 'These are all my funds. This is what I have. This is my business. I answered all their questions.

John: That's smart. I told Nick, "Shut up until you hear from me.' From what I hear, they're already all over Fred.

FJ: Yeah.

John: 'They're sayin it just doesn't add up. Some guy came all the way down from Port Hueneme to burglarize a home in Bixby Knolls?

FJ: Yeah.

John: And the Schockners are going through a bitter divorce. I guess the old man's got money and didn't want to share half of it.

FJ: I told Fred: 'Whatever problems you have between yourself and your wife, I have nothing to do with it.'

John: Other than you found Nick, you know.

FJ: I know Nick. The guy used to work for me.

John: You're right – at LA Fitness. Yeah, but I can't believe he killed that lady. He must have been really hurting for money. Well, he sure fucked himself up, but he thinks he was set up. He came out of the house and there were cops all over the place. Just like that! He felt like he was set up. I said to him: 'Why would they do that?' There's no gain in that.

FJ: No gain whatsoever. Send my respects to him, man, and you know...

John: I'll tell you what. He likes you, but he ain't too thrilled with that old man. You'd think Schockner would help him out. I mean, Nickie's got a girlfriend, and I think she's knocked up.

FJ: I don't mind helping Nick, but I really haven't had a chance to sit down with Fred and talk to him. Give me about a week or two and I'll see what I can do to get you some cash to help out the family or whatever he needs.

John: We're trying to find a better attorney for him. You know they gave him one of these public defenders…

FJ: …who isn't gonna do anything for him…

John: Well, you know the only deal he's got to really give is Fred.

FJ: Yeah.

John: I said, 'Don't do that. You gotta be standup in this shit.'

FJ: Give me a couple of weeks and I'll sit down and talk to Fred and see what we can come up with.

John: Be careful, because they're already looking at you.

FJ: Yeah.

John: All right. So you're the Cubano?

FJ: That's me.

John: Are you really Cuban?

FJ: Yeah.

John: No shit. Were you born there?

FJ: Actually, I was born here, but my full name is Francisco Fidel Jaramillo the 7th. It doesn't get any more Latin than that.

While trying to downplay his role in the crime and gain assurances "Uncle John" would keep a lid on Harvey, Jaramillo was stunned speechless when the detective told him he had received a call from yet another member of the Harvey clan: Nick's brother, "Casey," who left a message that he would call him back the next day. Nelson didn't tell him this would be yet another character interjected into the investigation – a fellow CCAT Det. John Bruce, to call Schockner as "Casey," Harvey's angry brother. At 10 am the next day, just after Bruce had called Schockner posing as Casey, Nelson called Jaramillo to pass along the bad news.

John: Hey Frank. We've got a problem.

FJ: Talk to me.

John: I hate to come to you with this, but I dropped the money off yesterday. His mom and his brother were still in town for the arraignment. I didn't tell her where it came from - I just gave her the money.

FJ: Uh huh.

John: But we got a problem. Nick talked to his brother. A little later Casey pulled me aside, and he said, 'Hey, Nick told me what's up. He's pissed off because he said Fred fucked up by not having his wife out of the house. I was supposed to get in there and set everything up, make it look like a burglary and not be fucking surprised.'

FJ: Okay.

John: I couldn't fucking believe Nick told him that whole thing. But we got him to put a lid on this crap. I had to calm him down, his brother. Do you know the guy – Casey?

FJ: No, I don't.

John: He's from up north somewhere, and he gets all emotional. He's been reading the newspaper articles, and they put Fred's name in the paper. He just wants to go over there and knock on his door. And I go, hey, don't do that, you know. That would really fuck things up."

FJ: Yeah.

John: I said: 'Nick told me what happened a week ago. I'm trying to get him some help. These aren't bad guys. You know, your brother messed up most of all.'

FJ: Okay.

John: I said, they're just watching those guys' bank accounts, and they can't come up with too much cash right now.

FJ: Just to give you a little information, I talked to Fred, and in about two weeks I can probably hook you up with some good cash.

John: Oh yeah?

FJ: Yeah.

John: 'Cause you know a good attorney on a death penalty case doesn't come cheap.

FJ: Of course.

John: Casey said, 'You know I'm not talking about holding this guy hostage for his entire life. I don't feel like I was set up but Schockner he didn't hold up his end of the bargain.'

FJ: I'll take care of the end that you're asking for, but you have to give me just a little time.

John: Well, that's another problem. Casey wants me to meet with Fred. I told him I would call you. He goes, 'Who's Frank?' And I said 'You don't need to know who Frank is.'

FJ: Yeah.

John: But, you know, it's unraveling. You know, I'm self-employed. I've got a business to run. As much as I like this family, I can't spend a whole lot longer down here. I need to get back up in the Bay area and take care of business this weekend.

FJ: Okay. Give me a couple of hours. I'll call you back after I make some arrangements.

Jaramillo drove away in growing unease. Bruce called Schockner a couple of times in character as Casey, hoping wire-taps would catch more admissions as Jaramillo and Schockner exchanged calls.

"It was like pouring gas on the fire," Nelson recalled of the call. "We wanted Frankie to need Uncle John more and more, anything to avoid Casey, and speed up the investigation." Unable to find quick cash to quiet the killer, and stone-walled by Schockner, Jaramillo found himself painted into a corner by his own lies. A few hours later "Uncle John" called back with more bad news:

Uncle John: Hey, Frank, I'm trying to handle these problems. Casey wouldn't listen to me and I wasn't where I could even grab him.

FJ: Uh huh.

John: I was talking to him, and he goes: 'Fuck Fred. I'm gonna go down and knock on his door 'cause I know where he lives. His address is listed, and I'm gonna tell him myself he needs to pay up.' Then I went, 'you're messing up – don't do this.'

FJ: Shit!

John: I don't think I convinced him. You might want to get word to Schockner or something and tell Schockner not to answer his door.

FJ: You gotta let Casey know there are a lot of cops around him right now. Shit. This is not the right time.

John: If I could, I would. But hey, if you can get word to Fred, give him a head's up. You know, to be careful cause we don't know what will happen.

FJ: Yeah, but try to tell them I'm trying to get everything clean and kosher. Now is not a good time.

Uncle John: I know, I know. I thought I'd better call you so you could warn Schockner not to answer his door.

Jaramillo left lots of messages on Schockner's cell phone, calling him between five and fifteen times a day that first week of December, but he ignored most of the middleman's calls and declined his pleas for more money when they spoke. He figured his longstanding generosity toward Jaramillo – more than $100,000 over the past year - had come to an end.

Jaramillo called "Uncle John" the next day, December 2, complaining he was getting drawn into the middle of a problem of which he claimed no part. Finally, Manfred was returning his calls, but now he wanted no part of the old man.

FJ: Hey, what's up, big man? It's Frank.

John: What's going on?

FJ: I just got a call from the detective.

John: Oh, you did?

FJ: They said a guy by the name of Casey [Det. Bruce] called Fred and brought up my name.

John: Oh shit.

FJ: He named me and you.

John: Oh, that fucking Casey. He must have really done it. But how did he have your name?

FJ: I don't know...

John: ...unless Nick told them.

FJ: You know my involvement in this is nothing, so if you can try to talk to him for me, I'd appreciate it.

John: Talk to who?

FJ: Casey.

John: I'll call him and see what I can do. Is that what you wanted?

FJ: Yeah, I'd appreciate it.

John: How'd you find that out? Did Fred call you?

FJ: Yeah, I just talked to him.

John: Oh, geez...What do you think they want from you?

FJ: The cops just asked me if I knew Casey, and I told them I didn't. We'll see what happens.

John: I'll try and get a hold of him right now and give you a yell back.

Schockner blithely claimed indifference toward his partner's problems, but Jaramillo was hanging by a thread. He tried to minimize his link to the killing, but the Harvey clan was banging at the door while the hateful millionaire was determined to squeeze the value from his loans. The wire-taps were especially critical after Thanksgiving, but Birdsall and Cardoza found themselves battling the brass again to sustain overtime and keep their investigation alive. The huge costs of the three-week undercover and wire-tap operation drained tens of thousands from the police budget, and something had to give.

The case broke wide open on Thursday, December 2 with Nelson's call.

Uncle John: Hey Frank. I got a hold of Casey.

FJ: Yeah. What happened?

John: He told me he contacted the old man. 'What good did that do?' He said, 'Schockner denied knowing what I was even talking about.' I said, 'What did you expect?'

FJ: Uh huh.

John: I said to him: 'I haven't even talked to the guy and now you've mentioned my name. Who told you about Frank?' He said Nick mentioned your name. I said, 'You know you guys are fucking it up.'

FJ: Uh huh.

John: I said, 'So you're going to end up with everybody in jail and your brother with no financial help at all.'

FJ: What'd he say?

John: I said: 'You're not thinking straight. Regardless of whether Fred was supposed to have his wife killed or stage a burglary, or whatever he's told you, Nick still messed it up.'

FJ: Yeah.

John: We can sit there and blame the golden goose, Schockner, all you want. But it's not going to help getting everyone thrown in jail.'

FJ: Yeah.

John: I told him you showed up, gave me some good faith money and said you would give up more. 'That guy didn't have to do that, you know?' I told him. 'You just gotta let this thing quiet down.'

FJ: Yeah, what happened is that the detectives called me; they're coming to my house in about a half an hour.

John: I wonder why that happened.

FJ: I'm going to just answer their questions. You tell Casey to keep his mouth shut.

John: If the cops called you then that means Fred called the cops.

FJ: Yeah.

John: You've got to tell Fred to stop doing that.

FJ: Yeah, what I'll do is take care of all the loose ends.

John: Casey assured me he wouldn't bother him anymore.

FJ: Okay, good, and then we'll take care of everything.

Thirty-seven minutes later, Jamarillo received his final phone call from "Uncle John," eleven days after the detective first called him to engage their conspiracy and expose the true crime. Jaramillo had spent the past 72 hours trying to contain crises and shore up the stories that would keep him in the clear, all to no avail. Finally, he found himself caught in a rush of events over which he had no control, inextricably drawn into deep waters and devilish currents far more powerful than anything he ever imagined.

Uncle John: Hey, Frank, it's me. I talked to Casey again.

FJ: Uh huh.

Uncle John: And he wants to call the old man to apologize.

FJ: Yeah, well, don't even bother calling him right now, dude.

Uncle John: Well, that's what I told him: 'No, don't do that.' He said, 'I didn't mean to scare him and wanted to apologize.' I said, 'You know, just let it go.'

FJ: Actually – wait - the detectives are right outside my door right now. Let me call you back in 30 minutes.

CHAPTER 10

Birdsall and Cardoza confronted Jaramillo at 12 noon on December 2 when the suspect welcomed the officers into his home and allowed them to record their formal interview. "Frank, I wanted you to know our investigation is pretty much over," Birdsall said. "Fred got a call last night. Some names were mentioned – Casey was one of them. We asked him [Schockner] to find out if you knew these people, because he claimed he didn't know them."

"Yeah, neither did I," Jaramillo said. "I never heard of them."

"The guy was named Casey, right?" Birdsall asked. "And there was another guy by the name of Uncle John."

"I don't know them," Jaramillo repeated.

"No? Well, okay," Birdsall continued. "So having said that, have you talked to Schockner today?"

"Yeah, I talked to him today," Jaramillo said. "We talked about the arrangements we were making to get him a car."

"Were you going to meet somewhere for an auction?" Birdsall asked.

"Yeah, next Thursday," he said. "We're going to Modesto. I'm trying to get a list of vehicles that will be available. He's thinking about a Volvo, or an Acura."

"Have you guys talked about anything beside the car? Maybe something about the case, or what's going on?" Jaramillo denied anything. "Now, you know Nick Harvey's been in custody for a while now. Has he ever been in contact with you, or tried to get a hold of you?"

"Not at all," Jaramillo said.

"The reason I ask is because his brother, this fellow Casey, he called Fred last night," Birdsall revealed. "Do you know why he would call?"

"I could not tell you," Jaramillo said. "I've never met Casey."

"Do you know a man named John, his uncle or something?" the detective asked.

"No," Jaramillo said.

"So you don't know anybody named 'Uncle John' who is related somehow to Harvey?" Birdsall asked. Jaramillo repeated his denial. "So you wouldn't have any reason to contact the Harvey family, or they wouldn't have any reason to contact you?"

"No reason at all," he said.

"Well, the reason we're here to talk to you – and I've told you this before – we asked you a couple of questions," Birdsall continued. "We already know the answers to those questions and they weren't the answers you just told us. You lied to us and you're in deep shit right now."

They stared at him with disbelief and then relished his anguish when Nelson walked into the apartment, his badge draped around his neck. When Frank saw him for the cop he was, his face sagged. "He looked at me and rolled his eyes," Birdsall said.

Nelson recalled the moment. "That was the first time Frankie didn't have anything to say." I looked him and said: *'Let me tell you something. You've got one play here and that's to cooperate with us. Anything else and the shit just gets deeper."*

"Yeah, I know," he said.

"You need to start getting things straight and thinking about yourself," Cardoza instructed. "Don't think about Fred. Don't think about Harvey. You need to think about Frank. I'm gonna ask you again – do you know a guy named John (Det. Nelson) who's related to Harvey?"

"No I don't," Jaramillo said.

"That's bullshit – he's standing right there. You must know we've talked to the Nick Harvey's family," Cardoza continued. "They've been quite open and have asked us for assistance. So we know they have reached out to you. Why would you lie about that?"

Jaramillo scrambled for an excuse. "I don't want to be involved in this," he said. "You've got to understand, I have had nothing to do with it. A man called me and said that Nick needed assistance. I told him I was sorry but there was nothing I could do for him."

The family reached out to you," Birdsall insisted. "They spoke to you and actually met with you. This is according to Nick's mother. We know that for a fact. Why didn't you tell us that?"

Jaramillo said he was "very intimidated" by their questions but was innocent.

"Fred's already involved you - that's a given," Birdsall countered, denying his assertion before laying out his case. "We didn't pull your name out of a hat – Fred's the one who brought your name up, the one who pointed us to you. You can't change that. And you're lying about a family member getting a hold of you, and meeting with you – why are you denying that part? You better start being honest about what's happening. No bullshit. What's going on right now with you and Nick's family?"

Jaramillo admitted "Uncle John" had called him on behalf of Nick Harvey to get money for a lawyer, but then said he only gave him $1,000 because Nick was a friend who needed help.

"You gave *who* a thousand dollars?" Cardoza asked. "When was that?"

"Detective Nelson," the suspect said. "Two days ago, November 30."

"That was Tuesday, and today's only Thursday. You had to refresh your memory for a check you gave him on Tuesday?" Birdsall countered. "That's all you're gonna give him? You didn't promise any more today?"

"No," he said.

"Okay, so when they tell us you promised them more money, they're lying, correct?" Birdsall demanded.

"I wouldn't say they're lying," Jaramillo replied. "I told them if there's anything more I can help them out with, I'd do my best, but I also told them there's nothing more I can do for them."

Birdsall pressed him for a straight answer. "Nick's mom told us you were going to call Fred to get more money for a lawyer. You are trying to minimize your conversations with these people, but we have talked to them and we know you know more than you are telling us. Now is the time to be totally honest or you are going down with all the rest."

Jaramillo desperately tried to deflect his role in the killing, but delivered a confession instead.

Birdsall: Lynn Schockner was killed. Did you do that?

FJ: No.

Birdsall: Did you want her killed?

FJ: No.

Birdsall: Did Fred want her killed?

FJ: I have a feeling that he did.

Birdsall: Come on, man, cut out that 'feeling' stuff. Your cooperation means everything right now. Did Fred want her killed or not? Yes or no?

FJ: Yes.

Birdsall: How did you help Schockner find Harvey? How did he enlist your aid? How did Nick get hooked up with Fred?

FJ: Originally, Fred asked me about getting some work done at his brother's house. He wanted some furniture moved, or whatever. At that time Nick called me for some money. I couldn't help him, but I gave Nick's information to Fred and they talked. That was the last time I heard about the whole situation.

Birdsall: So your involvement is only…

FJ: …transferring the phone number.

Birdsall: How did you get Nick's number? Did you meet with him? Did you talk to him in person, or over the phone?

FJ: No, I've had conversations with Nick.

Birdsall: Did you meet him at the El Torito Restaurant?

FJ: Yeah, I met him at El Torito for lunch, but it's nothing.

Birdsall: Okay, so you met him for lunch. You gave him Fred's information. 'He wants something done,' you told him, but you didn't know what he wants done?

FJ: Not the extent of it, no.

Birdsall: Don't minimize what's going. Just stop that crap. Did Fred say: 'I want Lynn offed because she's getting my money?'

FJ: Yes he did.

Birdsall: What, exactly, did Fred tell you he wanted done?

FJ: He said: 'this is the point where I'm gonna have to take care of that situation. I have to move on with my life.'

Birdsall: 'Take care of that situation?'

FJ: In plain words, that he wanted to get rid of her. He wanted his wife dead.

Birdsall: So this guy from Port Hueneme – Nick Harvey - is gonna help somebody in Long Beach just because you magnanimously feel you could set these guys up and they can mutually help each other? Think about how that sounds. You were told by Fred to find somebody to kill his wife, and you did. You chose Harvey.

FJ: I didn't specifically choose Nick.

Birdsall: Did you ask other people?

FJ: No.

Birdsall: He's the first person you asked?

FJ: Nick needed money, okay? I hooked him up with Fred because Fred needed some work done. And when I found out about the situation, it bothered me so much I didn't want to be involved.

Birdsall: How much money did you give Nick?

FJ: $2500.

Birdsall: Out of your own pocket? Why?

FJ: Because Fred said he'd pay me back when the job was done.

Birdsall: So you gave him $2500?

FJ: Yeah, and then I gave John a thousand dollars, and I offered him $1500 more. That's all.

Birdsall: So $5,000 for the total deal? And Fred would pay you back the money you put up front. That's your obligation?

FJ: Yeah, that's my obligation.

Birdsall: Okay. We understand. Have you ever been involved in any conversations between Nick and Fred?

FJ: No, not once.

Birdsall: So, if I were to say that on the day of the murder, Nick called you up in the morning, is that true?

FJ: Yeah, he did call me, but the conversation was very short.

Birdsall: I know it's short because I saw the timeline. What'd he tell you?

FJ: He said: 'Hey, I'm going to help out your friend, Fred. I'll talk to you later.' I said, 'okay.' Then, when I got the phone call from Fred, he told me: 'There's a homicide.' That's when everything just really bothered me.

Birdsall: Why didn't you tell us this from the very beginning?

FJ: Because I did not want to be involved, whatsoever.

Birdsall: But you were involved – you *are* involved - and you can't just talk your way out of it.

FJ: I'm involved in the sense of introducing one person to another; but I'm not involved in the situation, not in the sense of doing something wrong.

Birdsall: Let me spell it out for you. You found a murderer for a husband who wanted his wife dead. You not only found the person and worked as a conduit, but you furnished them with money from your own pocket, up front, with the understanding that you're gonna be paid back.

FJ: Yeah.

Birdsall: Do you understand where that puts you?

FJ: Yeah, I understand where it puts me, but you have to understand something: when I spoke to Fred, I did not know this was gonna happen. The conversation between Nick and Fred, that's between them. That's not my wrongdoing, whatsoever.

Birdsall: Well, listen to this: you are the middleman in this murder, because you recruited one man to kill for somebody else. That is the situation you're in right now. By lying to us from the very beginning, you're showing us you are conscious of your guilt, that you know you're involved.

FJ: I respect that, but I had no wrongdoing here. My standpoint is this: I have had nothing to do with whatever Fred and Nick have done. Fred's given me money. So if he asks me to do something, I'm gonna help him out as much as I can.

Birdsall: Here is the question: 'Did you do all this because of that money Fred has given you?'

FJ: No, not at all.

Birdsall: It's been over $100,000 he's given you. You're aware of that?

FJ: Yeah, I'm aware of that.

Birdsall: Okay, well, what's it look like to us? This person you borrowed over $100,000 from comes to you – and nobody else – and recruits you to find somebody to kill his wife. You front the first money, and you pony up more money, and you have talked to Nick Harvey. When I talk about the phone records, I'm not bullshitting you. We have those. We have Nick's cell phone. We have it all the way back to when you first talked to Nick about this. When was that?

FJ: Maybe about 45 days ago, say two months. But then again, I've talked to him more over times when he was at Ames.

Birdsall: When did you have lunch with Harvey at the El Torito restaurant when you gave him the money?

FJ: I would say three weeks before that killing. We met at the place in Thousand Oaks.

Birdsall: And that's when you gave him Fred's business card?

FJ: Yeah. Fred asked me to give it to him.

Birdsall: Did Harvey ever mention talking to Fred?

FJ: No, he didn't.

Birdsall: You're right – there are no phone records between Nick Harvey and Manfred Schockner, ever.

FJ: Okay.

Birdsall: So the only person that has ever talked to or directed Nick Harvey to commit the murder of Lynn Schockner is you. Period. So stop minimizing what you said, that you don't know what they've been talking about, because we know you have talked to them many times.

FJ: They must have talked, but I don't know what was going on.

Birdsall: We have taped exactly what you said. You're the middleman for this murder. You're the one that recruited somebody for somebody else. You're as responsible as the person that stuck the knife in her throat.

FJ: I'm not responsible for that. I'm not involved.

Birdsall: You gave money from Fred Schockner to Nick Harvey to kill Lynn Schockner. That puts you in the mix, and right now you're gonna have to start telling us how Fred approached you, how Fred expressed why he wanted this person, and what he wanted him to do. Your total honesty right now is gonna control your future and your fate.

FJ Understood.

Birdsall: Denying your acts and minimizing your involvement will hang you. Do you understand that?

FJ: Yes.

Birdsall: Start at the beginning. How many months ago did Fred contact you to find somebody to kill his wife?

FJ: First, he was telling me about the divorce and how she's gonna take like $2.5 million. Fred says to me: 'My friend back east won't be able to do something for me, in terms of helping me out with my money. Can you help me out? My life would be so much easier if I she was just gone. Then two months ago he told me: 'I hired somebody to kill my wife,' so I forgot about it. But then a week-and-a-half later he asks: 'Do you know anybody that would do any work for me?'

Birdsall: So you say, 'I found somebody who might help you, taking care of Lynn for you,' correct?

FJ: I did not say that. I said 'I have somebody that will help you with whatever. I didn't find out until a week later that he was using Nick for the same problem.

Cardoza: How did you find that out?

FJ: Fred said 'I'm gonna have him do what I asked. The thing my other friend couldn't do.' I said, 'You're kidding me, right?' And then it went downhill from there.

Birdsall: Downhill to what?

FJ: My involvement with Nick was to help him out with money. I gave him information about an individual that needed help. Whatever information was shared between them, I don't know.

Birdsall: But Fred communicated to you he's gonna give you five thousand dollars to give to Nick?

FJ: Yes.

Birdsall. And you decided to give him $2500 up front and then $2500 more when he completed the job, right?

FJ: I said all I could do is give him $2500.

Birdsall: And you knew you were giving him the money so he could kill Lynn. He told you that, right?

FJ: Yeah, about a week-and-a-half later. Schockner said 'I'm want Nick to kill Lynn.' And I said, 'I can't believe you're doing what you're doing. In all respect, whatever you're doing, that's on you. That's not on me, dude.'

Birdsall: Okay.

FJ: And that when he was saying, 'You know, Frank, you owe me money.' And I said there's no secret about that, but your actions are uncalled-for.

Cardoza: Did you ask for the $2500 back?

FJ: Yes I did.

Cardoza: And then what?

FJ: Schockner said: 'You owe me more than $2500 – I'm not gonna give it back to you.'

During the 90-minute interview Jaramillo relayed details about the timetable for the operation, including Harvey's two surveillance trips to the house before the murder. While he tried to downplay his role in the crime, Birdsall spelled out the plain truth: "Your credibility's in the shitter. You've lied from the very jump. You've minimized everything you've done, but that doesn't change a thing. We're just asking you – again – to start thinking about being honest, and totally up front."

"Oh, I understand," Jaramillo replied, explaining the instructions he passed to Harvey, specifying certain days he should scope out the Bixby Knolls residence. Jaramillo offered other obfuscations, insisting Harvey would relay Fred's instructions whenever they spoke. "I do not know how they communicated," he insisted.

"Let me drop this one final thing on you right now," Birdsall offered. "We interviewed Nick Harvey and he laid out everything to us. That's why we know you met at El Torito, where you gave him Fred's business card with hand-written notes on the back. We knew about the $5000 and how you told him what to do. Everything. He never talked to Fred, not once. You did, and you've just put yourself in a deep hole."

Jaramillo mumbled an affirmative and described how Schockner instructed him to tell Harvey how and when he should visit the neighborhood to scope out the job. He claimed Schockner must have talked to the killer because Harvey had the alarm codes and other information about the house that he had not provided. The detectives then produced their extensive collection of telephone records.

"You were the go-to guy, Frank" Birdsall persisted. "Fred's calling your marker and jacking you around for the money you owe him, and that's your motivation. Every time a crime's committed, there are always means and motivation. Guess what? Money's always the biggest motivator, and you paid the money.

"Fred told me the easy way into the house from the alley, and the code for the alarm," Jamarillo admitted. "He told me to warn Nick that if the dog's not in the backyard, Lynn is home. He told me to tell Nick to remember the code if he breaks into the house."

The detectives pretended surprise when Jaramillo admitted Manfred had called him earlier that day to tell him "Casey" called Schockner to extort money. When they asked if he would be willing to contact him again, he willingly agreed.

Although his confession now entered its second hour, Jaramillo still hadn't been arrested, and spoke freely and permitted five other LBPD detectives to search his condominium. As the search progressed, Birdsall asked the middleman to "walk us through the entire matter from the beginning to the end."

FJ: Fred called me about two months ago, telling me how ruthless the divorce was going to be. That was his description:

vicious. I knew it was going to be half the house, half the assets, equivalent to about two-and-a-half million dollars, maybe more.

Birdsall: He was angry at Lynn?

FJ: Yeah, he was angry because she got legal help, and they couldn't settle it themselves. He hated that lawyer, and hated Lynn for hiring her.

Birdsall: Did he ever talk about hiding some of the assets and doctoring some legal document?

FJ: I know he always used to say he hid a lot of money back East. I guess he has some friend in Atlanta who owns some bars or something.

Birdsall: What precipitated him calling you and saying, 'I want her out of the way?'

FJ: At first I thought he was blowing smoke, you know, but then he said what he wanted to happen. He was going to hire somebody from Atlanta or somewhere to kill Lynn, but then a while later he told me that didn't work out.

Birdsall: The deal to get her killed?

FJ: I guess. He told me to pay that money back I owed him, but then he said we could work things out if I knew of anyone who could help him out with a couple of things. That's when I told him about Nick Harvey, and he asked me: 'Do you mind fronting up the money because of how much you owe me?' I told him I would do that and I gave Nick the $2500. About a week later, Fred called to ask: 'Do you think Nick would take care of my business? Could he take care of Lynn?' That's when I got kind of defensive....

Birdsall: ...but what happened? Why did you have to ultimately decide to assist him in this?

FJ: Because he pushed in my face that I owed him money. He said, 'Kid, you got to help me out with this if you want to settle our debt.'

Birdsall: He basically threatened you?

FJ: Yes, and that's a formal threat, plain and simple. Absolutely.

Jaramillo recalled meeting Harvey when he asked him to help his friend with odd jobs: moving furniture, minor remodeling and some other things as well. The middleman remained coy about his explicit instructions, but had already admitted arranging the hit. "He wants to give you a little bit of money up front, and when the job is done, he'll give you the rest." He gave him Schockner's business card, the layout of the house, the alarm code and $2500 in cash. Almost in the same breath, he insisted he didn't know the nature of the tasks at hand.

"So Fred told you to give him $5000 for a job that you don't even know what it's about?" Birdsall asked, incredulous. "Did you find that strange?"

"I didn't know what needed to be done," Jamarillo said, but then admitted Harvey called him a week later and said: "You know, your boy Fred wants me to take out his wife. He wants me to kill her."

Jamarillo said he called Schockner immediately after this meeting, and told detectives he became hostile on the phone. He said: 'Don't worry about this because I'm gonna come out of this. You know what, Frank? You owe me money, so just get it done."

Jaramillo said Harvey called him back a few hours later to tell him he "wasn't comfortable with the environment." Jaramillo immediately called Schockner, who again demanded the contract be carried out right then.

"You said you felt threatened by Fred because you owed him a hundred thousand dollars," Birdsall commented. "He's gonna absolve all your debt if you took care of Nick? Fred made it clear if you paid him, your debt was gone?"

"Yes," Jaramillo replied, sealing his fate. "I have told you guys an honest truth of it – pretty much scripture – from A to Z. Just that, 100 per cent."

On that note the detectives pressed him to call Schockner. "When you talk to Schockner on the phone right now, you want to just simply do the right thing, right?"

"Yes," Jaramillo asserted, dialing Schockner from his wiretapped cell phone line. After complaining to Schockner that the police continued to demand details about his relationship with the killer and the widowed husband, he asked Schockner to meet him that day, as soon as possible. "There's no reason why they should point to you," Schockner said, agreeing to meet him that evening.

• • • •

Nelson coaxed Jaramillo to wear the department's denim vest, one equipped with audio and video feeds, the same garment "Uncle John" wore during their Macy's parking lot meeting when the middleman handed the undercover detective the balance of the money he owed Harvey. Still, Jaramillo denied his role in the crime and believed he would go free, Nelson said.

"I said to him: 'You're a bright guy, Frank. We want you to talk with Fred about Nick, and what went wrong, so we can implicate Schockner,'" Nelson explained. "I think, for some reason, Frank thought if he did all this, we were going to let him go. He's talking to his wife on the phone, and he tells her 'I'm gonna go help these guys - I should be back for dinner.'"

Years later Nelson and I shared a second beer in the noisy 11th floor bar at the Long Beach Airport Holiday Inn, that strange round motel with an unobstructed view of concrete and asphalt. Nelson chuckled at the memory. "He just didn't quite get it. Even afterwards, he insisted because he didn't commit the killing, he wasn't involved. Well, that was his fantasy, not mine.

I told him: 'You didn't stab her, but you found the guy, you paid the guy, and you told him when to go down there. You don't pay someone $5,000 just to rob a house. You paid Nick to kill Mrs. Schockner.'

"You can lie to your friends and I'll lie to mine, but let's not lie to each other," Nelson insisted.

But he also explained the subtle tactics he used to trap Frank Jaramillo and nuances of the investigation that never reached the public eye. Had Harvey escaped, Schockner's oblique strategy probably would have succeeded; but once police had the killer's cell phone, all their efforts to distance themselves from each other fell apart. The suspects forgot the first lesson of criminal success.

"That's the mistake they made," he stated, chuckling sardonically in memory of Harvey, Jaramillo and Schockner. "Three can keep a secret only if two of them are dead."

CHAPTER 11

More than three weeks after Lynn bled out on her back porch, Jaramillo's confession provided Long Beach police with probable cause to arrest their lead suspect - Manfred Schockner - and end their costly investigation. But that wasn't the way the detectives wanted to close the case. Birdsall and Cardoza prepped Jaramillo to meet Schockner while wearing a wire.

Their first call was to DDA Barnes, asking her legal approval for their plan, how to document their findings, and specific instructions for Jaramillo before he met Lynn's husband at an Asian seafood restaurant near the house. Barnes endorsed their plan to get Schockner on the record and gave her sanction for the undercover operation. "She never pulled a punch," Birdsall said with a smile. "Cyndi is one tough lady, a tenacious attorney who really watches the details. She'd worked dozens of hard-core criminal cases, and really knew her stuff. She wanted this one as bad as we did."

While the detectives developed their tactical script, assigned surveillance and stationed perimeter posts for the operation, they ignored calls from their boss. Anxious to wrap up their plans and trap the final suspect, they still wanted to play a trump card for the prosecution and insure convictions.

"We needed to talk to him [Schockner] now, we needed to get him [Jaramillo] wired up, and we needed to move fast," Cardoza recalled. "The gig was up that day. We took Jaramillo into custody and called our commander to advise him what we were going to do," he continued. "He immediately said: 'You can't do that – it's not legal.' We told him we had contacted our DDA, who approved the legality of the operation. As soon as Birdie got off the phone he looked over at me and said: 'If we're going to do this, we gotta move now!'"

"I've got to admit – Richard has some real *cajones*," Cardoza said of his partner. He was senior on the team and he stood up to the brass many times. "Our sergeant called us into his office and ordered the investigation closed: 'The command staff wants to wrap this thing up and arrest him (Schockner) tonight. We've got a press conference set for tomorrow morning.

"Birdie goes: 'We're not doing that,' and all hell broke loose," Cardoza continued. "The sergeant yelled 'I'm telling you to go fuckin' arrest him,' and Birdie shouts right back in his face: 'No. We're not doing that.' And the sergeant hollers back: 'How am I gonna explain to *them* that you guys don't wanna do that?' We told him we don't have everything in order to do it.

"Birdie whispered: 'You need to order me to do it.'" Cardoza continued, recalling his partner's precise demand. "The sergeant stands up tall, hitches his pants and says: 'I'm ordering you to make that arrest.' Birdie looked him right in the eye and said: 'Fuck you. I'm not doing that. I have the right to refuse an unlawful order, and I'm doing so.'

"Our commander didn't know what to do – he couldn't put it to paper because he knew Richard was right. The moment passed and we just split, but turned off our cell phones as soon as we reached the elevator. That was just another battle we had."

"You have to understand the pressure on the whole department," Cardoza said. "Some thought the officers screwed up at the beginning, even though the killer was apprehended. I'm sure they thought the department looked bad and worried about litigation. However it played out, but there was intense pressure to make this arrest for almost a month; but we knew if there were problems for the prosecution, the first finger would be pointed at us: *You guys screwed the pooch!*

• • • •

As the homicide team carried Jaramillo to the restaurant a half hour before Schockner was due, a dozen other detectives took assignments for their roles in surveillance, protection and even crowd control, if the situation warranted. Despite the discord with some of the LBPD brass, the department didn't hedge on the operation; fully manned, the Schockner investigation was about to reach critical mass. After donning the electronic vest, technicians checked the connections and sent Jamarillo on his way.

It was 7:30 pm that Thursday evening when Jaramillo entered the LV Seafood Restaurant at Carson and Lakewood Drive, only a half dozen blocks from Lynn's home in Bixby Knolls. Several undercover officers were already stationed in and around the restaurant. The tape began with an exaggerated, almost surreal image of Schockner showing a scribbled note to his friend: *Are You Wired?* Jaramillo shook his head, but then the camera failed. After that, the police relied on audio.

FJ: Hey old man, how are you feeling?

MS: Absolutely shitty. How're you doing?

FJ: I'm scared, man, I'm really scared.

MS: They tell me it's over. I told you not to worry.

FJ: I don't know if it's over or not. You know you and I would not be sitting here if you didn't want Lynn killed.

MS: I don't know what you're talking about. We're not gonna mention that again. I don't know anything about that.

FJ: You have to understand – Nick's family is calling me and

I'm getting hit with everything, and all kinds of information.

MS: Don't say anything. I'm not saying anything.

FJ: Tell me what you want me to do. I don't have any answers anymore, Fred. I'm scared.

MS: Well, don't answer them [the detectives] anymore. You've given them everything you have, right?

FJ: True.

MS: There are two things that make this go away. The first is the money trail. When the trail gets eliminated, and paid off, it just goes away.

FJ: So you think, just by paying off the money I owe you, that's gonna solve everything?

MS: No, it's not gonna solve everything, but that's where we have to start. They are trying to follow me and that's the problem for me.

FJ: You really think that?

MS: Yes, I'm not lying or anything for you.

FJ: Me either and on top of that I'm broke I need to get something solved here because I'm meeting [the detectives] again. They're coming to my house tomorrow.

MS: Again?

FJ: Yes. I don't know if Nick has talked or what.

MS: Like I've told you on the phone – I've gotten two calls and I don't know if they're from the police or from whoever it is.

FJ: They're looking at me as the main suspect. I'm scared.

MS: I'm scared, too, okay? Otherwise, I wouldn't be here.

FJ: We have to settle what's going to happen here, right now.

MS: Then have someone shoot me. That's the only way it'll go away.

FJ: So when they come to me, you think I should go to jail for your problem.

MS: What can I do?

FJ: We would not be here right now if it wasn't for Lynn, you know that.

MS: One way or another, I'm a dead man,

FJ: And that's supposed to make me feel better, right?

MS: I'm not saying anything, anymore.

FJ: Gee thanks, Fred.

MS: I'm not going to leave you high and dry. Like I said – they're pushing us from both sides. Nothing will happen if we both maintain our cool.

FJ: So what advice do you have for me? You tell you don't want to talk right now – when else can I talk to you? I can't go to your house – I don't now who's gonna be there. And you don't answer my calls.

MS: I know that. I don't know what the answer is.

FJ: You think that's the answer for me? Because I tell you right now – I'm leaving – I'll get out of the country.

MS: That might be the solution for you.

FJ: You think that's the easy solution for me? Leave my family?

MS: I don't think that's an easy solution, but I don't know how all this happened.

FJ: How all this shit really went down is because of you – we would not be here if it wasn't for Lynn. You and I both know that.

MS: Or if he [Harvey] didn't get caught. It's not just one-sided.

FJ: It's not a question of one-sided. He got caught for something you wanted done, not me. His family is coming after me for something that you wanted done, bud.

MS: Can we stop this conversation? It's not doing any good.

FJ: What should I do? You want me to just go to the detectives and tell them everything I know?

MS: What good does that do?

FJ: I don't know – you tell me. I understand you are thinking of yourself right now, but I have a family, too.

MS: I'm not thinking of myself…I was told not to come here.

FJ: Told by who? By your lawyer? So you're telling me you are covering your own ass and cutting me loose?

MS: He's not my lawyer – he's my friend; and no, I'm not just looking out for myself. I don't know what to say or do.

FJ: I'm scared. You're scared, too, I understand, but you have to understand we would not be in this position if it wasn't for Lynn. You understand, this young man's gonna do time because of you?

MS: That's true, and if it hadn't have been sloppy on Nick's part.

FJ: So we have to do this quiet. We have to make sure he stays quiet with his family.

MS: You can give him money or whatever, but I don't have any money to give you. I'm leaving.

FJ: We need to settle this now, Fred.

MS: We can't do it here. We need to go somewhere out in the open.

FJ: I want to settle things now.

MS: What do you want me to say? I can't make it go away. Can you?

FJ: So basically, you walk away and I get fucked, right?

MS: You don't get fucked.

FJ: Oh, really? The cops are looking at me pretty hard.

MS: They told me today, or yesterday, this whole thing is over, and you've answered all their questions. There's nothing to connect you, is there?

FJ: I know both of you – you and Nick – that's not just a coincidence.

MS: What do you want me to say? How do you want me to answer that?

FJ: We need to get this thing over and done. We would not be here if it wasn't for you – it's that simple.

MS: And we wouldn't be here if it weren't for the way Nick fucked up everything. That's what I'm trying to tell you – why do you think I wrote you a note like I did? They can't put anything together if you don't say anything more.

FJ: They're putting things together by putting my name to it, because I knew both of you. It doesn't take a brain surgeon to understand this. I need to keep Nick quiet to do a favor for you.

MS: Give him whatever he needs, but I can't give him anything now.

FJ: I'm broke. What am I going to tell the family?

MS: Look, the two phone calls I got from Casey were for money. [Harvey] apparently believes he hasn't been paid.

FJ: He needs a lawyer. Do you know what it is to pay a lawyer to get you off death row? Do you realize he is doing time because of you? Who'd he do the favor for? Not me. It was you.

MS: I don't even know the man

FJ: If the kid talks, I'm going down, because you wanted something to move forward.

MS: It's not my mistake.

FJ: You think I'm going down for your mistake? For what you wanted?

MS: It's not my mistake – I don't know what to say to you. Everything will be okay.

FJ: Can you guarantee that, Fred?

MS: I can't guarantee anything.

FJ: I can't trust any fuckin' thing you say to me. This young man's gonna do time, I'm gonna do time, all because of you. Thank you, Fred, why don't you go right now? Let me enjoy my fuckin' food and you can leave. If I have to, I'll talk to the cops.

MS: You shouldn't have to. There is no answer - do you understand that? What do you want me to do – go to the police?

FJ: The truth has to come out.

MS: What good does that do? You know what happens if the truth comes out? The same thing happens to all of us, no matter what.

FJ: Really?

MS: Isn't that the case?

FJ: We wouldn't be here if you didn't want Lynn killed.

MS: If you say that to me one more time, I'll just get up and leave. It happened, okay? You know, if I turned it around on you, it would be the same. What're you gonna do?

FJ: I would never do that to my wife, so you can't put me in the same situation.

MS: I know you're angry right now.

FJ: You know I'm angry? You must be some sort of goddam genius.

MS: So you shouldn't have done it. What am I supposed to say?

FJ: Just for grins, let's say Nick talks. So when the detectives come over tomorrow, it's bye-bye, Frank. Who's gonna take care of my family? Not you, obviously. You have to understand – this is your problem.

MS: No, it's not my problem. It's our problem.

FJ: You benefit more than anybody. It erased your problem – you saved millions. If you want to leave, go ahead. I'll wait for a friend to pick me up. I'm in the same boat you are, and I don't want to be followed.

MS: You understand what I said before about the trail of money – that's really what this whole thing is about.

FJ: Okay, so let me say in the hypothetical – I take a fall for you, for something you wanted done, right?

MS: How do you do that if you don't talk?

FJ: It's not a question of talking anymore – what about Nick?

MS: What's Nick gonna do?

FJ: He's gonna serve time for you, that's what Nick is gonna do, and he is doing that right now.

MS: Are you wired?

FJ: No I'm not.

MS: I don't know what to say – I can't say anything.

FJ: You need to take care of Nick's family.

MS: If I do that, they'll put all of us away.

FJ: It's not a question of putting us all away, Fred. It's something you wanted done.

MS: And it's something that you did.

FJ: Are you saying I killed Lynn?

MS: Nope, I'm saying you arranged things.

FJ: Who wanted her dead? Answer me that question – who wanted her dead? Who benefited from that, Fred?

MS: Nobody benefited. Come on, Frank, do you want me to stay here and try to resolve something with you or leave?

FJ: You have to resolve it. You wanted her dead - not me.

MS: You should back off right now. What am I gonna do? Give us a chance to think and talk together.

FJ: That's why I'm here.

MS: No, what you're doing here is trying to incite me to say things or do things. You keep saying this over and over again.

FJ: Okay, why don't you just go home? Thank you very much. And I'll tell Nick the same. Have a good evening, bud. Whatever I owe you, I'll pay you back. Don't worry about Nick and me anymore. I asked you a simple fucking question and you wouldn't answer it. That tells me everything I need to know.

MS: I can't answer it because I don't know the answer. You created this problem – not me.

FJ: Oh, really?

MS: Didn't I put cash in your pocket?

FJ: Yeah, but I don't have anything now. I'm asking you to do one thing – take care of Nick's family. Pay them.

MS: I can't do that now.

FJ: What am I supposed to tell them?

MS: I don't care - you give them some money. You can do whatever you want.

FJ: Really? I don't have it.

MS: Well, I don't have it either.

FJ: Obviously, our conversation's done. It's my problem, right? I'll tell you something right now – it's more your problem than mine, because it's something you wanted done.

MS: You know what, Frank? You can do whatever you want, but it's not going to affect me one way or another.

FJ: It already has. I've got to deal with a young man and his family because he is going away for life, maybe the needle, for something you wanted. Not because of something I wanted.

MS: I don't want to leave you high and dry. I don't have the cash flow right now.

FJ: Well, you need to find it soon, because I'm not going to take a fall for you. Sorry. No can do.

MS: I can't. There's no way I can do anything. No matter what I do, we all go down.

FJ: The fact of the matter is, I'm gonna go down for something you wanted. That's the difference. Why don't you just admit what you did was wrong.

MS: I haven't done anything wrong.

FJ: And I did everything, right?

MS: No, you haven't done anything wrong, either. That's what you told me on the phone.

FJ: I'm here because of your problem.

MS: And you know what? We're both here because of another problem.

FJ: You need to cover Nick from your pocket. I don't have a dime.

MS: I don't have the cash for Nick's family because you

have all my available cash right now. So if you just give me the cash you owe me, I'll give it right back to you and you can do whatever you want.

FJ: Huh? What the fuck? Just get out of here, you asshole!

• • • •

Manfred stepped away from the table as the waiter approached, pocketing the note he had flashed at Jaramillo, excusing himself to the restroom before making a quick detour for the door. When the waiter presented the bill, Jaramillo pointed toward his companion shuffling toward the exit. "My friend's gonna cover the tab," he said, taking a drink of water from his glass. When Schockner was out of earshot Jamarillo whispered into the microphone implanted in the denim vest: "That motherfucker came with a list with all kinds of questions from his lawyer (Later recovered, they were written on a narrow sheet of promotional note paper provided by Schockner's local realtor). The first thing he did before we started was to flip to the other side of the paper where he wrote: 'Are you wearing a wire?' He asked me and I answered him 'No' three times."

Unexpectedly, Schockner strolled back into the restaurant and to their booth. He mumbled a few words, incomprehensible even to the informant, and then stalked back out onto the street. He drove straight home, tailed discreetly by a pair of surveillance vehicles. Nelson de-briefed Jaramillo immediately after the operation and transported him to LBPD headquarters where he was arrested and interrogated a final time.

As the restaurant operation was coming to a close, Birdsall and Cardoza organized a thorough search of the area, hoping to find Manfred's scribbled note. Litter and trash revealed nothing of substance, and squad cleared the scene. They received another call from headquarters – the same sergeant repeating the same message - but the detectives held out hope for the note and had one last gambit to play.

"We were sure Schockner would call his lawyer that night. We figured the wiretap would give us more evidence against the husband and possibly implicate his lawyer, Neil Ivan," Cardoza said. "But our commander wanted Schockner arrested right then. They worried he might split," Cardoza said. As it turned out, both parties were wrong. Schockner never left his home that night because Neil Ivan arrived a half hour after his arrival and spent the night.

The next morning, Friday, December 3, Lynn's husband was arrested at home. Ivan opened the door when Birdsall and Cardoza arrived early the next morning, just after 7 am, along with a half dozen other detectives.

"He and his attorney were already up," Birdsall recalled. "We got Neil's statement, which was basically a bunch of bullshit, and then we got Fred alone, back in his bedroom office.

"I walked in and said: 'Hey, I understand you met with Jaramillo last night.' He just looked at me and said: 'Oh shit.' I looked at him and smiled: 'I guess we're not as dumb as we look - you're under arrest. The look on his face was classic: his jaw dropped, his eyes bugged out and the color literally drained from his face. His shoulders sagged in the chair. It was worth the wait.

"Chris and I jerked him out of his chair, hauled him upright and fixed the cuffs. He demanded his attorney." Birdsall recalled. "He didn't mean Ivan, who had surrendered license to the California Bar Association, but his "real" attorney, Jack Stennett. There is nothing more satisfying in life than confronting a scumbag and slapping cuffs on his wrists. It is one of the truly glorious moments in life, especially with an asshole like Schockner."

CHAPTER 12

A week before Manfred's arrest, he made good on his promise to send Charlie to our Georgia home the Saturday after Thanksgiving. I collected him late, near midnight, at Jacksonville International Airport and brought him north to St. Simons Island. Over a home-cooked meal, Susan and I offered to share our island lives without reservations or conditions; since Charlie didn't need much of an opening, he accepted without missing a beat. Whether he was so ready to distance himself from his dad or felt the connection of our strong recent bonds, I don't know; nor do I care.

When police finally took Schockner into custody almost a week later, Charlie was less saddened than relieved. "I told you so," he said. "I always knew he arranged her death." Even so, I saw my sister's eyes fearful in his face when memories crossed his brow, quickly erased as he regained his composure. Thanks to his father, his demons ran deep, but the world works in mysterious ways, and nature always strives toward balance, and usually finds an equilibrium.

Schockner, normally a shrewd and exacting negotiator, gave up his son without protest or complaint. Usually, any kindness came with some sort of condition, but he offered his son with no strings attached. It was the bargain of a lifetime, one that rewards me more every day, but Manfred made the deal without a second thought. I still can't measure the irony. We litigated over every aspect of the estate, but I would have signed over every cent for this life with my new son. He didn't even haggle. The man who had my sister killed gave me the greatest gift of my life, a son of my own, a boy of my own blood. Go figure.

On Friday my brother and I received an email from DDA Cyndi Barnes, followed by a personal call to field questions she knew we were sure to ask.

> *Manfred Schockner was arrested today (Dec. 3, 2004) by Long Beach Police Department for the murder of Lynn Schockner. Long Beach Police also arrested a third suspect, Frank Jaramillo, a friend of Manfred Schockner. The press does not know about these two arrests yet. I know that you will have many questions about these arrests and the evidence that has been developed since the murder of your sister. Because the investigation is still ongoing, I am not able to disclose those details to you right now. However, once the investigation is completed, I will answer whatever questions you have.*

Birdsall also reached out with a personal call that day, outlining the extent of the investigation before explaining why everyone, especially our family, was kept in the dark. "It had to be done," he said. The detective revealed other details of the LBPD "sting," some key evidentiary points, and how the case was closed. A couple of days later, the *Press-Telegram* stretched the story across the front page:

> **Police tell of fees for killer, go-between**
> Monday, December 06, 2004
> LONG BEACH — A former gym trainer was promised $5,000 to slit the throat of a Bixby Knolls woman on behalf of the woman's husband, but a

middleman in the plot was paid as much as $25,000 to broker the deal, authorities said Monday.

The alleged financial arrangement of the three men now charged with the capital murder of Lynn Schockner, 50, came to light four days after the arrest of Manfred Schockner, 64, who stood to lose half of the couple's cash and property in a pending divorce, according to lead detectives in the case. The estate is worth an estimated $4 million to $5 million, detectives said.

Schockner was scheduled to be arraigned today in Long Beach Superior Court on charges of first-degree murder for financial gain, second-degree robbery and first-degree burglary. The alleged middleman, Frank Jaramillo, 29, of Woodland Hills, appeared in court Monday on the same charges, but his arraignment was postponed until Dec. 16.

Both men as well as the accused killer, Nicholas Harvey, will be eligible for the death penalty if convicted.

The case gained national attention because Lynn Schockner was slain Nov. 8 just outside her back door while two Long Beach Police Department officers waited at her front door unaware that her life was in danger. The officers were responding to a call about a prowler in the neighborhood.

Harvey, a 22-year-old Port Hueneme man with no prior criminal record, was caught fleeing the yard, covered in blood, police said. He initially told detectives he intended to burglarize the home and cut Schockner's throat with a knife only out of panic, but later allegedly confessed to being hired as a first-time hit man.

While many in the community speculated about Manfred Schockner's involvement in the crime, police immediately began tracking possible connections between Harvey and Schockner, LBPD Detectives Richard Birdsall and Chris Cardoza said Monday.

They said they learned, for instance, that Schockner had frequented an L.A. Fitness gym on Carson Street near Cherry Avenue, where Jaramillo had been a manager. They learned that Jaramillo left the Long Beach location and transferred to a Ventura County gym, where Harvey was a personal trainer. And they learned that Schockner had known Jaramillo for two years and had been giving him small amounts of money over the course of the last year, they said.

About a week before the killing, Deputy District Attorney Cyndi Barnes said, Schockner gave Jaramillo $25,000. It's unclear, she said, whether all of the money was intended to be payment for the murder.

Harvey allegedly told police that he was promised $5,000 and was told to make the crime look like a burglary by taking some of the victim's jewelry from the house, which he did. Birdsall said Manfred Schockner was interviewed numerous times during the last month but was caught off-guard when police arrested him Friday.

"He felt he was smarter than us," Birdsall said.

The grisly death stunned neighbors in the 1100 block of Andrews Drive, where the Schockners had lived with their 14-year-old son, Charlie, before separating recently. On the morning of Nov. 8, LBPD officers were investigating a report of a prowler when they knocked on the door of the Schockner residence and asked to inspect the back yard. Lynn, alone at the time except for her dog, politely told officers she was going to get her keys to let them in a back gate. She shut the door behind her and never returned.

• • • •

Relief might seem like an inappropriate response to learning we had a killer in the family, but the ugly truth brought an end to the improbable story of Lynn's death. Our well-developed disdain for Manfred Schockner suddenly morphed into a reality show, but that didn't provide much solace. Knowing he was ineligible for bail and would remain behind bars until trial provided some consolation.

I could not forget the errors I made along the way and stewed over the absolution I'd given Schockner so freely just days after Lynn's death. I fell for his fake tears and sham embrace, and the foul realization at how easily I had been duped burned like acid. I had been a fool – even mistrusting the police – and welcomed the murderer back into our midst before the crime was solved. I don't know what kind of family man I thought I would be, but I would never be fooled by Schockner again.

DDA Barnes warned us to expect the criminal proceedings to stretch at least a few years, allowing a sufficient reprieve to see Charlie safe in a loving home where he could finish his education. Reassured that prosecutors would see the defendants held responsible for their crimes, I arranged every other legal filing to freeze all of Schockner's assets in his family trust and fight for Charlie's estate. In a belated jab from the grave, my mother's fears were justified and her estate provided the funds we would need for the fight. I eventually retained four different legal firms – each with its own expertise in family, probate, civil and criminal law – and spent the quarter-million and more on attorneys to deprive Schockner of his money.

This was the beginning of my legal education, but I would never be more than a barroom barrister; still, the lawyers were more than competent. They were considerate of Charlie's estate and how many hits it could take before the money was gone. I know this, because I paid all, gladly.

When Charlie was born in 1990, Lynn named me his godfather. It was gratifying then, and even more so fourteen years later when we asked him to join our family. Now, I was fighting for *him*, and that changed the game, but my son had to give up a lot. He relinquished his life in Long Beach and classes at Long Beach Poly High, a school where he thrived. Now we offered him small-town life on a south Georgia barrier island. Still, there was a perk: we had built a plantation-style house a few years after we were married. We lived on the ground floor, but, a huge second-floor great room stood vacant, a permanent place he could call his own.

The police and district attorney, along with many branches of California judiciary became allies, and we embarked upon a legal journey through family, probate and civil courts in California, Georgia, and even federal court in New Jersey, of all places. We used every avenue to foil Schockner's hold on Charlie's estate. Fighting over accounts became my roadmap to revenge, undercutting Schockner's fortune while he faced more serious criminal matters. I embraced the task with Charlie's blessing.

Within hours of the Schockner's arrest, I contacted Lisa Brandon. She filed for my temporary guardianship of Charlie the next day in Los Angeles County Family Court. Using a referral from another Long Beach attorney who would assist us years later, she recommended a tenacious probate litigator who became our key advisor and advocate, as well as a good friend – Eric Adler.

A Long Beach native raised in the south bay of Los Angeles, Adler heard the siren song of the Pacific surf as a young boy and never lost his passion for riding a wave. After high school graduation he headed to Massachusetts and studied under Nobel Laureate and Holocaust survivor Elie Wiesel at Boston University where he received his BA degree in 1994, and then matriculated to Washington University in St. Louis for his JD degree in 1997. He admits he "always argued" and figured the law offered a profession where his talents could flourish. It was his reputation as a contentious and irascible litigator that drew him to our attention.

"Lisa called me the day after Schockner was arrested," Adler recalled. "She wondered whether I was as tough as my reputation. I didn't know exactly how to answer her question, but then she asked if I would fight hard for Charlie and his mother's family. I told her I would do my absolute best. Then and there, she asked if I could start on the case. In two days we had Schockner's entire estate frozen."

A probate lawyer who routinely handles large trust and estate litigation, he also has a taste for high stakes poker. (Years later, after our criminal and civil matters were settled, poker winnings paid for a three-week, first-class trip to Bali where he was engaged to his wife. A big night at the table paid for his wedding.) A shrewd man who could read a bluff, Adler became our most vocal advocate in the usually sedate world of probate court. He served as lead attorney over the course of complicated, multi-jurisdictional negotiations that remained unfinished two and a half years after the killing.

"Your case was unusual, to say the least," he said. "Most of the time, the law deals with nuances: details, and insinuation, and some bluff. It is really odd to find such a clear distinction between good and evil, right and wrong. That made it easy to fight for you guys against Manfred Schockner."

Adler petitioned the probate court to have me named guardian of both my sister's and Charlie's estates immediately after Brandon filed similar motions in family court. Both were granted just a few days after Schockner was arrested. Adler's heated arguments would become most critical to our eventual negotiations, revealing Schockner's uncommon greed and abusive nature.

Our probate filings locked up the Schockner estate, accounts, trusts and investments totaling $6.5 million. He also managed his younger brother Ronnie's estate, his elderly mother's estate, and that of her late husband. Schockner even directed trusts his own father set up for his two grandchildren: Charlie and Ronnie's adopted son, Paul. He had grown accustomed to having funds within reach, but now he was destitute, begging for favors. The staggering slowness of the legal system, especially across the different court dockets, invigorated me in a malicious sort of way. I could be patient, and without his money, these delays would be excruciating for Schockner.

Brandon also recommended a prominent Santa Monica lawyer, Ian "Buddy" Herzog, to represent Charlie and our family in a wrongful death action against Schockner. Our lawsuit named Schockner a defendant, along with Harvey and Jaramillo, Manfred's brother, his cousin, a family friend, his business associate from college and his personal attorney, Neil Ivan. The foggy and convoluted trail of his financial transactions made it impossible to decipher who else could have been involved in the conspiracy, and we employed a "shotgun" strategy to find every participant in the crime. Schockner never left the top of our list.

Time and troubles became allies, if not best friends. The turmoil my team of attorneys brought to my life was nothing compared to the problems they created for my adversary. All of *his* money would remain frozen, just out of reach, because Schockner agreed to have me named "successor trustee" in their identical wills. Both outdated 1999 testaments were simple, innocuous documents that stipulated the surviving party inherit everything, with no mention of their son. Nor did it list any separate properties or assets.

Even though Lynn was remiss in matters of her last will and testament, especially considering Charlie and her impending divorce, this seemingly insignificant inclusion – my status as their successor trustee – was crucial to our case. Until all the criminal and civil matters were settled, I would have control Schockner's fortune. This was the essence of sweet irony, and offered me a chance to *hoist him on his own petard.*

• • • •

The Press-Telegram ran this update three weeks after Schockner's arrest.

Accused husband wants special treatment
Tuesday, Dec. 23, 2004

LONG BEACH - Even O.J. Simpson didn't get what murder defendant Manfred Schockner is asking for, a prosecutor says.

Awaiting trial for allegedly killing his wife, the 66-year-old Schockner requested that he be privately transported to the court, housed separately from other jailhouse inmates and given more comfortable quarters than the holding cell at the county's Twin Towers jail in downtown Los Angeles.

Schockner's request, filed in Superior Court in Long Beach a few days after his arrest, cited his arthritis and other ailments as well as a murder threat by a fellow inmate as reasons for asking for segregation.

"I fear for my life and well-being in such surroundings," Schockner wrote.

"O.J. didn't even get that," Deputy District

Attorney Cyndi Barnes responded. His request was denied.

• • • •

Who was this man, Manfred Schockner?

Despite twenty five years of marriage to my sister, he remains something of an enigma to this day. He was a shrewd, secretive person, cheap to a fault and rude almost beyond belief. Voltaire might have been speaking of Schockner when he perceived this trait: *There are some men who employ words only to disguise their thoughts.* He cultivated grievances like an oyster, forming layers of ossified insults, sharpened into acts of revenge. Wealthy since birth, he carried an obsessive sense of having been grievously misunderstood and eternally wronged, bearing a grudge against the world.

The Schockners were German Jews, exorcised from the Fatherland by the anti-Semitic plague that ravaged Europe during the Depression and morphed into Hitler's Holocaust. His father, Herbert Schockner, was the youngest of fourteen children born into the wealthy Schockner family, raised in an opulent household that included castles, servants, and even a family copy of the Gutenberg Bible.

There were many siblings in the Schockner lineage, but only two survived the Holocaust: Herbert and an uncle. All others perished in Auschwitz or camps on the Polish border. Herbert left Germany for America in the early 1930s. He arrived with little beyond the clothes on his back, but had probably secreted a collection of diamonds or jewels to help him start a new life. He became a naturalized American citizen in 1938 and married Charlotte, another German Jewish exile, and settled in New York City around Madison Avenue and 50th Street. Their first son, Manfred, was born July 5, 1940 at Beth David Hospital in

New York. Charlotte gave birth to a second son right about the time World War II ended, but that boy died as an infant. Ronnie followed in 1948 and would be their last child.

From the little we learned about their household, Herbert Schockner was a strict disciplinarian. Others might call him a brutal sadist. He selected his oldest son for the lion's share of abuse, sparing Ronnie, who never developed the sharp instincts or feral intelligence of his older brother. While Ronnie missed many of the beatings that were an integral part of Manfred's upbringing, the younger brother was also excluded from the family's financial matters.

Ten years after their first child was born, the Schockner family moved into a tenement apartment to save money. There Manfred became acquainted with a man he would consider his "half-brother," Edward Tynan, even though he was just a neighbor who befriended the boy. Tynan served in the Air Force in the Korean War, and claimed he returned to the neighborhood as something of a hero. Manfred idolized his "half-brother's" exploits, but also looked to him for a lifeline from the abuse. When I finally met Tynan at Schockner's trial in 2007, he recalled how often Herbert thrashed his son with a vicious whip – a cat-o-nine tails - an instrument guaranteed to make a lasting impression on the body and the mind. Tynan said he comforted the boy as best he could but was unable to stop the beatings.

Manfred's father also convinced the Tynan family to support Charlotte and the two children while he pursued his fortune in California, traveling west alone to search for property and prosperity. He promised to repay this debt to the Tynan, but obligations never assumed the same importance as debts to the Schockner patriarch. The habit carried down to the son. More than 50 years later, Ed Tynan was all but destitute and Manfred continued to defer this obligation, claiming "cash-flow problems."

I met Herbert only once, just before his death in 1999. He was a bitter, hateful miser who berated the world with almost every breath; by all measures a nasty man. But my sister loved Herbert's wife, Charlotte, a sweet, old-world woman who was always cheerful. She never openly disagreed with Herbert on any subject. The only other member of this family was a cousin from Charlotte's side, a surgeon in New York who had severed his ties with the Schockner clan when they left the city. Even Charlie only met this side of the family once and had nothing but an unpleasant memory of their gathering.

The Schockners followed their father to Los Angeles in the late 1950s. Ronnie finished high school on the West Coast, but Manfred remained in NYC and graduated from the Newburgh Free Academy in 1958. He matriculated to Middleton Community College, where he received an associate's degree in 1960 and then transferred his credits to the University of Denver, where he graduated in 1962 with a BA in Business Administration. He and his roommate, Marty Chernoff, renovated older homes in Denver and then southern California, clearing a nice profit for their efforts. Chernoff remained involved in Schockner's financial schemes long after they dissolved their partnership, and held the post-dated promissory note Lynn discovered during her divorce. Schockner also told Jaramillo he could find an old friend in Atlanta to "take care of his wife." At the time, Chernoff owned a nightclub in Atlanta, and despite their best efforts, police were unable to establish any criminal connection between Schockner and this man.

Manfred was easy to despise. Selfish, greedy and a thief, Charlie discovered his father stole money from his Boy Scout fund-raisers. Schockner pursued a disability claim after a minor collision with another motorist, and then claimed a lifetime handicapped-parking sticker. An angry driver who plowed his Cadillac loudly into front-door spaces all throughout Southern

California, Charlie remembered how Manfred viciously cursed a wheelchair-bound woman for taking *his* space in front of a Circuit City.

His eyes twinkled when he caused despair, and he giggled when others were embarrassed by his behavior. He believed in the efficacy of dishonesty, and valued lying as a tool. He considered honesty a form of blasphemy, an untenable state of affairs.

Now Schockner found himself on the receiving end of problems that wouldn't end. Enjoined in civil, probate and family actions, not to mention his criminal prosecution, we extended complete cooperation with law enforcement and the state's efforts to convict him of this capital crime. At the very least, his millions would be encumbered in the California courts while his life eroded in jail, interrupted only by brief monthly forays before the bench, shuffling chained in an orange jump suit while strangers argued his fate.

All three defendants were locked away for a long wait to trial, bail denied by reason of the combined murder and burglary charges. These provided "special circumstances" to the crime and added death penalty considerations right from the start. The trial or trials, most predicted, would take place in three to seven years; but if the state sought lethal injections, probably even longer. Even so, with Schockner and the pair behind bars in the LA County Jail, one of the most dangerous detention centers anywhere in America, every day would be a desperate affair.

• • • •

The next news about Schockner was provided by *The Press-Telegram*.

Accused husband wants LBPD to pay

Friday, May 13, 2005

LONG BEACH — A Bixby Knolls man accused of hiring a hit man to kill his estranged wife has filed a $3 million wrongful death claim against the Long Beach Police Department, alleging that officers negligently failed to prevent the killing.

Manfred Schockner, 64, is in jail awaiting trial in the murder of his wife, Lynn, whose throat was slit in November outside the back door of her home. At the time of her killing, two police officers investigating a prowler call were waiting at her front door.

The claim for damages, a necessary precursor to a lawsuit, was filed with the city May 6, prompting criticism from Long Beach City Attorney Robert Shannon.

"It's such a ludicrous claim," he said Friday. "I don't know if I wouldn't characterize this as an attempt to divert attention from the underlying criminal case."

But Schockner's attorney defended the filing as legitimate.

"Shannon's description of the claim as 'ludicrous' is undoubtedly based on his opinion that Fred Schockner was somehow involved in the murder of his wife," Lionel Albanese said in a written statement. "As Americans, we believe that a person is innocent until proven guilty, beyond a reasonable doubt, in a trial by jury, notwithstanding the opinion of the Long Beach city attorney."

Schockner's claim names Officer Efraim Cervantes, Officer Sean Irving and Sgt. Curtis Yee, and alleges that all three "failed to protect Lynn Schockner after assuming a duty to protect her."

> "It is based on the fact that numerous police officers responded to a call of a prowler behind the Schockner home, talked to Lynn Schockner in her front yard about the prowler, and let her walk alone to the back of her home where she was killed by the prowler," Albanese wrote.

In fact, Manfred's "personal attorney," Neil Ivan, called me the week before Schockner's lawsuit to inform our family that any civil action we intended to file must be submitted within six months of the crime, warning us that our window to seek damages against the LBPD would soon close. We had no intention of suing the city, but filed our own suit against Schockner et al within the same time limit. The police response may well have been questionable, but in the bigger scheme of things, as our civil attorney correctly surmised, we would be aiding and abetting Schockner's defense by accusing the police of poor performance in this uncertain setting. We allowed the deadline to come and go, leaving Schockner standing alone with his ridiculous allegations. Our wrongful death action against Lynn's husband said everything we would need to say.

Manfred Schockner graduated from the University of Denver with a BA in Business Administration (above right), and is pictured in his high school yearbook after graduating from Newburgh Free Academy in New York in 1958. Below, Manfred and his father, Herbert, are featured in this photograph from the early 1970s.

Charles Jicha holds his daughter close in this photo of our dad probably taken in 1956. Since dad was the photographer in the family, we have very few pictures of him. Below, the three Jicha kids squeeze together in a chair.

The Jicha family pose around the Christmas tree in 1956, while below, Marie hugs Charlie in this 1994 photo taken at her golf course home located in Lake San Marcos, CA.

Susan Shipman, my wife, stands at the railing of a fishing pier near San Diego when we visited my mother in 2000. Both Lynn and Charlie, who joined us for the family visit, are pictured behind Susan.

CHAPTER 13

I remember Lynn as a victim, not just in her death, but in many highpoints of childhood and life. We were a Czech family emerging into the suburbs surrounding Cleveland, an early crop of Baby-Boomers after both our sets of grandparents separately immigrated to America before and after World War I. Our parents grew up during the Depression, proud but poor. No one had stronger work ethics than mom and dad. Our father projected generous compassion and lived with a forgiving eye, while mom wasn't shy about enforcing discipline around the house, often with a hard hand. Still, that was the way of the world and our Buckeye childhood embodied the American dream. My brother and I bounced into adolescence with broad shoulders, while Lynn grew tall and slight, almost skinny. She always lived in our shadows, except when memories flash through frames of terror from her past, especially one bloody childhood episode in a grocery store: As I chased her playfully around an aisle of the A&P market mom shopped far down the next row in the back in the store. Lynn dashed and danced around the aisles, shrieking with delight. Turning the corner at a dead run, still only four or possibly five years old, she slammed dead center into a store attendant carefully carrying a broken glass bottle, the thick, heavy shards of an old-style milk jug. At least a quarter-inch thick, the sharp pieces showered over her head as the stunned clerk reflexively reached to cover his groin.

As the glass crashed to the floor, my baby sister was stunned to silence while blood poured into her eyes. That became terror when she pulled her hands from her head, cutting her hands. And then her howls echoed throughout the store, screaming until I thought she would die. It was a horror, alive to this day. Mom whirled around the corner, grabbed her up and tried to make sense of a dozen or more deep cuts in her scalp – directly on top of her head – and more on her hands. This bloody accident left a mark on everyone – the clerk vomited in the aisle, and it took a few dozen stitches to close the incisions in my sister's scalp.

Every child tastes a little trauma along the way, and, like most, she recovered. Even so, every family has its own dirty little secrets, and Lynn's was truly terrible, well beyond any lacerations to her head.

Almost thirty years later, just a few days before my wife and I were married in 1987 on Jekyll Island, my little sister ended another round of therapy to announce the source of her self-loathing and depression: she had been sexually molested as a child – not by anyone in the family, but a neighbor's grandparent. None save the two victims, she and her playmate, were witness to the crime, and no one said a thing. It was if it never happened, but the sexual shame became a lie she had to live with, a fear carved into the very center of her young soul. Trying to reconstruct that watershed event, we knew mom said she carried her only daughter across the busy Tuxedo Boulevard to a neighbor's house to play with their daughter. The kids were alone at the start, but then her grandfather joined them to enhance their fun and games. This is the way pederasts plunder young lives, a sin that cannot be forgiven.

Today, most parents would be more vigilant, and there would be remedies and ramifications with the police. Back in the day, children were more seen and less heard, and sexual topics were strictly taboo. Abuse was rarely acknowledged, and the crime never came to light. The incident passed without notice, but the truth finally emerged after thirty years. Her wound never healed and Lynn was never the same, injured in ways she would never overcome. The revelation also confirmed early memories of happy days with our baby sister who then regressed into a child with a tentative nature and fearful ways. The little girl shrank and withered right before our eyes, replaced by a hollow shell of the person she had been, but we didn't know a thing.

The years passed. By the time my brother ended his sophomore year at Kent State University in 1970, Lynn neared the end of tenth grade at Valley Forge High School in the expansive Cleveland suburb of Parma Heights. I was weeks from graduation at the same school, set for my senior prom and admission to Kenyon College. Lynn and I left for classes that Friday morning; my mother drove to work as an elementary school librarian, all of us jealous of my brother who stayed in bed. Our worlds dissolved that afternoon when we learned dad was dead from a massive heart attack, lying on a slab at the local hospital.

Fifty-eight years old, early coronary warnings all but ignored, he barely made his way to the emergency room before expiring on the spot. His untimely death that year orphaned each of us from a father we loved and admired. He was a good man, in the most elemental sort of way, and even to this day, I try to live up to his example.

Lynn's devastation carried well beyond the loss of her father and best friend. Already at odds with mom about typical matters mothers and daughter argue over, dad's strength had carried her through most days, but now he was gone. He had been the only man with whom Lynn could feel safe, and she lost her moorings when he died. We all faced our share of problems but had never suffered Lynn's confusion regarding her sexuality and trust. I retreated into my own grief and I shut out the world, selfish for myself. I can't imagine my little sister's lonely world with demons and devils of her own.

After plowing through the funeral ceremonies, I graduated and took a seasonal job while Mom stayed home with Lynn for the summer. Their grief was only the beginning of the disintegration of our family. The kitchen table became headquarters for recriminations and shattered lives. We all loved our dad in our own special ways – he was just that kind of man – but now we faced a life without a man we adored. As the leaves turned that autumn, my brother and I went off to college. Mom and Lynn fought over remains of our home life and we left the two women to work out things as best they could, never aware of our sister's repression and deep pain.

Two years later, mother and daughter embarked upon an extended cross-country summer vacation to visit friends in California. During those short weeks, Lynn met a fellow named Dan who pledged his love. She eventually married him back in Ohio, less than a year later, but soon went back to southern California, where the marriage dissolved. After a no-fault divorce, she found herself alone and jobless in Downey. In just a few weeks she accepted an entry-level position at Garrett Airesearch, then a subsidiary of Lockheed, and rose quickly from the secretarial pool; in less than a year, she was promoted to customer liaisons representative on weapons and guidance systems service contracts with the military, primarily the USMC air wing. This pleased her greatly – our father had been an old Marine, a World War II volunteer, always prideful of his service, as were we. It was easy for her to make friends in the Corps, regaling Leathernecks with exploits of her dad. She reveled in her technical accomplishments, thrilled to have found demanding tasks at which she excelled. Stunted by hidden child abuse and then cast adrift by the loss of our father, she had burrowed deep into herself to find a strength that every person needs, especially one so long tormented. Those first few months and years at Garrett were her salad days, a time when my sister finally found confidence and self-esteem, when she came into her own.

But those old emotional wounds must have been crystal clear to Schockner when he met her as a 24-year-old woman. Lynn and Manfred were introduced midway through her first year at the busy air research office, and he swept her off her feet after Neil Ivan arranged their first date at Dodger Field in LA. She was vivacious, attractive, and smart, and it took only a few dates for him to decide to make her his wife. Schockner was a man of means who used his funds judiciously, offering new comforts and adventures to a girl so long bound by tight money. I believe he recognized her fragile psyche, and seized on her weakness, correctly assessing her pain. Even as an anti-social and ill-tempered man, he hid his anger as he courted the girl, far out of her depths and oblivious to his true nature. No one would ever call him handsome, especially considering his most prominent features: a long, hooked nose framed by dark, hooded eyes and a permanent scowl. Initially, they shared the camaraderie of careers in the same thriving corporate community, sharing successes for the firm. Schockner showered her with expensive gifts and extravagant plans. They dined out frequently before moving into a domestic routine and were married in 1979 on a sailboat in Redondo Beach Harbor. It was a small ceremony attended only by my mother, Manfred's parents and his two friends – Neil Ivan and Marty Chernoff. My mother described it as a tawdry affair, and shared her low opinion of her new son-in-law while offering dire predictions for their marriage. We tried to dismiss her complaints as those of a bitter woman, but many years later, we discovered his abuse began within a few weeks of the ceremony and culminated with her brutal killing. Our mother had been right all along.

Older than his new bride by fourteen years, Manfred liked to think of himself as important, and he wanted other people to see himself this way. But he was fundamentally cheap, and played that hand at every turn. When the family got together, he'd spring for a cheap hamburger lunch to avoid paying for a pricey steak and seafood dinner that night. He would excuse himself for the restroom when the waiter promised the bill and usually fled for the parking lot before the tab arrived. This was just a portent of things to come: Lynn was finally reduced to thrift shops and Goodwill stores, living with an allowance measured for each and every dollar.

Finally, I almost lost touch with my sister because of the man she married. He was a twenty-four carat asshole, and still is. We drifted apart, not with high drama, but the inexorable passage of time and the purposeful alienations Schockner inflicted. She continued to rationalize his tirades and her timorous retreats and we all tolerated her excuses, avoiding conversations about their relationship. After her death we learned how he berated or beat her almost every day, Charlie said, and she often wore sunglasses or long sleeves to hide the bruises and scars. From the other side of the continent, the signs were hard to spot, but Lynn was a battered wife. Typical of the species, she steadfastly denied the abuse, made excuses for him and his misogynistic ways, finally easing into an over-medicated cocoon.

Married for twenty-five years, she spent that quarter century trying to fill empty corners, compensating for her husband's tirades and vengeful ways. He never forgot an insult, real or perceived, and could invent one on a moment's notice to box her into cowering submission, grinding her down like the savage Pacific surf. As a couple, they entered therapy before their second anniversary; more than twenty years later, she reported the same mindless platitudes offered by countless counselors in different settings. Invariably, he returned to his angry ways and she suffered in silence within their suburban home. She feared him greatly, and in her confusion, she never found a way to escape with her son and her life.

• • • •

Manfred ranted on almost any subject, but none more than his opinion on the legal profession, notwithstanding Neal Ivan's status as *his* lawyer and their best friend. Early in their marriage, he promised Lynn a divorce whenever she wanted on the condition she would never retain legal counsel in any dispute over their estate, warning her of dire consequences if she did. After he was arrested, I looked for every legal roadblock I could throw his way, relishing any opportunity to make him engage the services of many other lawyers who demanded substantial retainers and regular payment. He was going to have to spend his own money, and watch in dismay his own lawyers chewed through hundreds of thousands of dollars a year. My first lawsuit involved the investment firm where he kept the family accounts, embroiling those bankers and brokers with claims that froze the funds until other courts decided family and probate matters. Eric Adler handled the complicated and convoluted process, complemented by civil and family court pleadings by Lisa Brandon and Buddy Herzog. The probate ruling Adler secured effectively by-passed family and civil court jurisdictions, stipulating the estate of Lynn's son would supersede all other pleadings. It was a masterful plan, limiting Schockner's claims but not his complaints, brought forward by his civil attorney, Lionel Albanese.

Listed by the California Bar Association as an administrative & governmental lawyer with special practices, Albanese hung his shingle in a Torrance Boulevard office. I don't know much about his practice, but I learned more than I cared to know about his difficult personal life. Only a few months into our negotiations, he was diagnosed with a mysterious throat or sinus ailment that required surgery. Then his wife suffered a miscarriage. The traumas paled to his relationship with his client, Schockner, who abused him almost without end, as he regularly admitted to Adler. Albanese's personal issues and absences prolonged our negotiations for more than a year, and despite the adversarial situation, both my lawyer and I grew to pity the poor man. But when monthly hearings ran into a second year without progress, his routine had long grown old. Every few months the unfortunate attorney would arrive in court, hospital forms and medical statements in hand, pleading to avoid sanctions from the court and grant yet another continuance. When Albanese finally returned Adler's emails and calls, Schockner's lawyer often spent more time discussing his client's latest harangues and repulsive personality than terms of a settlement.

I set out to secure all Schockner's family funds, about $6 million dollars, for Charlie's estate. With grudging reluctance we shuffled everything Schockner owned back and forth across the bargaining table and held out for what we could get. I argued that Schockner was a one-man criminal enterprise - everything from insurance swindler to thief and murderer - and all his assets should be forfeited in light of these crimes. That goal was never realistic, and we finally split the family money into a convoluted pie, shaving points here and there until we reached terms I could endorse. Even then I balked at the final amount, reluctant to stack this pile of dollars against Lynn's life. Adler convinced me to see beyond my anger and place Charlie's interests ahead of my own, where they belonged; we reached a division of property roughly equal to what California courts would have granted under their equitable divorce parameters. Schockner could have granted Lynn's divorce and walked away with that much money *and* his life, but decided he needed it all.

He finally agreed to the terms but insisted all Charlie's assets would be held in a California trust during Schockner's lifetime and his boy wouldn't get a dime until he died. That wasn't going to fly, I told Adler. Those funds would settle where Charlie resided in Georgia and nothing would change my mind. This was a deal-breaker.

Poised at this unshakeable impasse, our next venue was the pending civil action in the wrongful death suit filed against Schockner et al, one which had eclipsed every deferral and was now front and center on the docket in California Civil Court. Al Israel, who recommended Eric Adler to Lisa Brandon for our probate pleadings back in 2004, now stood ready to present our case, while Albanese was denied another delay. Juggling court appearances in three different courts - family, probate and civil – I stood by my cell phone and fax machine while Adler, Israel and Brandon went to work, operating in concert to force Schockner back to the bargaining table. Albanese, on the other hand, shuffled from one unfamiliar courtroom to another, representing a client who believed he could stonewall the courts while treating his own attorney to rude behavior and raging tempers. A shrewd and devious litigant in many ways, Schockner was contemptuous of judicial tempers and ignorant of how a determined judge can exercise complete power from the bench. This would be the first setback he endured in a California courtroom, but it wouldn't be the last.

Charlie's guardianship and custody were granted to my wife and me in family court while Schockner's millions were frozen in probate court. Our wrongful death suit remained an active issue in civil court, where Judge Elizabeth White was forced to follow an accelerated timeline stipulated by California's Trial Delay Reduction Act, which dealt with the state's hopelessly back-logged civil court calendar

That law mandated all actions be heard within one calendar

year of the filing date. That deadline expired in June 2006, and each succeeding month her honor grew increasingly impatient. After six months on her active docket, and considering how little progress our negotiations had achieved, she allowed Schockner's lawyer one final deferral in September with a promise the civil trial would begin the following month. We would have been hard-pressed to force the state to release the evidence gathered in their criminal investigation of the murder conspiracy, but even so, Albanese was ill-equipped to defend Schockner against the murder charge at the heart of our civil litigation. A wonderful convergence of disparate legal rulings merged to provide me an opening that would undermine Schockner's ability to keep his money from the boy who had become our son.

• • • •

I called Adler on August 18, 2006 to offer Schockner an olive branch to settle our eighteen-month run of fruitless negotiations: I would back off on my demand for the death penalty with the DA if he settled Charlie's estate - an apparent concession on the state's capital punishment considerations. "Take the needle off the table," I said. Adler and I had been speaking almost every week for many months, and since I wasn't chained to a desk that day, I called from the 10th tee at Coastal Pines Golf Course in Brunswick. After a brief conversation, he affirmed Schockner's determination to retain control of Charlie's estate but promised to tender the offer. "Let me make a call, but don't get your hopes too high," Adler advised. "Lionel hasn't returned my calls for a couple of weeks. I'll get back to you as soon as I hear anything at all."

Many times during the protracted negotiations we were convinced an agreement was at hand, only to endure weeks, sometimes months of silence. I didn't figure to hear back from him for another week. Dozens of telephone and email messages from Adler to Schockner's attorney went unanswered, and even his secretary claimed she didn't know his whereabouts. Albanese failed to appear in civil court for a proscribed hearing in our wrongful death lawsuit, only to show up weeks later, another doctor's note in hand.

But the district attorney didn't have to endure such delays. LBPD provided reams of official documents while prosecutors steadily laid the cornerstones for three criminal trials, proceeding with deliberate but steady pace. The DA's Special Circumstance Committee met privately from May through September without revealing a thing. Any one or all three defendants could face lethal injection or life without parole, the capital alternative for felony murder with special circumstances attached. (Lynn's murder and burglary of her costume jewelry, valued just enough to meet the threshold for a second felonious count, satisfied the legal requirements for seeking the death penalty.)

Sometime in early June, DDA Barnes emailed to inquire about our opinions on the two prosecutorial paths, but warned that death penalty cases could extend for years. If any or all were convicted, each would also be provided special "penalty phase" hearings that would bring every character witness or childhood incident into play, and could drag out for months, even years. It was clear that our sentiments would be just one of many matters considered, and probably not a deciding factor. After polling Charlie and other members of the family, we decided only Nick Harvey deserved the death penalty, if for no other reason than the dangers he might pose to prison guards or nonviolent fellow inmates. We didn't believe Frank Jaramillo constituted a real threat to anyone other than himself, and we lobbied the committee to seek life imprisonment against Schockner, not death, hoping he would have a long and tortured existence behind bars.

Neither Schockner nor his attorney knew details about these deliberations, but Lynn's husband faced mounting legal fees that forced his hand. High-profile criminal defense attorneys post billable hours with the best and his lead lawyer was among the most prominent in Long Beach, a man known for a bare-knuckled defense and impressive retainers. Adler said he would try to reach Albanese in time to meet the latest deadline, but he wasn't optimistic.

I was stunned when he called me back before I reached the 12th green. "You need to establish a guardianship account at a local bank and the funds will be transferred there for Charlie," he happily advised. "Schockner agreed."

And that was it.

Eric quickly congratulated me and broke the connection: he had to run off to another court session while I picked up my golf ball and headed to the 13th tee, flushed with success. I nailed a huge drive down the left side of the fairway, the ball fading back to the center of the short grass, well within range of the gap wedge I flushed to twelve feet. I strolled to the green, stunned giddy by my successful ploy with Schockner and my sweet shot, sinking the birdie putt. The relief was palpable, almost intoxicating, an end to all these angry arguments and endless animus I had endured for almost two years. If I had not been alone, I believe a companion could have seen me glow. My new son and his money would soon be united; and my golf swing, normally the image of an angry man chopping cotton, was smooth as butter and pure as the driven snow.

Both were miracles in their own right.

I played the back nine to perfection, well beyond my normal abilities, especially around the green. I'd bluffed Schockner into a desperate agreement, one he would forever resent, and secured Charlie's financial legacy and my sister's estate while playing nine holes of scratch golf. I still don't know which is more improbable, but on that day, all were not only possible, but true. I was a man who didn't miss.

• • • •

The next few weeks were less pleasant and more problematic than that memorable day on the links. Without delay, my attorney faxed a draft of our final agreement to his counterpart, and I sent an affidavit certifying my request to the Special Circumstances Committee before close of business in LA. But Lionel Albanese took another powder, avoiding calls and message for a week; by the end of August all we had was Albanese's claimed consent with Schockner, a habitual liar. Eric finally fired off a fax, and sent me a copy:

> Lionel - It appears that settlement will not take place due to your failure to communicate or work toward settlement. I will file a petition with the civil court to let the judge know that you were dishonest when you told the court that you would work toward settlement. We will also begin to move forward on various pleadings in the probate matter and the trust matter. I have also advised Al Israel to move forward in the civil matter.
>
> It is a shame that your failure to work toward settlement will cause Manfred's estate to be further depleted by legal fees. Finally, we discussed the fact that Mark and Jon Jicha would ask the death penalty committee to refrain from authorizing the death penalty as part of the settlement agreement. Since settlement appears to be off due to your lack of communication, Mark and Jon Jicha are preparing a written statement requesting the state seek the death

penalty since the committee meets in the near future.

If you ever desire to discuss settlement in a substantive manner please call me. However, before I waste more time and money discussing settlement with you, since I have been lied to so many times during this process; there will have to be a good faith showing on your part before we re-engage in settlement negotiations. Eric Adler

Just before the Labor Day weekend, DDA Barnes updated our family on the status on SCC deliberations:

Mark,

Sorry I did not get back to you earlier, I was in and out with an eye infection and a trial, so I was not really checking my emails.

We had the committee meeting on September 6th. They told me late in the afternoon on the 5th that they could not do it on the 13th - so my choices were that day or in late October. I am trying to get the process moving along, so I said that I would do it on the 5th. Unfortunately that did not give me much time to prepare, but things went smoothly.

Basically, the meeting is just an internal District Attorney meeting, and is somewhat confidential. The committee chairman is the Assistant District Attorney. Approximately 10 people were present, including my boss here in Long Beach, and then all of the top administration of the District Attorney's Office. As you would expect, these meeting are very serious. I gave a presentation about the case, and then they asked me questions for about an hour

> about the case. No one from the public was present, and no transcripts or records were generated. The defense attorneys are not present either, but they are allowed to submit a letter outlining the position of their client, and the factors to consider as to why their client should not get the death penalty.
>
> I did inform the committee that we had discussed the issue of penalty, and that your family did not want to seek the death penalty against Schockner or Jaramillo, but that you did want to seek the death penalty against Harvey. We also discussed Schockner's age and his deteriorating health. – Cyndi

With all the delays and deferrals we had already encountered, it was heartening to see some sort of progress with the criminal case, especially if it ramped up pressure to get my deal with Schockner done. My attorney faxed another angry denunciation to opposing counsel, venting our collective frustrations:

> Lionel - Your last message to me was that you would call me no later than August 28 with an update. For some reason, I believe you each time you apologize to me and tell me that you will begin communicating and working toward settlement.
>
> Of course, you clearly have no shame at this point, since you are dishonest with me and in open court. You have not responded to my latest phone calls or faxes. You told me that settlement was close and to hold off on our punitive steps, but then you fail to even return a phone call with an update.
>
> If I do not hear from you by 12:00 p.m. on September 1, 2006, then we will move forward with

> our probate and civil pleadings and our letters to the prosecutor in support of the death penalty. I have never had an opposing counsel act in this matter. - Eric

A week later, on September 6, Barnes informed us the state would not seek the death penalty against any of the defendants, and tried to explain their decision without having been privy to their deliberations.

> I am not sure what they based their decision on - they do not tell us why. When we discussed it at the meeting, what everyone seemed to agree on, was that Schockner is the most culpable of the three. To him it was personal. He planned it and he paid for it. He even set it up so that Lynn would be killed in her own home - presumably Charlie would have been the one to come home and find her.
>
> In my opinion, the death penalty issue really hinged on Schockner. I think if they had sought death on Schockner they would have sought death on Harvey. Once they decided not to seek death on Schockner, then it became a question of whether or not to seek death on the less culpable if you are not going to seek death on the most culpable. I would imagine they considered other things as well - the lack of criminal record, etc.
>
> This case seemed to be an especially tough one for them. Usually the committee decision is made immediately shortly after the meeting. In this case, not only did they not make a decision right away, they called a few times to get more information and ask more questions. We still don't have the official

> letter, but the head of the committee called to tell us the final decision.
>
> You are always welcome to write a letter or call the committee chairman. I think I may have given you that information before, but if not I will be happy to email it to you. I am not sure how much they will tell you (they don't tell us much!) but they are all good people and will answer your questions. Does that answer your questions at all? Cyndi.

The committee's decision cleared the way for criminal prosecutions, but for reasons unknown to our side, the district attorney did not release the information for almost two weeks, creating a unique opportunity to continue our negotiations for Charlie's stake in the family estate. Neither Schockner nor his attorney knew the committee had already resolved against the death penalty for all three defendants, and I wasn't going to tell them.

Schockner's money was the only thing keeping him alive right now, or so I hoped. Taking something close to half the estate for Charlie was not my only objective; once deposited, I figured the litigation could continue as long as Schockner remained alive. Eight years later, the trust account was a living nightmare for the Farmers & Merchants Bank in Long Beach, the trustee battered with Schockner's endless written complaints and litigation. Better them than me.

• • • •

I gave up nothing in the ploy - from the start I hoped he would earn a life sentence, not the needle, to provide him years of fear and abuse behind bars. It was satisfying to know that vicious old wife-beater spent every waking minute trying to keep the gangs at bay, and that was just at the LA County Jail. Big and crowded, meaner than many state prisons, the jail was a house of horrors where Schockner would find few friends.

Before the *Press-Telegram* published the SCC's decision, Adler received the signed settlement at his office. We had finally locked Schockner into a deal, celebrating that seemingly insurmountable hurdle in September.

By Christmas 2006 we had galvanized into a real family: Susan, Charlie and I; my brother, his wife, and their kids, Amy and Dylan. The same was true for all of Susan's extended family: her brother and his wife, Bill and Cyndy; her sister and family, Linda, David, Keith and Virginia Landgraf; as well as a host of aunts, uncles, cousins and more distant relations. We went out of our way to reinforce filial connections, setting holidays aside for any members of the clan who could attend. Charlie stood tall through school at Frederica Academy, a friendly and robust academic prep school within walking distance of our home. Already an accomplished actor who excelled in FA's dramatic productions, he felt even more comfortable behind the scenes, building sets with creative backdrops. He also played fullback on the school's state champion soccer squad, and that spring he and his tennis partner, John Allen, claimed the state doubles title among Georgia independent schools. It was a pretty good year!

But Charlie had lived on the dark side, and the damage inflicted by his father over fourteen years of fear and sorrow would take more than a few months to heal. It took a while to appreciate the depth of his inner traumas; along the way, he helped me atone for the guilt I couldn't avoid over Lynn's death. We worked together and forged a bond as father and son. Still, during holidays, he recalled one terrible celebration when Schockner scooped up every present under the tree on Christmas Eve and packed them into the trash, all because his son insisted on sharing services with Lynn at the Methodist

Church instead of joining Manfred at temple. He shrank with that memory of that sad holiday season.

Back before I had double knee replacement surgery, we enjoyed spirited, if not especially skillful, tennis sessions on the local court. He had already developed steady ground strokes and could cover the court with quickness and agility, but when it came time to put away a point, he'd place the ball away from his opponent instead of hitting out on the shot. He played cautious tennis, always looking for a safe play. After time, I made the connection between this habit and his old man: Schockner railed against any kind of shortcoming, and instead of nurturing the joys of success, he pressed Charlie to avoid failure at all cost. I even photographed his matches and shared those revealing images with my son. They showed him how he hit off his back foot, placing his shots instead of swinging through the ball. I called him on every soft lob and dink in our rallies, often egging him onto furious tempers; I didn't berate his strokes, but tried to explain his tendencies during water breaks.

We took this subject to his therapist, Dr. William Furey of Savannah, who added the topic to his private conversations with Charlie. Children can be blessedly strong and resilient, but it would take many years to exorcise these demons. I finally developed a formula, and described it to him as I taught him to drive my car, an unnerving errand as ever was. I explained his life was filled with family, schools and support, but his father's tempers created a burden that would be hard to overcome. "I figure another fourteen years," I said to him one day. "It took fourteen years to get where you are, and it's probably take another fourteen to dump his baggage." Fortunately, we had each other and years of happy promise while Schockner had only his cellmates and his rapidly-approaching day in court.

By the time we celebrated New Year 2007 it was clear the Superior Court of Long Beach would be ready for three consecutive criminal trials: Nick Harvey, followed by Frank Jaramillo, and then Manfred Schockner, hopefully before the year was out. After more than two years, we would be there to see their fates resolved.

CHAPTER 14

Judge Ferrari's courtroom was at the far end of the main corridor. He would preside over all three criminal trials related to my sister's murder, while he also dealt with a steady progression of other cases. He was an energetic jurist and master of understated efficiency, a man who also gauged the investments of all parties - jurors, witnesses, court personnel, family members and attorneys – with equal respect. He conducted his courtroom with an even-handed professionalism that boded well for our unapologetic desire to see Nick Harvey go down.

On Monday, March 12, 2007 Harvey took the stand in his own defense. It was his 25th birthday. His lawyer mounted a desperate argument to link his long-term steroid abuse to the homicide in Bixby Knolls, but Harvey openly smirked and showed his intricate knowledge of martial arts. He bragged about the steroid cocktails he ingested to grow strong, and then broke down and cried on the stand. Every day of his trial the man seemed to shrink further into his cheap courtroom suit, withering as DDA Barnes intricately built the state's case against him. My brother and I watched the proceedings from beginning to end, as did Nick's mother and sister. Each day of the trial, visitors would drop in to see the accused killer and stay for a quarter hour, attracted by the headlines surrounding the case.

Harvey's tears came exactly two weeks after his trial began

in Long Beach Superior Court. Jon and I entered the municipal building that morning, passed through the security checkpoint operated by Los Angeles County deputies, and joined the morning rush to face three elevators, only two of which were in service. The cars were grimy from constant use. After disgorging its passengers, the vehicle lurched upward in the sluggish fashion, packed with attorneys and court personnel, plaintiffs, defendants and confused family members like us.

The car stopped on a lower floor before arriving at the 5th floor, and as we ascended we could hear a crescendo of strange sounds echoing from the shaft: squeals, moans, shudders and eerie sighs. A haunting, discordant song wailed softly, the tune sibilant and sad, something like a medieval chant of monks in prayer.

The 5th floor hall was lined with family members sour with fear on either side of many complaints or crimes. Parked on benches outside the row of six courtrooms, police and probation officers, attorneys, bailiffs and clerks mingled, all indifferent to everything but the neutral bounds of the court. The strange serenade echoed from our left, hidden by a wall. We turned that corner and found an old, sadly-worn escalator that carried passengers to the 6th floor. For some reason, the elevator only reached the 5th. The antique escalator was almost ruined – bearings complaining of wear, belts stretched and frayed, wheels ground down to mere shadows of their former selves. I learned to love and fear that haunting melody, a sort of soundtrack to the days and weeks that became our cause for justice.

Harvey's trial was to begin on Monday, February 26, but was delayed from the onset when the defendant's lawyer was unable to interview his expert witness: Dr. Ronald Siegel, a psycopharmacologist and associate research professor from UCLA. Judge Ferrari reluctantly re-organized his trial schedule to accommodate this last-ditch request by the defense, granting a continuance hours before the case even started.

Since the jury had not yet been empaneled, Harvey entered court in an orange jumpsuit. He was shackled, shrunken and sallow from more than two years in the bowels of a county detention complex so harrowing as to be the feature of true crime television shows. Facing a witness list numbering more than a dozen police and forensic specialists, not to mention his detailed confession to Birdsall and Cordova, the defendant grasped for straws. His defense was limited to a diminished capacity based on long-term steroid abuse endorsed by Siegel. We saw it as a desperate effort to deflect his guilt, but Siegel did provide a clinical name for the syndrome: the "steroid facilitated rage reaction."

This would become the essence of Harvey's defense, the only way a jury could excuse his crime: a technicality linked to his admitted drug abuse, not his homicidal nature. Even though Siegel's testimony raised interesting analytical arguments, especially in an academic setting, it was offensive to my brother and me, an insult to our common sense.

Defense attorney Anthony Patalono asked Siegel to testify about the physical and emotional side affects of anabolic steroid use and abuse. On Monday, March 5 the court heard his findings, and also considered the admissibility of his testimony for Harvey's last-ditch defense. Displaying charts, graphs and Power Point presentations, Siegel was an ardent academic, a clinical scientist who claimed research on anabolic steroids dating back to the 1960s. He said young Harvey "satisfied the criteria as a steroid abuser." Drug abuse has decimated many families, and steroid abuse can trigger the same downward spiral that other drug dependencies produce, he insisted.

This key element of Harvey's defense was debated before the trial was underway, but Judge Ferrari promised a ruling within a day. Capital cases require careful handling, but he welcomed this case into his busy calendar and didn't miss a beat along the way. Always careful to avoid a reversible trial error, Ferrari perceived potential problems and moved the Harvey case to the top of his docket, laying a foundation for the process of the trial. Though clearly skeptical of Siegel's expertise, Ferrari granted the defense another week so he could finish his interviews with the defendant, and stipulated the trial would begin with jury selection the following week. Dr. Siegel, if allowed, would be Harvey's last witness.

"My primary interest of study is the aggression we see as a result of long-term steroid use," he explained. "The effect on the brain is similar to PCP, and my studies suggest a correlation between use of steroids and outbreaks of aggressive behavior."

Siegel reluctantly admitted his papers had not been published in medical journals but said his peers consider him an expert on substance abuse. He insisted he was qualified to testify for the defense based on hundreds of patient interviews who admitted steroid abuse during his years of clinical experience. Harvey claimed constant moodiness, intolerance, frustration, and paranoia about his girlfriend and violent outbursts toward his mother, Siegel asserted, and said these behaviors resulted from his chronic steroid abuse and culminated with murder.

"When confronted by the victim in her own backyard, Harvey felt an over-powering fear," Siegel testified, calling Harvey's behavior consistent with a "classic steroid facilitated reaction." The wounds on the victim's body were consistent with a "rage killing," he said. Patalano would argue Lynn's killing was an accident because Harvey was "dissociated and his reaction was caused by persistent abuse of anabolic steroids."

The same sorrowful song met us in the hall when we left the courtroom, growing louder as we walked toward the elevators adjacent to the sad old conveyance to the top floor. The trial would begin the following week.

• • • •

During that week in California I discovered Alfred Alistair Cooke's observation about LA: *Between a quarter and a third of Los Angeles's land area is now monopolized by the automobile and its needs - by freeways, highways, garages, gas stations, car lots, parking lots. And all of it is blanketed with anonymity and foul air.* He seemed right – we drove long distances between destinations, meeting few friendly faces along the way. I missed my home life, stubbornly proud of my rural Southern ways. We were strangers in a strange land. But we also found kindred spirits in law enforcement and the courts, collecting a small cadre of companions among the professionals we met along the way: DDA Barnes, the cops, investigators, other specialists, our attorneys, the judge and bailiffs. Even the jurors, a casual cross-section of solid citizens. These were the same personalities we would call friends at home, men and women outraged by the crime. We wanted them to see us sitting in court, reflecting the brutality and cunning involved in Lynn's murder. Despite the overwhelming evidence in the case, we knew *justice* was anything but an obvious outcome; any verdict can hinge on a matter of law, an opinion or an error in trial procedure. Strong wills conduct business before the bench, and there are unexpected events, impossible to predict, unknown factors we couldn't realize until the verdict was revealed.

• • • •

Harvey appeared in civilian garb for jury selection on Tuesday, March 5, but wardrobe change couldn't hide how his body sagged in the clothes. He looked smaller in an oxford shirt that might have fit him three years earlier, and even Ms. Russell noted his "sullen" appearance in her coverage for the *Press-Telegram.*

Judge Ferrari held Siegel's testimony under advisement and promised a ruling on the admissibility of the witness and scope of his expertise, concluding the last pretrial matter. He dropped the gavel at 10:57 am for jury selection from a panel of about five or six dozen prospects, and the trial began. I took a hard look at the group, but it's impossible to gauge any character at a glance. That didn't prevent me from wondering how each would consider the defendant and react to the crime, or how extenuating circumstances could influence their collective minds. An attractive Asian woman explained she could not help but be biased by his arrest, and was excused. An 18-year resident of LA County, a gentleman of Hispanic descent, did not understand English. One man was stone deaf, and another believed the police treated a friend unfairly after he fired a handgun in his neighborhood, and claimed bias against all cops. All were excused.

By mid-afternoon Harvey's full jury, five men and seven women - along with four alternates - were in place. There were other interesting footnotes to the group: only two, both alternates, remembered hearing about the crime two-and-a-half years earlier; and every juror had been victimized by burglary or criminal theft, many more than once. The final alternate, an unnotable actor from Beverly Hills, was selected at 3:04 pm. "This is a long way from Beverly Hills," he said after being named, and the jury was advised the trial would begin promptly at 10 am the next day.

• • • •

DDA Barnes may have enjoyed an extra cup of coffee that first trial morning, a snap in her step as she took the state's table, closest to the jury box. Dressed smartly in black, her sandy brown hair brandished with streaks of burnt copper, she presented an attractive counterpoint to the sad defendant at the opposite table. Harvey's public defender arranged his papers while the court reporter settled into her seat before the bench. The bailiff stood near the rail, his back to the secured door reserved for prisoners awaiting entry into the court. Barnes looked energized and ready; and when a passing attorney swiped her pen from her papers on the table and made a dash for the side exit, she chased the culprit across the room and reclaimed her property, flashing angry eyes at the man. Composed back at her table, she busied herself with the progressive list of exhibits she would present, held in cardboard boxes stacked behind her and supplemented by reports on the table. She had a lot of evidence and the law on her side.

There was a subtle but unmistakable shift in the court's temper when Ferrari settled his papers and asked the bailiff to call the proceedings to order. The judge waited pointedly for almost a minute before declaring the matter at hand on Wednesday, March 6. Then, as the jury entered the court, the judge carried on a light-hearted banter with attorneys and clerks; he even singled out a cute co-ed at the press table, a pre-law major from Cal State Long Beach, and asked after her studies. She responded with slight embarrassment and delight. Jurors wore casual clothing, many in sandals, and others in tank tops and t-shirts. For those featured in the court's process - the judge, bailiffs, clerks, attorneys and police - the routine had become mundane. Even horrible crimes, or gaffs in the system, hold some element of black comedy endemic to any legal affairs, and the parties were privy to their share of sadly humorous anecdotes.

Before Barnes could present her opening argument, there was still one last bit of judicial housekeeping to perform: the prosecution's request to present crime scene photographs, including those of the bloody victim.

"The defense objects to the display of the crime scene photos," Patalano argued when she asked to admit the stack of prints. "There is so much blood - they are so gruesome - as to incite the passions of the jury and prevent a more rational verdict." His objection was overruled. "I find the probative value of this evidence outweighs the prejudicial effect upon jurors. Motion denied," said Ferrari before turning back to business. The defense passed on an opening statement and Barnes took the floor.

To preface the case, Barnes outlined the charges and crime for the jury, describing Lynn's brutal murder in deliberate, impersonal language. She chronicled her exhibits in confident and coherent terms, but also explained why our family needed closure to this horrendous crime in this LA County court. Never hesitant to unleash a full court prosecutorial press, she remained reluctant to let anyone - victims, cops, criminals or even the family - become part of a personal crusade. She was a consummate professional; and as our trial experiences unfolded, I realized how well-suited she was for the job. Sharp and smart, she reminded me of my wife when we were married many years earlier, and I was happy to have both women in my life that day.

"The evidence will show you this defendant killed Lynn Schockner for five thousand dollars. It was a job. Harvey received $2500 as a down payment and he took the job," she said. "He didn't just take it - he relished it. He went to her house three or four times, he learned her son's schedule at school. He knew about the dog and that it would be in the home when Lynn Schockner was home. He went out and bought a dagger, and he also bought a Taser. He knew the alarm code to the house. He hired a driver to take him to the residence and to pick him up when he was done. He dressed in black - completely black - and he wore gloves. Then he went into her backyard and killed Lynn

Schockner."

Her first witness was a stranger: LBPD Officer James Foster, who arrived on the scene at 1:20 pm that day, about two hours after the murder. "I was assigned to write the main report," he testified. "I think of it like the trunk of a tree. It sets the stage and general timeline - other reports become branches of that tree." Barnes brought out maps, photos and an aerial layout of the neighborhood showing the house bracketed by the street in front and the alley in back. She displayed panoramic views of the house from front and back, the pool, porch and backyard. Others showed adjacent homes. The officer verified her presentation, explained the limits of the Schockner property in relation to the streets and alley, as well as the neighbors.

"As you can see," she said to the jury, "this was a family of some wealth and means." She introduced more photos depicting blood found in the bedroom along with pictures of the master bedroom closet showing jewelry cabinets and dresser in burgled disarray.

Officer Cervantes, the first officer at the scene at 11:05 am, testified next. He had been on solo patrol when he received the call. "A neighbor saw a male suspect dressed in black get out of a car the in the back alley," Cervantes said. The witness heard the suspect tell his driver: "this is the one."

"We formed a perimeter, front and back," he continued. "Other officers had been called and two more units arrived in front of the house with me. That would be Sgt. Yee and Officer Irving. While we're talking to the neighbor - Scott Rider - a woman [Lynn] walked up to the window in the house in question to see what her dog was barking at. That was Mrs. Schockner. She stayed in the house and looked confused."

Cervantes didn't even need to look down to his notes. "She walked to the front door and finally came outside. I was standing behind the back corner of the car and I yelled to her to come toward me. She walked to the middle of the yard, about halfway, and stopped. Mrs. Schockner asked what was going on. I told her what her neighbor had told me," he said of Rider's call. "She said she had been sleeping. Sgt. Yee told her we needed to search the yard and had sent an officer to the back gate. Then she said: 'Hold on, that door is locked. Let me get the key.'"

Without another word, Lynn turned back into the house, the officer explained, allowing the door to swing shut behind her. She walked away from the officers at the door toward the patio and pool. They soon lost sight of her. For some reason I still can't fathom, she didn't want the police to walk through her house. She disappeared into the family room and out the back door to unlock the gate from inside so police could search her yard.

"Our officer at the gate couldn't see much of the backyard," he said. "We waited another minute, and it might have been a little more, but not long after she left us at the front door, Sgt. Yee ordered me to go into the house to check on her," Cervantes said. "I opened the glass front door and yelled to her: 'Ma'am, where are you?' Then I heard Officer Radcliff yell from the back alley: "There's someone going over the fence."

"We still didn't get any response from Mrs. Schockner, and we ran through the front door. The dog was still there, barking at us, but we made our way toward the back porch," he said.

LBPD Officer Donald Radcliff testified next. "I rolled up behind Cervantes. I saw him talking to the neighbor, and then I cruised around back and took up a position behind the house in the alley. I stepped out of my car to have a clear view of the fence, garage and pavement. I stood there for a few minutes and heard the conversation with Mrs. Schockner over the radio, and then she was gone. I knew one of our guys was waiting for the key, but then I heard somebody yelling.

"All of a sudden I saw a subject dressed in black jump over the fence and land in the alley. When he saw me he ducked behind the trashcan in a space built into the block wall. I gave him numerous commands to come out and show his hands. I must have called out fifteen or twenty commands at him – stop, hands-up, other things - I know I shouted at him a lot.

"Finally he came out, and at first he seemed very compliant," Radcliff said. "Officer Carranza searched him, and found a black cap, a 'beanie; stuffed with jewelry. She also found a hand-held Taser. Then she tried to handcuff him. After she fixed his right wrist, Harvey pulled away. He resisted being moved, and he was a very strong man. She warned him once again, but he continued to resist. Officer Carranza had to use her Taser to get him on the ground and the second cuff on his other hand."

After lunch, LBPD Officer Leticia Carranza, the state's next witness, explained how she assumed a perimeter position on the northwest side of the alley a few minutes after Radcliff arrived. "I saw a man in black with a shaved head, black shirt, black jeans," she said. "I searched him after I cuffed him. He had a little black beanie half-filled with jewelry, a Taser and a cell phone in his left jacket pocket. I also found a dagger and bloody latex gloves. He seemed a little squirmy at first, and then he was okay," she added. She was modest about her efforts, minimizing the pacifying effects of her own non-lethal Taser, judiciously applied.

The first day's testimony ended with LBPD Officer Eduardo Saladano, who reported the suspect appeared calm at the time of his arrest, and then an evidentiary report by LBPD Detective Dennis Robbins regarding jewelry found on his person. The judge allowed Barnes to admit scientific analysis of the blood found on the dagger, that of the victim and the clothes she was wearing when she was killed. The court adjourned.

After packing her files to leave the almost-empty courtroom later that afternoon, less than ten minutes after jurors departed, Barnes stopped by our seats in the shallow gallery. It was a small courtroom with comfortable seating for only a few dozen, and she approached my brother and I with a pleasant smile and self-assured air.

"I just wanted to tell you I will use many photos in my case," she warned. "There are photos of the house and the alley, others of the interior and even an aerial shot. Some of these photos depict Lynn, your sister. They are not at all pleasant. There are others from the autopsy. I just wanted you to know."

My brother was clearly shaken - I watched the blood drain from his face - and she quickly assured him all photos would be displayed toward the jury and the court. Spectators like us would not see the images. My brother was obliged, passing his chance to view the grisly images. "I don't think I can see those," Jon said, letting his words trail off. I was of an entirely different mind – I would be a complete and willing witness to every outrage and see the deliberations from beginning to end, fulfilling the promise I made my little sister and her son just a few years ago. I wanted to see each violation and hear every excuse. I wanted to know the people involved, the processes served, the choreography of actors and advocates and their debates over the pieces and parts of Lynn's death. I wanted to hear their conversations and read their lips, see every detail and feel every nuance, everything these men had done.

• • • •

The following morning I sipped my coffee at the Hilton courtyard of the World Trade Center Plaza, devouring Thursday's edition of the *Long Beach Press-Telegram*. Twenty-eight months after the crime, the story still topped the front page. The banner headline stretched across the March 8 edition promised details never before revealed by the police.

Police Testify in Murder-for-Hire Trial
Bixby Knolls mom found dead after telling officers she'd get keys.

LONG BEACH – An inexperienced hit man from Port Hueneme killed a woman in an affluent Long Beach neighborhood "for $5,000 and a handful of jewelry" and then inadvertently jumped right into the custody of Long Beach police, a prosecutor told jurors Wednesday at the start of the man's trial.

Nicholas Harvey, now 24, is charged with the robbery-murder of Lynn Schockner, 50, who had been helping police investigate a prowler call in her backyard just moments before her death on November 8, 2004, in Bixby Knolls. The defendant allegedly agreed to kill the victim at the behest of her estranged husband and a middleman, both of who face future trials on the same charges.

On Wednesday, Harvey appeared thinner than he had at the time of his arrest two and a half years ago. Sitting alongside his defense attorney in Long Beach Superior Court, he listened calmly as a cadre of Long Beach police officers detailed the crime, showed jurors the bloody murder weapon and discussed graphic crime scene photographs taken of Schockner's home and body.

Deputy District Attorney Cyndi Barnes promised to present a case of overwhelming guilt – including DNA evidence and a tape recording of the defendant's own confession. She said Harvey was approached by an acquaintance named Frank Jaramillo to kill Lynn Schockner for $5,000 - $2,500 up front and $2,500 upon completion – and all the jewelry he could grab. She said Jaramillo was

> a "middleman" for the victim's husband, Manfred Schockner.

• • • •

I had the courtyard to myself, sharing the space with a black stone monolith, and after a second reading, my attention drifted off to the polished granite totem. I've always had an affinity for stones, an interest in lapidary and crystals I shared with my dad. I collect them to this day, looking for answers in the complex compounds and forces recorded in solid rock. The black stone matched my mood but revealed no secrets - a Hollywood hack would have been hard-pressed to come up with what we had learned of the case: a sad little woman slashed to pieces by a hired thug; a killing in a sleepy suburban home surrounded by police.

From my seat in the courtyard I could see the shining split skyscraper of the ARCO Towers, home to the *Press-Telegram* as well as our attorneys. The towers are impressive, even beautiful, but our destination was the Long Beach Courthouse, a strictly functional edifice. We perfected a twice-daily pilgrimage to the anonymous high-rise, the most important place in our lives. Still, my sister was dead and I felt like I was dying a little more each day, trading away a piece of my humanity with each session in court.

• • • •

The prosecutor began the next day at 10 am by calling Deborah Kruek from the Long Beach Crime Lab, a forensic specialist who photographed the crime scene at the Schockner home. She also presented a series of print showing Harvey's Nissan Altima after it had been towed to the impound garage.

Kruek documented evidence located by Birdsall in the car, including two walkie-talkies, three other knives and the empty box which had contained the murder weapon. The detective also found a small case containing medical equipment, including both new and used syringes, three vials of testosterone, medical receipts and a small bottle of pills.

Inside Harvey's wallet, investigators noticed a critical piece of evidence connecting him to Lynn's husband - Schockner's business card, including his hand-written address and information about his family. LBPD Identification Technician Carmen Moncure, an 18-year veteran of the force, said she found one latent print from Harvey's right thumb on the card, establishing this connection. Less than an hour into that second day of the trial, Birdsall took the stand.

"I've been a cop for twenty nine years, and an investigator for nineteen years," was the opening line of the detective's extensive testimony. "I spoke to the suspect on the day of the murder. He waived his rights and wanted to talk about the case. He said he was there to commit a burglary. Mrs. Schockner surprised him in the back yard and he panicked."

A soft-spoken man with concise diction and a ready command of his facts, Birdsall testified in a low voice. He is a big man with a big presence – tough to the core "I had another conversation with the suspect the next day, and he gave me the same story. But then on Wednesday, November 10, we received new information from his telephone records and got his confession." The hour-long taped confession proceeded while Det. Birdsall sat patiently on the stand, attesting to the verity of every word spoken. Extracted a few hours before charges were filed in court, Harvey's final confession was the handiwork of detectives Birdsall and Cardoza.

When he was done, Barnes introduced LBPD Sgt. Richard Conant, one of Birdsall's former partners, another member of the homicide squad, who offered wiretapped contacts from Harvey's cell phone, including key evidence against the co-conspirators. Conant documented 118 phone calls between the defendant and Frank Jaramillo, and more to the point, a dozen calls between them on the day Lynn was killed.

CHAPTER 15

Anxious as we were to see Harvey's verdict delivered, we passed our days in fits and starts. Court sessions seemed to begin late and adjourn early, stretching our California stay at every turn. The days away from home morphed into weeks, and despite all the urgency Ferrari imparted to the jurors, a few invariably trickled into the courtroom after the 10 am deadline. Until they convened, the quick-handed judge impressively juggled all sorts of other cases - parole violations, deferrals, denials, and all the minutiae that make up his full criminal docket - combing his calendar for matters he could handle until the murder trial resumed. He ruled his courtroom with a keen sense of his people's time, a considerable skill in the casual but complicated world of southern California criminal justice. Ferrari paced the proceedings purposefully, patient with any objection yet decisive in his rulings. When Harvey's trial resumed, bailiffs closed the doors during testimony or pleadings, eliminating random intrusions.

Harvey's murder trial proceeded in spurts, stretching five trial days into a two-week span. Lunch breaks ran beyond the stipulated 2 pm hour, and testimony never extended beyond 4 pm. Ferrari seemed unwilling to overload the jury or rush to justice; he allocated six hours per day for the trial, including lunch, in his daily calendar, and that was it.

The third afternoon session of the trial ended with LA

Medical Examiner Dr. Pedro Ortiz who offered the most unnerving testimony yet. The state's fifth and final witness that day, he was quite different from the police officers who preceded him. Ortiz defined the crime upon Lynn's person, an antiseptic analysis of her wounds and violent death. An animated crime scene investigator whose articulated English was heavy with a Caribbean accent, he described nothing but facts about the traumas to her body; clipped phrases that narrowed the killing to precise, anatomical terms.

"The victim, Mrs. Schockner, suffered ten sharp-force injuries and seven blunt force traumas. Of the ten stab wounds, seven were incise wounds and the other three were puncture wounds. The puncture wound in her left upper back was potentially fatal, and the incise wound on the other side of her neck was also fatal," the veteran of 4,500 autopsies reported. "There were at least six and as many as ten blows to her body. She died in minutes from the wounds."

A dozen or more autopsy photographs were presented to the jurors, all directed away from our view, but we could see men and women jurors wince involuntarily at images of Lynn's wounds and traumatic injuries.

Like all others on the 5th floor, Judge Ferrari's courtroom is paneled in blond hardwood, a subdued effect appropriate for institutional atmosphere of the chamber. Mounted prominently on the rail that separates the audience from the court, two permanent plastic signs warn against unapproved contact with anyone across the aisle:

TALKING, COMMUNICATION WITH PRISONERS
IS PROHIBITED
PENAL CODE SECTION 4570
ES PROHIBIDO HABLAR O CUMUNICARSE
CON LOS PRESOS.
ARTICULO NO. 4570 DEL CONDIDO PENAL

'The Host' offers delightful horror U

Playoff wins for Artesia and Poly

SPORTS / B1

Press-Telegram

www.presstelegram.com

Long Beach, California | FRIDAY, MARCH 9, 2007 | 25¢ (plus tax)

Story of killing caught on tape

Law: Interviews with murder suspect are played in courtroom.

By Wendy Thomas Russell
Staff writer

LONG BEACH — Two days after allegedly killing a Bixby Knolls woman on her back patio, a 21-year-old man told police that he was hired by the victim's husband but had been reconsidering attacking her just moments before she surprised him.

The statement was part of a taped police interview played for Long Beach Superior Court jurors Thursday during the trial of Nicholas Harvey, now 24, who is charged with the Nov. 8, 2004, murder of Lynn Schockner.

"I know this is gonna sound ridiculous to you guys — it may or may not," Harvey told Long Beach police detectives during the hour-long interview. "I did the job that I was hired to do, but I did it unintentionally. ... I was contemplating, you know, 'Should I do it?' ... I sat down in the bushes when I got to the door, thinking about it. And then she came out, and what happened happened."

Schockner | Harvey

Harvey's often candid and sometimes jarring interview seemed to offer a rare glimpse into the mind of an inexperienced killer.

At one point on the tape, he even talked about how he feared he had been set up by his co-conspirators and was quietly vowing revenge if he could get away with second-degree murder and make parole.

Unbeknownst to Harvey, the killing of Lynn Schockner occurred while at least six Long Beach police officers — summoned to investigate a possible prowler on Andrews Drive — surrounded the victim's house.

Just moments before her death, Schockner had been speaking with officers on her front porch and had gone inside to retrieve a key to a side gate. She was killed as she stepped onto the porch to scan the yard herself.

Authorities believe Harvey was hired by Schockner's estranged husband, Manfred, using a middleman named Frankie Jaramillo to negotiate the deal. Both men face separate trials later this year, and all three face life in prison without

PLEASE SEE TRIAL / A10

Early in the proceedings, Ferrari had taken pains to warn the entire gallery, pointedly advising my brother and me that no infraction would be overlooked. That day we happened to be sitting just three rows – about eight feet – behind the defendant. His honor's admonitions notwithstanding, the blood rushed up my neck in anger as Ortiz revealed the horrible details of her slaughter, the back of Harvey's head almost within reach. It wouldn't be the first time I found murder in my heart, nor the last; I nurtured hard hatred that envisioned a terrible end for Lynn's killer, but let it pass.

DDA Barnes rested the state's case after the coroner left the stand, and Ferrari adjourned Thursday's proceedings with a three-day weekend to follow. Friday had been set aside to allow the killer's expert witness, Dr. Siegel, his chance to appear for the defense. Patalano had interviewed his witness and prepared his testimony. A week into our stay, we faced another long LA weekend on our hands.

With the court's permission, I examined all photographs entered into evidence, including those from the crime scene and the autopsy. They were stunningly gruesome, progressively worse as the camera focused on Lynn's corpse, a half dozen shocking incisions on her hands coupled with three or four deep wounds in her neck and upper torso. No one could have survived Harvey's silent assault, and just outside the fence, police didn't hear a thing.

• • • •

The next day I sat down with my first cup of coffee and Friday's edition of the *Press-Telegram* to corroborate what I remembered from the previous day's testimony.

> **Story of Killing Caught on Tape**
> **Interviews with murder suspect played in court**
>
> LONG BEACH – Two days after allegedly killing a Bixby Knolls woman on her back patio, a 22-year-old man told police he was hired by the victim's husband but had been reconsidering attacking her just moments before she surprised him.
>
> "I know this is gonna sound ridiculous to you guys – it may or may not," Nick Harvey revealed during his jailhouse confession. "I did the job that I was hired to do, but I did it unintentionally…I was contemplating, you know, 'Should I do it?' I sat down in the bushes when I got to the door, and then she came out, and what happened, happened."
>
> Harvey's often candid and jarring interview seemed to offer a rare glimpse into the mind of an inexperienced killer. At one point on tape, he even talked about how he feared he had been set up by his co-conspirators and was quietly vowing revenge

if he could get away with second-degree murder and eventual parole.

"I might as well break it down for you guys," he said. "I was hired to hit the house." According to his own words, Harvey was chosen by Schockner largely on his tough-guy image. "Not to sound macho," he said, "but I'm kind of, like one of the local, like, bad-asses in the area. No one f---s with me. No one bothers me."

"They wanted the burglary staged," he added.

Harvey said he was about to try to jimmy the home's sliding-glass door with his knife, which is why he had it out of its sheath at the time Lynn Schockner opened the door. He described the killing as a chaotic event where he tackled Schockner and then accidentally grazed the back of her neck and cut her hands.

"That's not what I was going to do," he said of the stabbing. "I didn't plan to hit her in the neck. And I didn't plan for it to happen in the backyard. That's when she came out and we tackled and she fought a little bit, and what happened happened.

"I mean it would be stupid for someone to kill someone right up in her backyard," he continued. "Making that much fucking noise, for one. You got the dog barking. You got the shit breaking. She's screaming, you know."

Then his description becomes nearly unintelligible.

"My right hand came over and at that point we were still struggling. She ... it was some kind of ... I don't know ... it ... all I know is ... it cut something and blood was just ... and then I felt my knife ... my

> blade hit her neck. And I guess, from that point, it was like, well, f---."
>
> He said he thought about leaving but then figured that the man who hired him was a "crooked guy" who might kill him if he didn't complete the job as agreed. So he said he found his way into the victim's bedroom, overturned a couple of drawers and stole a bunch of jewelry before fleeing over the back fence.
>
> He jumped right into the custody of the Long Beach Police Department.

• • • •

I'm sure he was a sociopath, possibly a psychopath, and who knows what other labels social scientists would apply. To me, Harvey was the man who cut the life out of my little sister, a killer without conscience or remorse. It seemed we would be better off with Nick Harvey behind bars forever, but I was hardly an unbiased observer. He would have to convince a dozen strangers to find him guilty of a lesser offense, opening the door for eventual parole. When the court permitted his tape-recorded confession, I studied each juror, trying to gauge his or her reaction. I couldn't divine their sentiments from facial gestures or frowns, and waited anxiously for their decision.

• • • •

When Nick Harvey finally took the stand Monday afternoon, March 12, my brother and I were thinning our trousers on the court's wooden benches to help him mark his 25th birthday. After the long list of state witnesses who detailed Harvey's connections to the crime, Patalano faced an uphill fight. Barnes sat confidently at her table during his opening remarks, attractive and attentive in a tailored black suit; only her hazel-gray eyes flashed angrily when the court-appointed counsel contradicted her chronicle of Harvey's crime, but she never raised an objection. The lawyer's only hope for Harvey hinged on any juror who would excuse his psychotic lapses and believe his four-year "addiction" to anabolic steroids that made him "more intense and aggressive." Harvey laughed while he described how he became quick to anger. "You develop a very low tolerance for B.S," he said.

His attorney led him through his relationship with Jaramillo at the LA Fitness Center and explained how the he offered him the job. "He [Jaramillo] asked me if I wanted to make some money, and I said: 'Yes.' He laid out the proposal," Harvey testified. He described his bodybuilding efforts that progressed to great strength and bulk, and bragged about victorious street encounters against others who got in his way. Finally, he made an observation about Lynn's husband. "Just by telling me what he wanted done gave me an idea about Schockner," Harvey said. "He's kind of a scumbag."

We had developed a mutual friendship with Wendy Russell of the *Press-Telegram*, but I also felt a kinship with the woman, not only because of my own background in newspapers, but also because her dispatches were invariably in synch with my own take on the trial. The newspaper topped its March 13th edition with another fifty-six column inches on the killer's testimony, and as always, there was a surreal aspect to the tale.

Body Builder Dreamed of Becoming Hulk, Hit Man; Defendant charged in alleged murder-for-hire cites damaging steroid abuse

LONG BEACH – A body builder charged with the murder-for-hire of a Bixby Knolls woman told jurors Monday that he was a fitness buff who idolized comic-book heroes, collected knives and took excessive amounts of steroids – the basis for what could become a "roid rage" defense when the trial wraps up today.

Nicholas Harvey took the stand in his own defense Monday afternoon – his 25th birthday. He appeared at ease, even comfortable, on the stand in Long Beach Superior Court, especially under questioning by his own attorney. At one point he turned to address jurors directly while talking about how steroids work. And he seemed eager to offer personal information about himself such as his father's interest in knives and his mother's Christian faith.

"I was one of those kids that was always into the comic book heroes – the Hulk," he said. "I always wanted to be the big guy, the strong guy."

He said he had a knife and sword collection and even named his young daughter, Katana, after a Japanese sword. Harvey said he worked as a personal trainer, bouncer and loan officer after graduating from high school, but had bragged to his friends about wanting to become "a hit man." His steroid use, he said, began at age 18.

Harvey said he was contacted by Jaramillo. He described him as "a charming and flashy guy who acted as a middleman for Manfred Schockner. He asked me if I wanted to make some money, and I said, 'Yes,' and he laid out the proposal," Harvey testified.

While he didn't take the job seriously at first, Harvey said he was later paid $2,500 – with the promise of another $2,500 upon completion of the job – and that Jaramillo started getting "pushy," calling Harvey's cell phone daily. Schockner "wanted it done.

"Did you feel pressured to do it?" Patalano asked.

"Yes," and he described how he bought the double-edged dagger and a stun gun, promised to pay a friend $1,000 to drive him to Long Beach, and then hopped the fence in Schockner's backyard, adding that he wore latex gloves to protect his identity. He said he unsheathed the dagger to jimmy the sliding glass door to enter the home when the victim walked out onto the patio and startled him.

"She just came and saw me, yelled something along the lines of 'Oh my God'…and I panicked," he said, claiming Lynn's murder was some sort of accident.

"Did you go after her?" Patalano asked.

"Yes. My first impulse was to keep her from screaming…I tackled her down, and the next thing I remember was there was a whole lot of blood," he said. "At that point, I jumped up because that was the last thing I expected to see. But she was still moving. I remember that."

As soon as the defense attorney reached his seat, Barnes challenged Harvey's contention that he didn't remember the stabbing, and that it was unintentional during her cross-examination.

Using autopsy photographs as a backdrop, the DDA drilled the defendant on his previous statements to police on Nov. 8, 9 and 10, 2004 in which he described stabbing Schockner in the neck with one hand while trying to cover her mouth with the other. He testified that he had lied to police in those interviews.

"You are willing to lie when it helps you?" Barnes inquired.

"At the time, yes," Harvey answered.

"You lied on Nov. 8, correct?"

"Yes."

"You lied on Nov. 9, correct?"

"Yes."

"And you lied on Nov. 10?"

"I believe so."

Now that the jury has been impaneled to make a determination of guilt, she asked, "don't you have a motive to lie?"

"It depends on what I'm lying about," he answered.

Barnes said she found it difficult to believe that someone could stab or slash a woman 10 times accidentally.

"One. Two. Three. Four," Barnes said as she pounded her fist into her palm for effect. "Six, seven times. Nine times. Ten times. You don't remember any of that?"

"No, ma'am," he answered.

• • • •

Judge Ferrari was determined to see the proceedings withstand the appeal process, which he knew would follow. After Harvey left the stand, he adjourned the session and advised the jury to expect one "possible" additional witness before closing arguments on Tuesday and instructed them to return at 11 am that day. When the jury was gone, Ferrari explained how he remained unconvinced Dr. Siegel qualified as an expert witness for the defense, and he pointedly recalled the DDA's objection on these grounds. Despite his skepticism, he scheduled an early hearing to review Dr. Siegel's planned testimony at 9 am before granting him status as an "expert" witness. If he did not, he would disallow the witness entirely, and the trial would proceed to closing arguments later that morning.

The Section 402 hearing opened Tuesday when the judge explained his indecision about the qualifications of the witness and the specific scope of his testimony. "The issue with Dr. Siegel is whether he will be permitted to testify about his claim that Harvey had a 'steroid-facilitated rage reaction.' The question is simple – how does he know?" he asked. Ferrari wondered aloud about other plausible reasons for Harvey's actions, including the completion of a contract for murder. There were many nuances that distinguish first-degree murder from all other killings, but impairment by self-induced intoxication was not one. Even so, he listened carefully to Siegel's credentials and encouraged his claim.

"I've studied anabolic steroids since the late 1960s and seen the effects of these drugs: paranoia, hallucinations and violent behavior," Siegel testified. "My primary interest is in the aggression we see as a result of long-term use. My first encounter with the phenomenon of 'steroid intoxication' came in 1968, and my clinical experiences have shown a correlation between the use of steroids and outbreaks of aggressive behavior.

"Nick Harvey satisfied the criteria as a steroid abuser and I believe he experienced a 'steroid-induced rage reaction' when he killed Lynn Schockner," he said. "He was at a confluence of very bad things happening in his life, and he felt invincible, like he could do anything."

The clinician seemed well-versed in human reactions to various compounds and chemical agents, and comfortably claimed this extraordinarily violent act as an aberration brought about by pharmaceutical abuse, not the killer's nature.

"The human brain employs different operating systems, like computers we use today," Siegel testified. "The most primitive system within the brain is the limbic system, the animal functions of the organism, and when that system is activated, we respond like reptiles. We refer to the 'four F-words of survival:' *fear, flight, fight and fornication.*' When that happens, the higher cortical areas of the brain are shut down, disconnected. This is a momentary reaction to the threat."

Siegel described effect of steroids on Harvey's brain in a crisis, when the primitive corridors of neural pathways take over. "The limbic system operates by influencing the endocrine system and the autonomic nervous system, and is highly interconnected with the brain's pleasure center, which plays a role in sexual arousal and the *high* derived from certain recreational drugs," he claimed.

"I cannot rule out the role that steroids played in Nick Harvey's crime against Lynn Schockner," he said. "Steroids enabled the process to go forward."

Ferrari remained unconvinced. "Voluntary intoxication is not a defense," he repeated, but after additional arguments, he admitted the witness but limited the scope of his testimony. "I find the admissibility of Dr. Siegel's testimony to be infinitesimally small and I was not impressed by his expertise on steroids," he said while the jury remained sequestered. But he would allow the witness to explain how Harvey's behavior was consistent with what happens when somebody abuses steroids, but prohibited any suppositions about Harvey's emotional state at the time of the killing. "I think the doctor's testimony would be confusing and misleading," Ferrari said, and forbid him to testify that Harvey was suffering from a 'steroid facilitated rage reaction' when he committed the murder. He would only allow him to speak on how steroids affect human beings in a general manner – nothing about the defendant.

• • • •

During closing arguments, the public defender portrayed Harvey as a naive young man who was pressured into becoming a hit man by his two conspirators. "They took advantage of his heavy steroid use, which transformed him into a would-be junior commando. They abused his abuse of steroids." Patalano said. Without denying the murder, he told jurors his client had kicked his habit and found religion behind bars. Harvey could be rehabilitated and emerge from prison a new man, his counsel claimed, pleading for something less than first degree murder.

Barnes dismissed Siegel's testimony as irrelevant and described Harvey as a man who repeatedly lied to the police, as well as the jury, in an attempt to place himself in the best possible light. She pointed out that, by his own admission, he was a self-styled hit man who idolized comic-books characters, such as the Hulk, and bragged about his ability to beat up three to five men at one time.

"This is not some naive innocent kid who was manipulated by two older men," Barnes said. "He took steroids to get bigger, stronger, faster and meaner, and that's what he did. He bought a dagger and a stun gun, and then he hired a friend to drive him down to Long Beach on the day of the murder."

After her summation, Ferrari dismissed the jury with instructions to return at 9 am the following morning: "Being so late in the day, we're going to recess," he said. "You should avoid discussing the case or viewing any of the media coverage after your leave, and then return here in the morning to begin deliberations."

But the jury didn't retire when they recessed. The group retired to the jury room, a few offered comments, and they didn't need more than a few minutes to make their decision, deliberating briefly before surprising the court with their verdict. Russell reported the stunning news the next day.

It's easy being GREEN

P-T Career FAIR
BUSINESS / A19

Council pioneer in Cerritos
Joseph Cho LOCAL NEWS/ A3

Press-Telegram

www.presstelegram.com

Long Beach, California — WEDNESDAY, MARCH 14, 2007 — 25¢ (plus tax)

Sunday parking meters OK'd in the Shore

Council: In a unanimous vote, members also agree to extend metering hours to 7 p.m. daily.

By Don Jergler
Staff writer

LONG BEACH — The City Council voted on Tuesday to expand parking meter enforcement in Belmont Shore to Sunday and shift hours to later in the evening, a move that has received broad support from businesses there.

The unanimous council vote means hours at the meters on and around Second Street will be expanded to include Sundays. The hours of enforcement will also be shifted to 10 a.m. to 7 p.m. Holidays will remain an exception.

The current hours of operation for parking meters are from 9 a.m. to 6 p.m. Monday through Saturday.

The change could take effect within two months.

Two groups working to improve the Second Street neighborhood — the Belmont Shore Business Association and the Belmont Shore Parking and Business Improvement Area Advisory Commission — endorsed the proposed changes.

Councilman Gary DeLong, who represents Belmont Shore, supported the change.

"It's good for the district," DeLong said after the vote. "All the dollars that are generated are invested back into the community."

The city estimated the change would bring a 15 percent revenue increase, raising $529,000 in fiscal year 2007 compared with $460,000 in 2006.

Under an agreement with the city, an advisory commission oversees the Belmont Shore Parking Revenue Fund, which collects parking revenue in the area. By law, all of the fund's money must be used for infrastructure improvements in Belmont Shore and cannot be absorbed into the general fund.

PLEASE SEE COUNCIL / A5

CARE TO COMMENT?
At www.presstelegram.com, scroll to the end of this story, click the link and type away.

L.B. HONORS ITS VETS
■ Many city employees have served in the war on terror in Iraq or Afghanistan / A7

Hit man guilty in Schockner killing

Twenty-five-year-old Nicholas Harvey listens to a jury's guilty verdict Tuesday on charges of first-degree murder for financial gain in the 2004 killing of Lynn Schockner, 50, of Bixby Knolls.
Sandra Jay / Press-Telegram

Crime: Panel needs only half an hour to convict man in alleged

Nicholas Harvey, 25, appeared sullen but showed no other emotion as the seven-woman,

SUPPORT FOR POLICE

Police show new video of suspect in child rape

Crime: Surveillance tape image shows man walking with victim of attack in Long Beach.

By Hanna Chu
Staff writer

The Long Beach Police Department released a video Tuesday of the suspect in the alleged rape of an 11-year-old girl on Feb. 28, in the hopes of identifying and finding him, authorities said.

The footage from a business on the 1100 block of Loma Avenue in Long Beach shows 31 seconds from two different cameras that show the suspect walking with the victim, whose image has been blurred.

Police are seeking the public's help in finding the man who allegedly raped the Long Beach girl at knifepoint in an alley about a block from Jefferson Middle School.

Letters were sent home with every student at the school, including 1,000 copies of the suspect's sketch.

Police did not release the business' name because the owners did not want to be publi-

PLEASE SEE RAPIST / A5

TODAY ONLINE
PRESSTELEGRAM.COM

Hit man guilty in Schockner killing

March 13, 2007

LONG BEACH - Faced with what they described as "overwhelming evidence," Long Beach Superior Court jurors deliberated for less than 35 minutes Tuesday before convicting an inexperienced hit man of first-degree murder for financial gain in the 2004 slaying of a Bixby Knolls woman.

Nicholas Harvey, 25, appeared sullen but showed no other emotion as the seven-woman, five-man jury returned its verdict just as the courthouse was closing for the day. In the audience behind him, Harvey's family sobbed quietly and held their faces in their hands.

He faces a sentence of life in prison without the possibility of parole when he returns to court next month.

The quick verdict stunned attorneys, court staff and the victim's brothers - who attended every day of the trial but missed the verdict because they were slated to fly back to their respective homes in Georgia and North Carolina after closing arguments Tuesday.

"We are gratified and appreciative of the thoughtful and incisive verdict delivered by the fine men and women of the jury," brother Mark Jicha said by phone Tuesday evening. "I had hoped I would be able to be there to thank each and every one of them personally, but we had to leave."

Jurors interviewed after Tuesday's verdict said they felt no need to draw out the deliberations after being dispatched to the jury room about 3:40 pm. Shortly before 4:15 p.m., a bailiff entered the room

> to tell jurors they could go home and was informed that the jury had managed to reach a verdict.
>
> "The evidence was overwhelming," said juror No. 1, a Torrance man who spoke on condition of anonymity. He said jurors "tippy-toed" around the issue for a while after convening, then re-read a few specific jury instructions before polling themselves for the first time. It was immediately clear, he said, that further deliberations were unnecessary. There was no one who had a qualm about it," he said. "It was unanimous."
>
> In a statement released to the Press-Telegram, Mark Jicha expressed deep appreciation to the police officers involved in his sister's case. And, in an interview, he stressed that they bore no responsibility for his sister's death. "They did their level best to protect residents and apprehend a criminal," he said. "Putting responsibility on anyone but the killers is absurd."

• • • •

Unfortunately, we weren't in court when the jury returned with their verdict. We had already booked an evening flight back to the East Coast and instead of paying a hefty rebooking fee we decided to keep our reservations and leave town. We checked out of the hotel as planned and opted for an early dinner before boarding our plane. Setting our schedules between Long Beach and our lives had become something of a crapshoot, and we didn't know how long deliberations would last. Our jobs demanded personal attention but we looked forward to returning home for more than business reasons - we just wanted to go home. Trying to plan our travels to and from Long Beach according to the whimsy of courtroom schedules, deferrals and other delays had been incredibly frustrating. We convinced each other our role in the courtroom drama was done: our presence had put a face on our family's loss, but we would have no further influence on the proceedings.

We were jammed in traffic in a sluggish, rented PT Cruiser when I received a garbled call from the court. Juggling the phone, I scrambled around a five-car snarl at Ximeno Avenue and East Vista Boulevard and took the call from a detective: Harvey was guilty! Finally breaking free from traffic, I cruised north along Ocean Boulevard while Det. Dennis Robbins explained the unexpected verdict. I finally found shelter in the parking lot of the Long Beach marina, eased the car to the curb and cut the engine. My brother and I jumped from the car and hugged in celebration and sorrow, our blood almost flowing back and forth between us to wash away the loss. Our lives had been defined by fits and starts all through the courtroom drama, and the outcome of Nick Harvey's trial was no different.

CHAPTER 16

We arrived in Jacksonville at 6 am, driving north on I-95 into light Georgia traffic, more relaxed by the mile. There's nothing like returning home where my wife, son and dog welcomed me warmly. Once there, I fired up my computer and found the *Press-Telegram's* website leading with the Harvey verdict and a sidebar that featured a photograph of my brother and I on the balcony outside Judge Ferrari's 5th floor courtroom.

> **Family praises work of officials**
>
> This statement from Mark Jicha, on behalf of Lynn Schockner's family, was released to the Press-Telegram on Tuesday.
>
> "Despite the terrible circumstances surrounding the brutal murder of our sister, we have become acquainted with some of the finest people we have ever met, especially in the law enforcement community. The citizens of Long Beach should take pride in the jobs performed by the police, the district attorney's office and the judiciary.
>
> "Due to circumstances beyond the control of anyone but the killers, our sister died in Harvey's savage attack. Every officer acted in a thoroughly capable and professional manner, and the investigating officers followed through with a

> thorough and sophisticated effort to identify and incarcerate the three men who perpetrated this crime, and did so with concern and compassion for the family.
>
> "The deputy district attorney (Cyndi Barnes) has been a stalwart advocate for our murdered sister, and we are proud to have her prosecuting those responsible for the crimes. We are confident that justice will prevail and all those associated with this savage killing will be held responsible for their crimes."

There is a phenomenon many journalists discover early in their careers – many people seem to believe an event lacks substance unless they see it reported by the media. I discovered this reality not long after I took my first newspaper job as an eager (but not especially talented) sports reporter for the now defunct weekly, the *West Columbia Journal* in South Carolina in 1980.

This was a "community" newspaper in the purest sense of the word; a weekly that covered the high school pageants and featured special sections for local festivals: everything from the dogwoods in bloom to chitlins fried in pure pork fat, and a few in between. But none hitch their wagons more firmly than sports-minded moms and dads, all cheering for their children and quick to find fault when the local rag didn't headline the youngster's heroics, or a reporter didn't find the time to cover every minute of every game. Back in the day, readers confirmed their lives in the pages of the public record, and when involved in some event outside the ordinary, they wanted ratification in ink. I dismissed their small minds and provincialism, but in the end I was no different than all those I had disparaged.

It was comfortable, even gratifying to read my words and return to the mundane matters. I enjoyed preparing meals for my wife and Charlie, and embraced familiar surroundings and welcome routines. This was a reprieve from the daily anxieties of court room, but it couldn't last; the court agreed to fast-track Frank Jaramillo's trial, bumping it up to March 30, 2007. What seemed inconceivable just a few weeks earlier had become marching orders for a new day. I packed for another fortnight in California, my business in shambles and my life on hold.

That wasn't the least of it: I had been summoned for jury duty in Glynn County Superior Court where we lived, and I had already been excused from a summons in February because of the Harvey trial. When I received another summons in March, my request for another exemption was denied. I tried to explain my situation and beg pardon from a stony clerk, who reluctantly granted a final excuse. A few days later Barnes emailed news that Jaramillo's trial had been set back to April 11, the same day I was to begin jury service in Georgia. This time, there was no chance of an extension. The clerk was furious, warning me I better show up that Monday morning ready for my duty, warning of dire consequences if I failed to appear: a bench warrant would be issued for my arrest.

I just laughed. My life was completely beyond control. Incarceration would be the only reason I would miss a day of my sister's trial, and I wouldn't be arrested in Long Beach until I returned home. I would turn myself in after Jaramillo's trial – I couldn't see a local deputy flying clear across country to track me down and resigned myself to these conflicting court calendars. Luckily, the court date was set back once again, now into May, and I was able to fulfill my April jury service in Georgia without a hitch.

• • • •

I was selected to serve in the first pool assigned to the criminal court: a 20-year-old woman charged with child endangerment for hot tub sex with a teenage girl as they frolicked in the motel's hot tub. Joining me on the jury was one of our own superior court judges, the Honorable Amanda F. Williams, who happens to be a personal friend. I figured she would be first to be excused, but no one in the court voiced an objection, reaffirming my reluctance to claim understanding of any jury.

The prosecutor called a couple of cops to the stand, and then the defendant before resting his case; but he neglected a key witness because he assumed the defense would call the cop. Before he got settled in his seat opposing counsel rose to rest his case, calling for a summary judgment. The novice ADA didn't recognize his mistake for at least a minute, and even though Superior Court Judge Stephen Scarlett considered the motion, he declined but charged our jury with specific instructions regarding the point.

Ensconced in chambers, we set out to elect a foreperson. I nominated Judge Williams, primarily to avoid the job. Everyone seemed agreeable, but she politely declined, citing her position on the bench. Since I was the first idiot to open his mouth, they nominated me, closed the ballot and gave me the job. I accepted, but insisted I would side with Amanda on any points of law. They were fine with that.

We acquitted the defendant, who was clearly guilty, but not for the reason one might expect. After we got acclimated to our seats, I called for a quick vote. To my surprise, it came back 11-1 for conviction, only a single holdout for the defense. But as soon as I announced the ballot, Judge Williams admitted hers was the dissenting vote and said we had to acquit. Now retired, Williams enjoyed a fearsome reputation on the bench, and we listened to her explanation with care: the defense listed a GBI agent as their primary witness who had interviewed the teenage girl (the victim), an eyewitness and the suspect. Without his testimony, the charges lacked substance. The ADA dropped the ball when he failed to call the agent to corroborate the charge. Apparent guilt and innocence were irrelevant, Williams insisted; we were required to determine if the state had proved guilt beyond a reasonable doubt, which it had not. We had no choice but to acquit.

This episode illustrated the tenuous ground we still walked, the real-life ramifications of any sort of error or technicality. Two Long Beach trials remained, and one false step in either could bring a mistrial, which would drag out the proceedings at least a year *and* jeopardize the outcome of ensuing prosecutions. An acquittal was too much to consider, but we were confident in what we had seen so far of California's courtroom personnel. Even so, I had to acknowledge the fallibilities of our criminal justice system, the narrow restraints placed on the state and the many ways criminals are protected under the laws of our land. I was still determined to see Jaramillo follow Harvey into a long penitentiary sentence, but we considered both minor players compared to Manfred Schockner, whose trial was scheduled later that year.

Nick Harvey was sentenced to life without parole that same month. Judge Ferrari passed down the penalty to an empty courtroom and Lynn's killer became a part of the penal system, a life without hope, incarceration without end. Within a few days, he announced that Jaramillo's trial would begin on Monday, May 21.

One down, two to go.

• • • •

My business, a regional humor publication named *EVENTS Magazine*, finally went bankrupt after ten years of monthly publication. During those salad days my motto had been: *We're*

Serious About Humor! I prospered for a while, but then the banks brought prosperity to a halt, the housing market crashed and marketing dollars dried up. Those were the obvious reasons for closing shop, but advertisers fled from my calls with good reason - my *own* sense of humor had turned black. Animosity and anguish are tough sells in the trade - and in the last few months before my magazine folded, I was running on negative cash flow and antacid. As every week seemed to bring a new California court date forcing immediate flight plans and hotel reservations, my publication deadlines became a joke. My enterprise died with more of a whimper than a bang, but I was relieved to shed the monthly deadlines, sales calls and computer tasks.

CHAPTER 17

The escalator's haunting melody serenaded us up to the fifth floor and followed us down the corridor to Judge Ferrari's court, squeals and moans from the public conveyance. Long Beach Superior Court is a minor monolith standing in stark contrast to most of the modern buildings on Beach Boulevard; just a block from the water, the ugly building offers sullen reminder of the hard process of criminal justice in southern California. The halls are bleak and scarred, the stone floor polished smooth by wear. Life's no beach in this building.

The morning crush brought more than 100 prospective jurors to Judge Ferrari's countroom, many anxious for a quick exit. From a distance, it seemed a strange mix - court professionals and cops, reluctant citizens and a smattering of family, victims and friends who shared criminal sorrows and hushed voices. Furtive glances slipped through the room like spirits flirting in fluorescent lights.

Frank Jaramillo was unknown to our family, even Charlie. No one knew of the defendant's friendship with Schockner. No one had seen his face. What little we did know came from dispatches in the *Press-Telegram*, and those details were sketchy. My brother and I arrived on Sunday afternoon at LAX on May 20 and resumed our lodging at the Long Beach Hilton. The jury had been empanelled the previous week, and, barring some sort of procedural delay, the trial would begin at 10 am the following day.

. . . .

Ferrari performed "house-keeping" chores to keep his calendar open for the proposed two-week trial, ruled on two motions and then read the jury instructions he had prepared. He spoke with great clarity, carefully enunciating his words, even correcting himself a few times during the eight-page recitation, sipping water along the way.

He ended with a stern warning to the panel: "I'm going to issue a media warning to all jurors and alternates," he said, tipping his head toward Ms. Russell sitting alone at the two-chair press table. "Please, I say again, please do not read or discuss any media coverage of this trial. This is very important."

Barnes strode confidently to the podium and opened the state's case by describing the defendant as a "broker" in a deal to arrange the murder. She encouraged jurors to hear his confession and "follow the money trail" that would convince them of his role in the crime. "The evidence will prove the defendant's guilt. Manfred Schockner faced an expensive divorce and he didn't want to give Lynn his money – he wanted her killed. Frank Jaramillo was the broker of that murder, the hub through which the conspiracy flowed. He found Nick Harvey, he paid him and he gave him instructions."

The personal relationship between the defendant and Schockner was nothing like a usual friendship, she advised jurors. She described their association in terms of bank records and thinly-veiled loans. "Jaramillo and Schockner had a strange relationship," Barnes said, citing Schockner's habit of disguising payments as personal loans. "There are four things you should remember: First, you need to hear Frank Jaramillo's own statement when he admitted delivering $2,500 to Nick Harvey to kill Lynn Schockner. He admitted doing that so his debt would be excused.

"Second, Schockner and Jaramillo talked on the telephone all the time in the weeks leading up to the murder, but Manfred Schockner never, ever talked to Harvey," the DDA said. "Frank Jaramillo also called Nick Harvey all this time, and the phone records show the defendant called both parties back and forth.

"Then you've got to consider the third point," she continued. "When an undercover police officer contacted Frank Jaramillo, he not only agreed to the meeting, he paid some of the money he still owed the killer, and then admitted he owed him more. Frank Jaramillo adopted a nonchalant attitude toward the deal – he couldn't care less about the woman who had been killed.

"And finally," she said, "you need to follow the money trail. There you will find a direct link of payments from Manfred Schockner to Frank Jaramillo and to the killer, Nick Harvey. This was all about the money and nothing more. It was a business deal to Frank Jaramillo."

The defendant's lawyer, Alternate Public Defender Richard Caillouette Jr., admitted most of the state's assertions before outlining two defenses: either his client was ignorant to the true nature of the job; or Jaramillo was "scared to death" of Schockner's threats to his family, who were ready to testify that they were stalked by strange men after Harvey was arrested. Caillouette stipulated most of the state's case in his opening statement.

"In most cases, my client would categorically deny allegations like this, but you will find I will agree with a lot of what the district attorney says," he conceded. "But I would disagree with the DA when she says my client would get money for this crime. Sure, he received watches, and bought cars for the Schockners, Lynn included, but he only participated in this conspiracy because of his fear of this evil man."

"Schockner said he 'needed something done.' Jaramillo arranged for him to meet Nick Harvey, ostensibly for home repairs or routine work," the defense attorney argued. "When he learned of the plot to kill Lynn Schockner, he begged and pleaded Nick Harvey not to do it. Then he called Manfred Schockner and begged and pleaded and cried to prevail upon the husband to abandon his plan, all to no avail.

"The only reason he participated in this crime was from fear of the evil, insidious Manfred Schockner," Caillouette swore. "This man is a monster. Frankie begged, whined and cried to prevent the murder from happening, but Schockner was having none of it – he wanted his wife dead. My client was threatened by Schockner, who knew where his family and in-laws lived. He was convinced Manfred Schockner hired other henchmen to threaten his mother. My client did participate in the crime, but he did so out of fear for his family."

That was Jaramillo's defense: at first he didn't know Harvey and Schockner planned to kill our sister; but when he learned their true intent, he was forced to participate out of fear for family. That argument held water until the Barnes ran the table with police and forensic witnesses, testimony from an LBPD undercover officer and evidence showing the defendant's willing participation in a wiretapped meeting with Schockner weeks after the murder. Jaramillo's claims unraveled when Barnes ended her arguments with his tape-recorded confession.

We were intrigued by the details, and offended by the revelations how he and Nick Harvey tried to distance themselves from the murder they planned and committed. We were encouraged by Barnes's conservative approach to the prosecution, beginning with testimony with five LBPD officers from the scene or later assigned to the case.

LBPD Patrolman James Foster had been assigned to compile the comprehensive, overall report from the crime scene three hours after the killing. He described the crime scene, identified each officer's location on a map, and placed the victim and killer. While he testified, Barnes ran through a list of nineteen overhead images, maps and photographs from the scene. As with Harvey's trial, the images were hidden from our view, shots of Lynn's blood on the doorway and other forensic evidence. Foster distilled the crime to a series of interactions and events. Patrolman Cervantes testified about a brief meeting with the victim, and then his growing concerns when the housewife failed to appear at the side gate, followed by the confused clatter of radio traffic as the killer ran out to the back alley.

Laying the foundation for her prosecution with facts from the killing field, Barnes finally revealed the full extent of the LBPD investigation when she escorted Detective Kris Nelson to the stand, a grizzled veteran who groomed himself for deep cover and excelled in the assignments.

"Early in our investigation we realized there were three people responsible for Lynn Schockner's death: Nick Harvey killed her, Frankie Jaramillo arranged the killing, and Manfred Schockner paid to have the murder done," the 21-year veteran said. "Posing as a family friend, I cold-called Frankie on November 22 (fourteen days after the murder). I told him I came down from San Francisco when I heard from Nick's mom, and when I spoke to Nicky in jail, he told me Frank still owed him half the money for the job.

"My job was to infiltrate the conspiracy and collect money still on the books," Nelson explained to the jury, advising this would be a "positive action" by the defendant in furtherance of the crime. "I introduced myself as 'Uncle John,' a close friend of the Harvey family. I told him Nick asked me to reach out to Frank and Fred for the money still owed. Jaramillo was careful – he admitted to knowing Nick Harvey, but little else. I played it loose, but told him if something *didn't* happen for Nick he would talk to the cops."

Barnes changed gears after more than an hour of Nelson's

riveting testimony, asking permission to introduce yet another police investigator: LBPD Det. Brian McMahon. Respected as one of the most astute detectives in the department, McMahon prepared the court orders for wiretaps on the phones used by all three defendants. He chronicled that interplay of dozens of phone calls between the trio as they planned, executed, and then tried to conceal the conspiracy. McMahon also laid the evidentiary foundation for the deputy district attorney, who also asked him to explain techniques used by the police to "stimulate" interaction among the criminals to be used for their prosecution.

Barnes specifically asked McMahon to elaborate on any threats made by Schockner during their wiretapped conversations, to which he replied: "There were no such threats made against the defendant – they mostly talked about Frank Jaramillo paying back the money he owed Fred Schockner."

He described calls Jaramillo made to another friend with street loan connections when he tried to secure quick cash, ostensibly to deal with a pregnant girlfriend. The police knew he needed money to keep Harvey from implicating him in the murder, but that admission came less than two days after the killing and allowed investigators the opportunity to stalk their final suspect.

Recalling Det. Nelson, Barnes quizzed him about his tactics and techniques on this assignment, prompting him to apologize for his language during his recorded conversations with the defendant, which would soon be presented.

He described his cover as a former longshoreman who had seen his share of hard knocks, and then explained the profanity. "I swear a lot when I'm nervous, and I was nervous back then because I knew what we had to prove. The first thing I did with Frankie was try to make him need me, and involve me in the crime. I kept throwing gasoline on the fire, stimulating interaction between the Jaramillo and Schockner about Nick's need for money and his threat to confess the conspiracy. I tried to make myself the only person who could prevent this from happening by *handling* Nick Harvey."

Donning the electronic vest to videotape their meeting, Nelson also apologized for technical problems with the images, although the audio portion of their meeting was clear as a bell. Barnes asked him to describe other telephone conversations recorded via their wiretapped telephones, which he did, and then testified to that fateful meeting when Frank Jaramillo passed him $1,000 for Nick Harvey's legal defense, an *affirmative act,* that would hound him all the way to verdict. That payment confirmed his active participation in the conspiracy, and Frank Jaramillo was a doomed man.

Under cross-examination, the defense attorney asked Det. Nelson to describe how willingly his client assisted police and how he wore a rigged vest to record his meeting with Schockner at LB Seafood. He asked the detective to explain how Jaramillo had cooperated with LBPD during the final hours and minutes of investigation, which would end the following morning.

But Nelson stumped Caillouette when he inserted a final comment about his dealings with the defendant: "Frankie never said he was afraid of Schockner or afraid for his family during the time I talked with him," the veteran cop insisted. "He never said he had been threatened." That knocked the legs out from Jaramillo's defense.

Finally, Barnes called Det. Birdsall, now an arson investigator, the senior detective on the team that "caught" the case. His partner, Det. Cardoza, left the LBPD after the case and never appeared in court. Birdsall revealed details about the conspiracy we didn't learn until the coming moment- his testimony explained sordid elements of the killing, and portrayed a conspirator who would say anything to distance himself from the crime.

"Manfred Schockner told me Frank Jaramillo owed him more

than a hundred thousand dollars," Birdsall testified about his early interview when Manfred tried to explain his acquaintance with the middleman. Schockner said he had loaned Jaramillo various amounts of money over recent years and then fronted him twenty-five thousand to buy a used BMW and watches. The funds were transferred directly between their accounts, and there were no promissory notes or loan agreements to document the debt. Birdsall and Cardoza doubted his explanation early in their inquest, but couldn't prove Schockner's link to Harvey until Jaramillo confirmed their mutual plan, connecting these three very different men who lived in far-ranging cities of southern California: Bixby Knolls, Port Hueneme and Woodland Hills.

When Barnes asked the detective to verify Jaramillo's tape-recorded interview, everyone in court heard the suspect prevaricate, back-peddle and try to deny his complicity in the killing.

"The questions we asked you, Frank, sometimes we know the answers. You need to start getting things straight and thinking about yourself. We know the Harvey family has reached out to you and now you're denying that you talked to someone from the family. Why would you lie about that?

"It's not a question of lying," Jaramillo insisted. "I don't want to be involved in it. You've got to understand – I have had nothing to do with this."

The interview with the suspect ran almost forty-five minutes as Jaramillo danced around the facts. *El Cubano* admitted he introduced Schockner to Nick Harvey, then agreed that he knew Schockner wanted his wife eliminated. He also confessed to passing money between the two men to kill Lynn Schockner.

"You found a murderer for a husband who wanted his wife dead," Birdsall summarized during their interview. "You found the person and worked as a conduit so they could talk to each other, you also furnished him with monies from your own pocket, up front, with the understanding that you were going to be repaid for it. By lying to us from the very beginning, you're showing us you are conscious of your guilt. You refused to get a hold of us because you didn't want to be in the middle of this crime. That tells us that you know you're involved."

• • • •

That ended testimony for the day. While Ferrari dismissed the jury with another admonition regarding trial conversations or media coverage, my brother and I sat in place while the courtroom dissolved. As usual, the end of the court session seemed abrupt, empty and early. As we waited to speak with our favorite DDA, I noticed the defendant's mother and daughter sobbing quietly as the jurors departed. The old woman's shoulders heaved with anguish, her daughter cried in silence. As the totality of Frank's guilt became clear, the women realized just how they would share his sentence. Another family forever marked by murder, not altogether unlike us.

That left Jon and I alone with Cyndi Barnes. Approaching the rail, we congratulated her progress and fished for details about upcoming testimony, eager to learn her strategy to overcome the defendant's claims. Always conscious of protocol, she dropped her customary reticence and accepted our favorable reviews of her efforts, enthralled by this beautiful, steely woman hitting her stride in the second of three trials. In an unguarded moment, she voiced cautious optimism for Jaramillo's trial, but warned us that her case against Manfred Schockner would rest, to a great extent, on the successful prosecution of this fast-talking middleman. Anything but a conviction would make Schockner's conviction that much more difficult.

• • • •

Dr. Ortiz, the deputy medical examiner for Los Angeles County, took the witness stand to begin Tuesday's session. He recounted Lynn's autopsy and death in less than fifteen minutes, a killing so quiet even a half dozen police officers around the property didn't hear a scuffle or scream. There was no cross examination.

Birdsall returned to the stand to offer additional evidence against the defendant, including corroboration of taped interviews that spelled out Jaramillo's willingness to broker the deal, including the murder of a woman he said he had liked. "There were numerous times Lynn would fix me lunch, or a snack, things like that," the defendant willingly confessed. He had visited the Schockner home at least a half dozen times and considered Lynn a friend. "She was a really nice lady."

LBPD Det. Dennis Robbins, now lead detective on the case, produced documents from two briefcases police recovered at the Schockner home, and offered various financial records to verify transactions between Jaramillo and Schockner. Robbins had spent a year helping collect, organize and assemble the chain of evidence that would be crucial in all three prosecutions. He was the DDA's right hand man – literally sitting to her right at the table – and kept the records coherent for the court and jury in three major trials, no small task by any means.

Barnes introduced telephone records between the three men in the six-month period before the murder, documenting sixty-seven calls between Jaramillo and Harvey, and another 268 between the defendant and Schockner. No calls between Schockner and Harvey were ever discovered – Jaramillo was their only link. Even as Jaramillo tried to dismiss his role in the crime, he couldn't explain away sixteen phone calls from his own cell phone on the day of the murder: six to Harvey and another ten to or from Schockner.

In his 2004 confession, Jaramillo was evasive about the

amount of money he received from Schockner, but finally spelled out the real reason. "What happened? Birdsall asked Jaramillo during his taped confession. Why did you ultimately decide to assist him (Schockner) in this killing?"

"Schockner pushed it in my face - he said I owed him money. *Frank, you've got to help me out with this if you want to settle our debt*," Jaramillo explained. Later in the same interview, Jaramillo said he delivered $2,500 to Harvey on Schockner's behalf, gave him Schockner's business card with his home address and alarm code written on the back, and instructed the killer to commit the crime on a Monday or Wednesday because Lynn volunteered as a school nurse on Tuesdays and Thursdays and would not be home.

Jaramillo's attorney hardly interjected himself in the onslaught of damning details, finally rising to cross-examine Birdsall after Barnes stepped aside. "During your interviews with my client," Caillouette asked on cross, "was Frank Jaramillo consistent with his remarks? Did he tell the same story again and again?"

"No, he did not," the homicide detective insisted. The public defender seemed confused by Birdsall's answer and walked back to his table without comment, taking his seat. Without warning, Barnes rested her case and court adjourned for the day.

• • • •

Attorney Caillouette opened the defense May 23 by calling the defendant's mother, Rosalie Aguilar, to support her son's claim that strangers were stalking his family before the crime. Mrs. Aguilar testified that she noticed a white convertible parked across the street from her Santa Clarita home "three or four times" during the weeks between Lynn's murder and the arrests of Schockner and her son. She said she called the police "many times" about the suspicious car but officials failed to respond or refused to search their neighborhood for the car. She also claimed that her daughter believed she was being followed by men in a white car that made a U-turn and tracked her movements on the road. The younger woman pulled over to let the car pass, but she was unable to get the license number. That was all they could say about the menace they felt.

Then Frank Jaramillo took the stand. He was so nervous he botched his own name: "J-A-R-A-M-I-L-L-E," he spelled out for the clerk, reddening slightly at the gaffe. Caillouette claimed his client valiantly tried to prevent the killing but ended up as another victim in the crime. He led Jaramillo through a litany of admissions, recounting the number of fabrications he told during his interviews with detectives, some of which, he claimed, were orchestrated by officials seeking to implicate their main target, Manfred Schockner.

When Caillouette asked if he had been used as a "pawn" in the police investigation, Jaramillo sadly agreed. He had worn the LBPD electronic vest to meet Manfred and elicit incriminations, following a script formulated by the police. He was looking for a break, he admitted. His attorney insisted his lies were concocted to assist the investigation, and the police who promised him lenient treatment for his cooperation, failed to live up to their end of the bargain. His complaint seemed weak, but I couldn't read the jury.

Finally, he admitted he recommended Nick Harvey when Schockner asked for a handyman's services. He described the husband as a "good old man" to the young bodybuilder, but balked when Harvey told him "he wants me to fucking kill his wife."

"Nick told me he agreed with the deal," Jaramillo testified, "but I told him 'No!' I tried to talk Nick out of the murder. I even called Fred and told him I knew what he wanted Nick to do, and I said he should not. But Fred got mad and told me I had no right to interrupt his business with Nick Harvey," he said. "When I told him [the murder] was not going to happen, he got very irate, and told me to leave it be. Then Nick called and told me he needed the money, but I can't tell you how many times I tried to talk him out of it – a dozen times or more, at least."

Barnes asked Jaramillo why he didn't back out of the deal or, at the very least, end his own role in the crime?

"I had no choice," Jaramillo answered.

"You don't expect us to believe that, do you?" Barnes asked.

"Fred told me if I did not agree with the plan, the same thing could happen to my family," he said. "I was obligated to Mr. Schockner and I was frightened for my family – if I had it to do over again, I'd change it."

With that, Caillouette rested his defense.

• • • •

I welcomed the next morning with coffee, cigarettes and the *Press-Telegram*, and then braced for the final chapter in Jaramillo's trial, churning with a now-familiar mixture of anticipation and dread. An acquittal seemed unlikely, but a mistrial was always possible. That would suck.

The previous evening I discovered another strange fact about southern California: when the choppers fly, you shouldn't drive. News-hungry helicopters raced to any sort of calamity - anything from a minor traffic accident to an armed robber on the run – creating a stretch of gridlocked highway from which no one but a cop or a criminal can escape. That evening we were back on the road to another restaurant in another indistinct city in the suburban sprawl, stalled in a typical, inexplicable standstill. Every driver pushed his or her way into any car-length space available, seemingly ready for all other cars to levitate out of their way. It took three cycles of the traffic light to unsnarl the confusion, and after we cleared one intersection, the routine began again.

When we returned to our hotel, I completed my evening ritual by calling my wife and Charlie to share experiences from our respective days. After my synopsis of the trial, I tried to explain the nuances of procedures and the anxieties we endured. I probably complained more than I should have, but the calls were more about contact than communication, and I reached out to my wife and new son every day. Regardless of the outcome, we were going to have the kind of personal relationships that required a family bond strong enough to withstand any setback, however unpalatable. Win or lose, we shared the ramifications of every verdict. Even behind bars, Schockner never lost the power to cause pain or shame.

Looking back on my notes I found the word *scared* scrawled deeply across the top of that day's journal, but the adroit prosecution coupled with a gratifyingly thin defense allowed an uneasy confidence for Jaramillo's conviction. We hoped for another slam-dunk, like the stunning, twenty-minute consensus in Harvey's ruling, but couldn't comfortably predict the outcome.

• • • •

Barnes began her closing with an outline of the law. The state sought a conviction on the ultimate charge of First Degree Murder with Special Circumstances, the same as Harvey's. Beginning at 9:35 am on May 24, she explained that anyone guilty of aiding and abetting a capital crime is equally culpable for the killing.

"First, the defendant must have knowledge of the crime," she stipulated, "and Frank Jaramillo not only paid for and provided instructions to Nick Harvey, he also planned the crime and served as the go-between. Second, the defendant must have the intent to commit and facilitate the crime - he knew what was going to happen and he helped make it so.

"Finally, in order to aid and abet the commission of a capital crime, the defendant must perform an act that promotes the crime. Frank Jaramillo paid the killer to commit his crime, and that makes him a principal in the crime," she said. "These three men acted as a unit, and in every sense of the law, this was a conspiracy – he bought Lynn Schockner's life for $50,000 and found someone to take it for $5,000. He profited $45,000 from the deal."

After Barnes retired, Caillouette introduced his closing with a cautious description of the jury's job: "You have to be *real* sure before convicting my client. You must remember the police officers and prosecutor wear glasses of guilt, and they see my client in this light. They have a record of fifty-two phone calls between Frank Jaramillo and Nick Harvey, but Ms. Barnes doesn't know what was said during any of those conversations.

"The only thing you have to remember is that evil, insidious Manfred Schockner threatened my client and his family," he said. "Frank Jaramillo didn't know what to do, but he didn't want this to happen, he did not want this woman to be killed."

By foregoing her right to open the trial, Barnes used her option to close with this final statement: "Even if you believe everything Frank Jaramillo has said, he has admitted to First Degree Murder with Special Circumstances. He is guilty. But we also know he is a liar, and he keeps lying to get around the evidence. He needed this money to perpetuate his lifestyle, and so he brokered the murder of Lynn Schockner to profit from the killing."

By 10:10 am both sides had rested. Ferrari delivered his final instructions, a carefully crafted statement that took him six minutes to read. The jury went out less than an hour after the proceedings began that day and retired for deliberations until noon, when they broke for lunch. Fifteen minutes after they resumed their task at 2 pm, a juror asked to review a key statement in Jaramillo's testimony. From what we later learned, that single statement was all they needed to hear. It was his own admission he knew Schockner planned to have his wife killed.

Russell's story ran across the top of the next day's edition of the *Press-Telegram*, reporting how the jury deliberated four hours before finding Jaramillo guilty of first-degree murder. The foreman, a 36-year-old Long Beach man who spoke on the condition of anonymity, said those on the panel believed Jaramillo lied repeatedly in an attempt to distance himself from the crime.

"The evidence," he said, "was overwhelming. The funds were there, the means were there, and it just kind of made sense."

The article also described how my brother and I reacted to the verdict, and how we nodded to each juror as they left the courtroom and mouthed "thank you" again and again. When Ferrari imposed the prescribed sentence a month later, Jaramillo still claimed he had no real role in the murder, but the judge didn't buy his story.

Summer thrills for U

Strike up the L.B. Municipal Band

TIM GROBATY / A2

Press-Telegram

www.presstelegram.com

Long Beach, California — FRIDAY, MAY 25, 2007 — 25¢ (plus tax)

Middleman guilty in wife's murder

Crime: Second conviction follows guilty verdict for hit man; only husband's murder trial remains.

By Wendy Thomas Russell
Staff writer

LONG BEACH — A jury deliberated for four hours Thursday before convicting a former gym manager of first-degree murder in the stabbing death of a Bixby Knolls mother.

Despite his contention that he was forced to participate in the crime under duress, Frankie Jaramillo, 32, was found to have willingly acted as the middleman in the November 2004 murder-for-hire of Lynn Schockner, 50.

L. Schockner

As the verdict was read in Long Beach Superior Court, Jaramillo tilted his head back and looked at the ceiling. His mother, seated behind him, leaned forward, sobbing.

The victim's older brothers — Mark and John Jicha — briefly clutched each other's hands and then wiped tears from their eyes. Then, as jurors walked out of the courtroom, the brothers nodded to each of them and mouthed "thank you" again and again.

The verdict is the second murder conviction associated with Schock-

PLEASE SEE VERDICT / A8

Convicted — Awaiting trial

Nicholas Harvey — Frankie Jaramillo — Manfred Schockner

Middleman sentenced for role in killing
By Wendy Thomas Russell, Staff writer

LONG BEACH - A man described by authorities as a "sociopath and a pathological liar" proclaimed his innocence one last time Thursday before being sentenced to life in prison without parole for arranging the 2004 murder of a Bixby Knolls mother.

Frankie Jaramillo, 32, appeared in Long Beach Superior Court wearing a bright-orange jumpsuit and shackles and carrying a written statement in his hand.

"Do you mind if I stand?" he asked.

"No," Judge Gary Ferrari answered. "You can do anything you want." Jaramillo read from the statement, asserting that he had been "used as a scapegoat" and unjustly convicted for the murder-for-hire of Lynn Schockner - who was stabbed to death by Nick Harvey in November 2004 as police surrounded her home to investigate a prowler call.

"The truth of the matter is that I didn't do it, nor did I want it done," Jaramillo said. "God willing, the truth of this travesty will come to the light expediently to prevent an innocent man from [being] unduly convicted for a crime that I absolutely am not responsible for."

But overwhelming evidence during last month's trial showed that Jaramillo was something other than a scapegoat and truth-teller.

A debt-ridden, unemployed former gym manager with a taste for expensive cars and rare watches, Jaramillo was paid upwards of $50,000 to find a hit man to kill Lynn Schockner. Among other things, he provided Harvey directions to the victim's home, information about her habits and schedule, and the security code to her alarm system.

Phone records show he called Harvey six times on the day of the murder - Nov. 8, 2004 - and exchanged calls with Schockner nine times. Furthermore, by his own admission, Jaramillo knew the victim, thought she was a "nice lady" and let her make him lunch several times while he visited her husband over the years.

Given the facts of the case, Judge Ferrari seemed astonished by Jaramillo's remarks in court. "Mr. Jaramillo," he began, "I think you are in denial. You are in absolute denial. What you did to that woman - she befriended you - and to suggest that you were somehow not responsible for her death is absurd."

CHAPTER 18

By Memorial Day we were wrapped up in plans for the summer with Charlie, who approached his senior year and began to consider college. We welcomed the campus visits with our son. When we first came together in 2004, I promised he could attend any college he chose, and stuck by the bargain. I wanted him free to find his own way in the world, despite his old man, and make his own choices in life while my wife and I provided all the love, support and structure we could muster.

But then there was the money, and by securing my sister's estate, I could guarantee him the wherewithal to accomplish his vision and build a new life. Money might be a necessary evil, as my sister sadly discovered, but also solves a lot of problems along the way. Charlie endured a fearful childhood those fourteen years under Schockner's thumb, his home ruled by a tight-fisted man with an unquenchable rage, invariably directed at his mother. There were more than enough miseries to go around, and we didn't crowd him.

When he came home to Georgia he found sanctuary and security, a life of options and choices, and the resources to meet those ends. Given the imponderables, that financial security would allow him to prosper and survive a few mistakes, but I promised he would never be held hostage to the money that was his birthright and his due. My sister bought that with her blood.

We celebrated our first Christmas with our son in Georgia

just a few weeks after his father had finally been arrested, ratifying his fears. Just before that 2004 holiday, when he and Susan began clamoring for a tree, I dug up an eastern cedar I had picked out in the yard, potted the sapling and moved our Christmas tree indoors. (After the New Year, I planned to transplant it to another spot beside our house.) Charlie laughed at the puny tree, and reminded my wife and me of the perfectly awful blue artificial tree they used for holiday celebrations. He then grew somber as he recalled the "Christmas from hell" his father inflicted on his family when Charlie was a child. Schockner's parents were Orthodox Jews, and, like so many parents, they yearned to have their grand children follow their faith. For any number of reasons, including Herbert Schockner's horrible temper, those Hebrew holy days became a time of family strife, as Manfred demanded observance and obedience in Talmudic traditions. When Lynn returned to her Methodist roots, Schockner was incensed.

Sometime back in the mid-1990s, when Charlie was five or six years old, Lynn and Manfred came to loggerheads over the way they would "celebrate" the season. My sister insisted on attending the Methodist service, foregoing the inevitable duress of Schockner family traditions and tempers. Her husband grudgingly agreed to her plans, but demanded their son accompany him to his temple. Charlie refused. Even as a young boy, he held firm to his feelings, aligned with his mother. Unfortunately, that allegiance cost him Christmas that year. When Manfred realized his son's intentions, he scooped up the presents under the tree and dumped them in the garbage can in the back alley, forbidding any trespass in the trash. That was Manfred's way of showing displeasure with those he claimed to love.

These thoughts entered my mind as we faced the summer of 2007 – an exciting adventure for our young man and as we grappled with our roles as late-term parents. We had college visits in South Carolina, Florida, and New York in the works, and couldn't wait to hit the road. I watched Charlie closely, mostly because I had experienced the crises first-hand when a beloved parent dies, but he was a resilient fellow; still, I worried about the flinty toughness he acquired as he watched his mother whittled away in pieces.

• • • •

As Georgia's summer reached its full intensity - a repressive combination of heat and humidity that can take one's breath away - we prepared to return to Long Beach for the final trial in late August. I cleared my calendar and revived the foreboding that began when Harvey's trial date was announced before Christmas, an underlying fear that something, anything could go wrong. Despite the resounding verdicts delivered against the killer and the middleman, as well as the civil suit we had won, Schockner's conviction was everything, and the outcome was anything but certain. I didn't believe Charlie could truly become a free man if his father didn't end his days behind bars.

Assurances from police and the prosecutor's confidence notwithstanding, I could only perceive distractions and pitfalls that would prevent him paying with his life for the crime. Rival politics in the LA District Attorney's Office provided a perfect opportunity for the kind of snafu that could jeopardize Schockner's prosecution.

Just after Jaramillo was convicted, Barnes, at her own request, transferred to a different office to work with a gang violence task force in east Long Beach. Even though prosecutors were traditionally allowed to finish active cases after the transfer was confirmed, the Schockner prosecution was removed from her calendar. Without explanation, the DA informed us a new prosecutor would assume the Schockner case. We later learned the decision had nothing to do with the trial; it was a payback, staged to avenge an old grudge between two division supervisors in the department. Years earlier a different DDA was removed from the prosecution of an altogether unrelated crime, breaking that tradition; and in the real world of city politics, the Schockner prosecution was held hostage to settle this score.

I immediately called Barnes' boss. He apologized for the situation, but I told him the reasons were immaterial to me or my son. We wanted Cyndi Barnes to prosecute our family's murderer, insisting she be allowed to handle the Schockner case to closure. To date, our family had been quietly steadfast in support of the city's efforts, including the DA, but this was bullshit. Even though he didn't make the decision, I told him my protests would move to the media if she were prevented from sitting first chair, and I would become an overnight pain in the ass.

I don't know whether our prayers or promises had any influence over the inter-office rivalries, but Barnes remained the state's advocate when Schockner came to trial later that summer. We were glad to have her onboard. On June 29, she emailed information about the upcoming court calendar:

> Mark
> The trial was originally set for August 20 - but the judge is not available that date. We agreed to start on August 27. I personally spoke with the defense attorneys and the judge about your travel plans - everyone is aware that your family will be purchasing tickets. I do not see any reason why the trial would not go that date, but they are to inform me immediately if something happens.

> As you know by now, jury selection usually takes between 1-2 days. If you want to make sure you are here for the testimony - I would say the August 28 is the safest bet. We won't start testimony before that date.
>
> Because Charlie is a potential witness, I can fly him out here on County expense, with a guardian. I can also pay for the hotel room. If you guys are staying in the Hilton again, once the trial is over you submit the room bill to me and I submit it to the court. The court then approves the amount and a check is sent to you. Jon is a potential witness also, so I can do the same with him.
>
> There is one catch, however. If we list someone as potential witnesses, then the defense may try to exclude them from the courtroom. If that is done, I will have to decide if I am going to take you guys off the witness list so that you can sit in for the trial. If that happens, the defense may object to the court paying the witness fees/expenses. Let me know your thoughts on that. I will talk to you soon. - Cyndi

. . . .

The trial date would remain a moving target until the very last moment. Motions and last-minute scheduling matters would all but guarantee nothing less than a mid-trial delay or unexpected interruption. As a long-time adherent to "Murphy's Laws," I envisioned problems at every turn before trial, and nothing ever proved me wrong. Still, I never filed for any compensation for Charlie's costs because I understood how many millions of dollars Long Beach had already pumped into the investigation and the prosecution. My brother and I lived on daily briefings, ready to see jurors selected and the entirety of the case against Schockner, and the rest of the family planned to arrive when the trial actually began. The logistics of family travel and personal calendars guaranteed uncertainty, but then Barnes emailed an ominous warning. She predicted contentious, combative tactics from Schockner's legal team: Frank Perlo and Jack Stennett. She didn't know anything about Stennett, but was familiar with Perlo: he was a 25-year veteran of the LA Public Defender's office who moved into private practice in 2002. Ironically, Perlo penned an opinion piece published in the March 1996 edition of *Los Angeles Lawyer* magazine, warning other attorneys to enter private practice with care:

> "Twenty years ago the specialty of felony criminal defense was a small but viable area of legal practice," he wrote. "Today the attorney supporting a practice on a complete diet of criminal defense is often akin to a starving person looking at a banquet.
>
> "Don't let the media-crowned 'Dream Team' fool you," he said, alluding to O.J. Simpson's notable team of lawyers and monster legal fees. "With few exceptions, attorneys doing criminal defense today must have a firm grip on reality if they are going to be able to support themselves in this limited and specialized field."

Despite his published opinion, Perlo had earned a reputation as an effective criminal attorney with a resume dotted with high-profile cases, including the cop-killer Jose Luis Orozco, who was convicted of the 2005 ambush murder of LA County Sheriff's Dep. Jerry Ortiz. He must have possessed his own "firm grip on reality" when he moved across the aisle, because his practice drew prominent clients, like Schockner, capable of paying substantial retainers. Barnes welcomed the opportunity to face the former public defender, but she didn't underestimate his abilities or courtroom savvy. Even though they'd never faced off, she used her courthouse connections to learn more about the man and his tactics, and emailed a report:

> Mark - I just left you a voicemail - I have a new work cell phone. I figured that money would not be your concern, and that your family would prefer to sit through the trial. At this point, my intention is to not call Charlie, but I want you guys to be prepared if we do need him to testify. Also, the defense has the right to subpoena him as well. I don't see why they would, but I don't trust them. This will be a much different trial - I anticipate this trial will last longer and they will be extremely aggressive. Please feel free to call me or write me back when you get a chance. - Cyndi

The DDA seemed determined to prepare us for a different type of trial, not the steamroller she steered over Harvey and Jaramillo; it would be more of a street fight or a smear campaign - anything to prompt a mistrial or avoid a guilty verdict. Barnes shed some light on Perlo's track record, but even she still didn't know anything about Stennett, second chair for the defense. We learned he was a Torrance criminal attorney, Schockner's first call after his arrest, and an associate of Lionel Albanese, Schockner's civil attorney who represented him in the probate and civil litigation we pursued for Charlie's estate.

Finally we learned Schockner's trial would begin as advertised on August 27 and made airline and hotel reservations accordingly.

Since Charlie's senior year classes would be underway, my brother and I opted to travel west for jury selection while our families would arrive the next week for the trial. Past experience indicated jury selection would take up to two days, and as other matters arose, there would be other delays. It wasn't foresight but common sense, and I was right. The trial was pushed back two days for pre-trial motions and jury selection, and would begin with the state's prosecution followed by a probable break for Labor Day weekend. We booked new round-trip flights for the families to arrive at LAX on Sept. 3 to minimize school absences and accommodate work schedules.

• • • •

Pre-trial motions were set to begin at 10:30 am on August 27, but Judge Ferrari was forced to delay proceedings right from the start. The prosecutor could not be found. Frantic phone calls finally located Barnes stuck on the southbound shoulder of I-405 where her car suddenly expired. Det. Robbins used his blue light to bully his way to her location, where she abandoned her car on the side of the road. She jumped into his cruiser and they raced downtown, dashing into court thirty-five minutes later. During the delay, defense attorney Perlo affirmed Judge Ferrari's plan to select a jury pool of 90 prospects from which 12 jurors and four alternates would be drawn.

Schockner entered the same courtroom as his co-conspirators with a look similar to Harvey and Jaramillo: he was gaunt and prematurely aged, hair and body haggard. He sat stiffly and focused only on the judge for many minutes before finally revolving slowly to scan the gallery, glancing my way. Attired in the now-familiar jail jumpsuit, Schockner's hooded eyes still burned with the hatred – they were the same eyes I remembered from our introduction almost thirty years ago. Judge Ferrari gaveled the hearing into order.

"Before we begin jury selection," he advised, "we need to take care of a few house-keeping items." Schockner was to face three felony charges – murder, murder for financial gain, and burglary – but Barnes had agreed to drop the burglary charge and settle on the two most serious counts, a combination that made him eligible for capital punishment. Judge Ferrari then announced his expectations for a two-week trial, with morning sessions running from 9:30 am to 12 noon, and afternoon hours from 1:30 to 4:30 pm.

After approving the stipulation and the schedule, Perlo rose to comment upon "inflammatory" issues that could prejudice the jury. "I'm concerned about statements that may come in under hearsay," he disclosed, referring specifically to the extensive list of police officers prepared to take the stand. "I'm concerned jurors could hear testimony that goes into all the blood and gore of the crime, but does not acknowledge the guilt of anyone. Allowing this detailed information will be highly prejudicial, but irrelevant to the charges facing my client."

Perlo offered his concerns in a soft voice, never demanding; he asked the judge to see the wisdom of his words. The veteran public defender projected an earnest, almost self-deprecating manner; his bushy eyebrows bobbing to enunciate the points he found pertinent, his eyes downcast when denied.

Barnes, on the other hand, was all business when it was her turn to argue for the state. "For heaven's sake, your honor, this is a murder trial," she exclaimed. "The people have a right to hear the details of the crime which have a probative value in the case. There are three individual cases involved in this crime: Nick Harvey, Frank Jaramillo and Manfred Schockner. There is one common factor in all three, and that is the murder that happened. Those details are ultimately pertinent because this *is* a murder trial."

But Perlo claimed "some officers have a tendency to volunteer information. I have a problem with that."

Judge Ferrari took Perlo's objection under advisement, and asked each attorney to estimate the time they would need to present their case. Barnes predicted three to four trial days while Perlo proposed he would need only two; but then co-counsel Stennett rose to address his own series of objections, including a motion to move the trial to a new venue, claiming pre-trial publicity and coverage of the previous two murder trials had prejudiced so many potential jurors so as to make a fair trial for Schockner unlikely. Luckily, that wasn't the way the judge perceived the situation.

"Based on what I've seen in terms of media coverage, coupled with the lack of juror knowledge about the crime or the defendant, I'm going to deny that motion," Ferrari pronounced. Even though the 2004 murder in Bixby Knolls never garnered the kind of coverage OJ Simpson's celebrity prosecution featured in 1995, Lynn's killing and three trials were fixtures in the local media for a month. The *Long Beach Press-Telegram,* however, featured dozens of front-page stories on every trial through completion.

Judge Ferrari's pronouncement signaled the success of our media strategy. By ignoring the national press and celebrity news anchors that strangle California airwaves, we dragged our feet long enough for the story's "shelf life" to expire. Later, as the months evolved into years, we developed a friendly, almost symbiotic, relationship with Wendy Thomas Russell of the *Press-Telegram,* to whom we promised and provided exclusive details for the duration of all three trials. She withheld background information we provided until after testimony made those revelations part of the public record, and we explained what Charlie and Lynn had endured under Schockner's tempers.

Stennett voiced yet another objection to the state's case,

asking the court to disqualify items police found during the search of Schockner's home, as well as wire-tap records of his incoming telephone calls in the days and weeks preceding the crime. "Speaking generally for the most part, but also on specific items, I would ask you quash the results of the search of my client's home," Stennett requested, designating documents regarding personal loans Schockner used to hide $500,000 from his wife during their divorce as well as monies that changed hand between the defendant and his middleman, Jaramillo. "I ask you disallow a note found in the waste basket. That officer had no right to go through the wastebasket, because it was not specifically named in the warrant.

"Beyond that, I would ask you quash evidence regarding Mr. Schockner's telephone records. In my review of the records, there is no evidence there was any communication during those calls, and beyond that, there was no valid reason for that search warrant." Stennett expanded his exceptions to the search, claiming there was "no evidence anywhere that this was payment for hiring somebody to kill his wife. They were loans, nothing more. All were payment made through a bank paper trail, and this evidence does not enhance the DA's position. These were payments."

"As to the personal loans," he continued. "Lynn claimed at the time Mr. Schockner was going to cheat her out of a share of money. Unfortunately, this is a normal circumstance in a divorce. There is no evidence he paid anyone to kill his wife."

Finally, the defense insisted Nick Harvey's confession should be excluded, claiming that it would be inappropriate for the jury to hear this particular statement: "Mr. Schockner wanted his wife killed."

"You must consider the source," Stennett said. "Harvey is a confessed murder who received money from Mr. Jaramillo to kill her. Neither Mr. Jaramillo nor Mr. Harvey are what we would consider 'reasonable sources.'"

His protests notwithstanding, Ferrari denied the wide-ranging objection. Barnes didn't raise any legal challenges, but insisted the defense disclose their witness list and the nature of their testimony. Her list named a dozen or more police officers, the coroner and other crime scene investigators, providing reams of transcripts, tape recordings, and prior testimony that would have overflowed a four-drawer file cabinet. As the cases progressed, the load grew larger. When Schockner came to court, Barnes, Det. Robbins and Clerk Rose Kazuski managed the collection of documents and exhibits required; staff used handcarts to assemble the files, occasionally requiring assistance from Judge Ferrari's fulltime bailiff, Los Angeles County Deputy Eric Elder.

Finally Ferrari turned to the prosecutor for her complaints and requests. Barnes wasn't shy about pointing out shortcomings from the defense.

"We have no witness statements aside from those we have submitted on our list," she stipulated, indicating almost two dozens potential witnesses. She complained that the defense failed to provide statements from four character witnesses called on Schockner's behalf. "I need those statements to accept these witnesses."

Stennett was quick to offer profiles of four unlikely witnesses:

- a Long Beach physician who performed a minor hernia procedure on Schockner a few days before his arrest and would testify his patient was suffering from extreme pain and prescribed painkillers during this time period, hampering his mental abilities;

- the second, another physician, was prepared to testify Schockner had experienced a stroke or stroke-like symptoms after his surgery;

- the third was a Bixby Knolls realtor who would testify Schockner planned to purchase his own residence a few blocks from Lynn's home;

- finally, there was an enigmatic man from Schockner's past, Ed Tynan, a character witness who would evidently attest to the defendant's "non-violent" personality.

Despite Mr. Stennett's impromptu description Judge Ferrari ordered he produce witness statements for the state and gaveled the session to a close.

CHAPTER 19

Ninety prospective jurors were empaneled for service on the Schockner trial at 10:45 am on Tuesday, Aug. 28. Juror number one stipulated he had been arrested on two burglary charges and his brother had been murdered in LA. Four of the next seven candidates reported relatives killed in crime: two unsolved murders, a third killer convicted and the fourth shot dead by police. Once again, I couldn't help but wonder about the cold realities of life in this warm and sunny place, mean streets so close to the beach.

Before Ferrari could begin the proceedings, Perlo hunched to his feet, molded his face into an earnest expression and reiterated his primary objection regarding the "inflammatory nature" of hearsay testimony. The judge noted his trepidation and seemed to appreciate the performance, but quickly ruled all of the state's crime scene photos of the victim admissible, including the most horrific. The defense attorney suffered these setbacks in silence, but his shoulders sagged, suggesting something like betrayal as he returned to his seat.

The bailiff escorted Schockner into the room in civilian clothes. He wore a shiny gray suit draped loosely on his bony shoulders, a pale shirt opened at the collar, too large for his frame. The vintage fabric shined with a sliver of silk in the weave, framing the casual, old-style shirt, perhaps something he wore in Las Vegas. I wasn't sure if the look was affected or random, but coupled with his tinted aviator glasses and a shock of long gray hair carelessly arranged to cover male pattern baldness, he looked almost like a caricature of the man I had known. His features appeared more outlandish than shrewd. Expecting something more polished and prepared, I wondered whether his unimpressive grooming and disheveled bearing figured into his legal strategy or a careless decision. Wardrobe and personal appearance aside, the court clearly didn't want to hear Schockner's first request.

"Your honor, because my client still suffers from serious physical ailments and has a regular schedule of medication prescribed through jail, I would ask that his pain medication be administered during the noon hour here in court," Perlo attempted another apologetic expression. "My client is concerned he will not obtain his pain medication."

Immediately incensed, Ferrari snapped a pithy reply: "I intend to conduct a courtroom, not a pharmaceutical counter," and nodded dismissively toward his bailiff to handle the matter. Immediately back on keel, the judge cast a reassuring glance at the jury when the prosecutor chose to address the jury pool that filled the gallery. Barnes identified two specific charges: deliberate, pre-meditated murder and murder for financial gain. She stipulated the state would seek capital convictions for special circumstances against the defendant, crimes that could merit the death penalty even though the state would seek a life sentence if he was convicted.

As Ferrari predicted, only four of the ninety queried during *voir dire* had any recollection of the 2004 murder, and none remembered any specifics. For those seeking excuses from jury service, his honor warned: "Not wanting to be here will not fly for an excuse." The process began at 11 am, and by 2:45 pm, with a 90-minute lunch break sandwiched in between, twelve jurors had been selected.

Once again, we not only tried to divine their inclinations from their brief biographies, but also fathom the defendant's strategy from Perlo's endorsements and preemptory strikes from the pool. It took another hour to select three alternates to round out the panel, and, just before the afternoon session ended at 4 pm, attorney Perlo raised an objection to our presence in the courtroom:

"Your honor, I object to the proximity of the victim's family members sitting in the front row so close to the jurors," he claimed. "They could communicate with jurors or unduly influence them."

Ferrari's eyebrows betrayed just a hint of disbelief, but he dismissed the objection without serious comment and gaveled the session to a close. What the defense attorney didn't know was that we had been ushered there by the bailiff. The prosecutor employed a portable screen to display exhibits that faced the jury and bench, one that effectively blocked any view of the court proceedings from those seats. The blackboard wasn't used during jury selection, but would be back again in court for the Schockner trial. By habit, we usually opted for seats behind the defense table, on the other side of the aisle, where we could watch the judge, witnesses and jurors while the attorneys argued the case. After arriving early for the session, we selected our usual seats, but Elder approached us before the panel was wheeled into place and suggested we take seats in the front row behind the banister. We had obliged.

• • • •

The screen was in full view when we arrived just before 10 am for the trial on Wednesday, August 29. We took up our usual positions behind the defense without prompting an objection. Two print reporters, Ms. Russell and another woman from a small community weekly newspaper, shared the press table. The only television cameraman arrived 20 minutes after the trial began, but had to leave after learning his camera was only allowed with a signed court order, which he did not possess. He looked blankly at the judge for a moment, packed up his gear and was gone. The networks decided trial coverage wasn't worth the time it would require and never appeared again.

After the jurors and alternates were ensconced in the jury room on his right, Ferrari asked if both attorneys were ready to proceed. He looked up with a little surprise when attorney Perlo rose to raise "two quick matters."

"First, I would like to notify your honor that my client did not receive his pain medication during the lunch hour yesterday. He remains in great pain and this may affect his ability to participate fully in his defense. Secondly," Perlo continued, "I would ask all counsel be admonished to refrain from gratuitous comments upon the case."

Judge Ferrari smirked as he tossed an affirmative nod his way. The judge ushered jurors to their assigned seats courteously and provided the same instructions he used in the other cases, and then gave Perlo the floor for the defense.

"The evidence will show an ongoing financial relationship between Frank Jaramillo and my client for more than a year, and Mr. Schockner also provided an additional $75,000 to Mr. Jaramillo in previous years," Perlo said. "But Mr. Jaramillo was conning Mr. Schockner, and took advantage of my client's generous nature."

This money, as well as the promise of more for an import/export business scheme, prompted Jaramillo and Harvey to plan the murder without Schockner's knowledge, he said. When his pending divorce threatened to cut off their supply of cash, the pair acted independently, drawing his distraught client into the criminal conspiracy. Perlo explained how police and prosecutors misinterpreted the evidence and refused to follow a perfectly reasonable alternative theory of the crime.

"The state will also tell you about a number of phone calls between my client and Frank Jaramillo, but I would ask you to consider how little those telephone records show. They are calls from one cell phone to another cell phone, but the state cannot tell you a single word spoken on those calls, or who was using the device when the call was made.

"Finally, my client was amenable to a divorce," he claimed. "He set out to purchase a home where he and his son could live, at least part time, after his wife was determined to end their marriage. What he offered his wife was a very favorable settlement - he was ready to get on with his life while taking care of his son."

Not surprisingly, Barnes argued alternate theories in her opening: the defendant planned and paid for his wife's murder to avoid a costly divorce settlement, enlisting the two co-conspirators to complete the crime. "Ladies and gentlemen, the evidence we are going to present will prove this defendant murdered Lynn Schockner on November 8th, 2004," she said. "There will be three men you will hear about throughout this case: Manfred Schockner murdered his wife to prevent an expensive divorce; Frank Jaramillo was the middleman who set up the events of that day; and Nick Harvey was the man who killed her in her own backyard.

"The evidence will show Schockner deposited $50,000 in Frank Jaramillo's bank account in the weeks before the murder, and then Jaramillo called Harvey to carry out the killing of Lynn Schockner," she added. The DDA explained how the police investigation proceeded in four different directions, and that solving the crime was like "putting together the pieces of a puzzle."

"Bank records prove Schockner deposited $50,000 in

Jaramillo's account in October, and then Frank Jaramillo called Nick Harvey to provide instructions to the killer. The investigation followed the phone records between these three men. We will present wire tapped telephone conversations between this defendant and the middleman, and recordings of Schockner's own words with Jaramillo," she promised. "Then we will show you that videotape and let you listen to the defendant's own statements on tape. The defendant is not the man who repeatedly plunged a knife into her body, but he did hire the killer to murder his estranged wife."

• • • •

On the stand, LBPD Officer James Foster, a thirteen-year veteran, claimed authorship of the main incident report, which encompassed statements from the on-scene officials who cooperated to chronicle the initial blueprint of the crime. Within two minutes Perlo objected twice to his descriptions of his effort and the details he discovered. Then he complained about the position of the podium from which the DDA directed her examination. With an audible sigh, she moved it fifteen feet to the side, inquiring whether "defense counsel could now see everything he needed to see?"

Using a detailed drawing of the property, Foster identified multiple locations where police arrived and established a perimeter on their initial response to the prowler call. The prosecutor retrieved a folder from her table and turned back to display two dozen general and detailed photographs from the location, culminating with six photos of Lynn lying dead on the back porch. These images were not in view from the gallery, but I had seen them during Harvey's trial and recognized the jury's reaction to the shocking images. Offset by a ring of keys fallen next to her outstretched hand, they were of her head, neck and body in a pool of blood, as well as close-ups of the awful wounds the killer inflicted with his dagger.

Perlo raised another series of objections, demanding to be heard once again on the admissibility of nearly half the photos, claiming the images were having "an unnecessarily inflammatory effect on the jury." Stennett popped up to pose his own problems with the procedure, essentially reiterating his colleague's objection, but Ferrari overruled both with a flick of his wrist. "We've already discussed this matter," he advised. "The photos are in."

The defense attorney bounced back with another objection to the sequence DDA Barnes would use to introduce each photograph of the dozen or more photos, and wondered aloud whether they would be brought out in numerical order or by random chance. He told the court he "may want to object to specific photographs" and would need to know each image before it was revealed to the jury. "I'm sorry, your honor, I don't mean to fluster opposing counsel, but these are matters I need to know," he said in his most apologetic tone.

"I'm not getting flustered at all," Barnes replied, rising to the slight, but Judge Ferrari silenced both with a quick ruling that ended debate. Speaking gently, as if to children, he suggested the defense attorney move closer toward the bench where he could view each photograph as it was pinned to the board and then noted Mr. Perlo's objections to each of the six shots of the victim lying dead on her own patio.

It was obvious Perlo intended to bedevil Barnes with distractions, and planted this random barb in hope she would retaliate, or that it might catch some juror's fancy. The reason or rhythm didn't matter – all he needed was an opening. He also maintained a steady stream of complaints about the state's case, hoping to incite his attractive opponent into an angry outburst or error. Perlo's partner, Stennett, coordinated their strategy with loud interruptions from the table: moving papers from one pile to another, a noisy scrape of his chair, or a loud cough. Co-counsel's irritations were almost theatrical in their timing, designed to give Perlo a break and provide Stennett an opportunity to earn his keep. Stennett raised himself awkwardly during her slide presentation to retrieve a folder, tottering around and back, before sitting with a audible sigh. It seemed he would do anything to draw attention to himself during the DDA's time on the floor, but Barnes never faltered.

She shot him an angry glance and even some jurors seemed to grow impatient with their endless protests and interruptions. The defense strategy may have backfired – many seemed to find their methods obvious and increasingly tiresome. Ferrari allowed Barnes a wide berth as she cast dispersions on Perlo's contentions, and he seemed slightly amused as her color rose and her usual smile dissolved into a scowl. He inevitably ruled in her favor, time and time again.

Finally, after Perlo had exhausted Judge Ferrari's patience, Barnes was allowed to question Foster on the relevance of each photograph and how they described the police findings. The witness testified that the eleventh image showed "cheap jewelry" dumped from a jewelry cabinet on the floor of the master bedroom's walk-in closet. Perlo immediately objected to his description of these ornaments.

"Officer Foster, would you tell me how many times you have shopped for jewelry?" he inquired. The witness indicated five times in the past five years. "Are you a certified gemologist, or an expert in precious metals?"

"No I'm not, but the jewelry looked cheap to me."

The defense attorney challenged his ability to identify the bloody smears on the sliding glass door, asking him if he was a certified criminologist, which he was not. Finally, Perlo demanded to know the exact number of police officers or officials at the scene – twenty five – and also asked if the door showed signs of forced entry. "It did not," Foster testified. The attorney shrugged his shoulders toward the jury during his reply, muttering "really?" or "is that a fact?" as the witness answered, intimating this testimony had some particular relevance for the defense. Foster was then dismissed.

LBPD Officer Efrain Cervantes, the first cop at the crime scene, was the second witness called by the state. "I was working alone when the dispatcher radioed a possible burglary in progress at the Andrews Drive address," he replied after Barnes asked him to explain how he came to be there that day. "I coasted up to the house next door to the residence in question, and within a minute or so Officer Radcliff pulled up in the alley behind the house."

Attorney Perlo immediately rose to challenge this assertion, claiming the witness could not possibly know Officer Radcliff had arrived at that location because he could not view the alley from his post. Judge Ferrari looked inquiringly to the uniformed officer seated in the witness box.

"I moved to a spot between the two houses and could see him in the back alley." Cervantes explained how he traveled to the residence quietly, without his siren. Police procedures dictate officers should approach suspected burglaries in progress with stealth, allowing time for other officers to set up a perimeter and apprehend suspects at the scene.

Perlo objected again, again overruled, and then Radcliff took the stand, another familiar witness from previous trials. "At about 11 am on Monday, November 8, 2004 I responded to a 'suspicious person - possibly burglary' call in the 1100 block of Andrews Drive in Bixby Knolls," he said, immediately prompting another objection from the defense, again overruled. "I rolled up in my unit in front of the residence, observed Officer Cervantes in position in front of the neighbor's house and went into the alley so I could watch the fence line."

"My goal was to be the 'eyes in the back.' Within two or three minutes, the subject jumped over the fence from the backyard into a little alcove where the trash cans were placed. I thumbed my radio and drew my gun from its holster, placing a quick call before delivering verbal instructions for the suspect to come out. He had dropped down into this little alcove and I couldn't see him behind the garbage cans, but finally he came out with his hands in the air. At that time Officer Carranza came forward to make the arrest – I was the 'covering' officer when she applied her handcuffs.

"The first thing I noticed was he looked very muscular, very strong. A white male about 5-foot-10, and in very good shape. When Officer Carranza began patting him down, he resisted her search, trying to shield his left side. When she got him stretched over the back of the patrol car, I could see rubber gloves covered with blood in his pocket, and then Officer Carranza found a bloody dagger hidden in his clothes."

Following his testimony, Barnes introduced sixteen additional exhibits, including photographs of the items found on Harvey and aerial maps of the location that depicted the location of both police officers when they teamed up on the arrest.

Perlo raised a "philosophical" objection about the need for additional photographic evidence, quickly overruled, and then LBPD Officer Leticia Carranza took the stand. She quickly reinforced Radcliff's depiction of her takedown and search.

Just a minute or two from the noon hour, Judge Ferrari tried to adjourn for a ninety-minute lunch break, but before he could drop his gavel on the morning session Perlo renewed his objection to the display of crime scene photos, and added another objection to the press photographer who had joined the reporter from the *Press-Telegram* in the courtroom. "Photographs should not be allowed."

Judge Ferrari was ready with a quick comeback, allowing the press "could use photographs taken of the defendant dressed in his prison garb" for their coverage if the defense so desired. Perlo demurred, but then persisted. "Your honor, the prosecution has an embarrassment of riches and emotionality in the case. I renew my objection that the prosecution has been allowed to introduce inflammatory evidence into evidence."

Judge Ferrari held firm. "I've already made my decision in this matter," he said. "Your motion is denied."

Officer Carranza concluded her testimony less than ten minutes after the lunch break, telling the jury how she approached the suspect after he was lying facedown on the pavement without elaboration. She locked him in handcuffs and searched his body, finding a black hat, phone, Taser and jewelry in his right pocket, the dagger and gloves in his left. She stepped down after a brief cross from the defense attorney and was excused, making room for another on-scene LBPD policeman: Officer Eduardo Saldana, who testified how he responded to Radcliff's radio call and assisted with the arrest. While Barnes interviewed Saldana, Perlo made a deliberate production of rising from his chair, shuffling to the front and moving the lectern out of his way. The prosecutor eyed him with evil intent from her seat at the table and wouldn't resume until he sat down. Barnes finished by asking the officer to corroborate the bloody evidence recovered from the suspect, which he did.

Dr. Pedro Ortiz, deputy Los Angeles County coroner, was the state's next witness. As he had done in previous trials, he testified about Lynn's autopsy and his findings. When Barnes asked him to specify the victim's cause of death, he confirmed "three sharp-force wounds to her neck."

Perlo was satisfied with Dr. Ortiz's report, but inquired whether the coroner had conducted toxicology tests on the victim's blood, and if so, what were his findings. "I found the presence of five or six drugs in her system, including a painkiller, a barbiturate and other prescription drugs," he testified.

These were her addictions, I thought to myself, the chemical fog she allowed to envelope her consciousness, the narcotics she found necessary after half a lifetime married to Schockner. I assumed Perlo would save these nuggets for his defense, claiming her confusion contributed to the killing, even suggesting she shared culpability in her own crime.

But he reserved his most contentious cross-examination for the state's next witness, attorney Lisa Brandon, the Long Beach family law practitioner who represented Lynn in her divorce. "Lynn Schockner first contacted me in August 2004," Brandon explained after she was called by the prosecution. "I filed a summons to her husband, a petition for Lynn's legal separation and other documents on her behalf, including a list of assets."

The defense attorney bobbed to his feet to object to her testimony. He was quickly overruled, and then the prosecutor resumed her examination.

"Did the defendant have his own lawyer?" Barnes inquired.

"No, and given the size of the estate, I considered that very unusual," Brandon replied.

"Did you file a petition for divorce on behalf of Lynn Schockner?" Barnes asked.

"No," the lawyer admitted. "I prepared the preliminary papers for the divorce, but it was not completed. Lynn instructed me to take a slower pace with the proceedings. We had four or five meetings between August and late October 2004, and she was apprehensive at every meeting, obviously afraid of her husband. Other than that, she was a pleasant woman, but uncertain about many things and fairly naïve. She was not financially sophisticated at all, and very reliant on her husband for just about everything."

The prosecutor asked if she had prepared a summary of joint

family assets, the bottom line in any divorce. Brandon affirmed the tally: a million-dollar home, bank and trust accounts exceeding $2 million, two promissory notes for $1.2 million from Schockner's friend in Denver, along with antiquities, jewelry, and expensive collectibles. "I estimated the community property assets to value about $6 million, but Lynn didn't have any control or management of the family money," Brandon said. "I also had a perception there were other assets that weren't identified."

Barnes asked whether Schockner had prepared a similar list of assets, and after Brandon answered in the affirmative, she posed another question: "Was his accounting consistent with his wife's?"

"Not at all," Brandon replied. "Manfred had a copy of a promissory note for $1.2 million as a separate property asset, but Lynn had the original note payable to husband and wife. "His copy of the note was obviously altered and I disagreed with the defendant's accounting of their assets."

Defense attorney Perlo came at the witness from an oblique angle, questioning Ms. Brandon's billing practices.

"What was your fee for representing Mrs. Schockner?" he inquired.

"I required a $3500 retainer and bill $350 per hour for my services," she said.

Perlo almost gasped. "Three hundred and fifty dollars an hour?" he reiterated, letting his incredulity hang heavy for jurors to ponder. "Does that mean the rougher the divorce, the more money you make?

"No," replied the witness.

He immediately switched to another subject, tangential to questions he had raised with the coroner. "What kinds of medications were Mrs. Schockner prescribed when she was your client? Was she taking psychotropic medication?

"I don't know," Brandon replied. "I do know she was seeing a psychologist and was in counseling to escape her marriage." Perlo looked at the witness doubtfully, shot a glance at the jury and ended his cross-examination of Lynn's lawyer.

Barnes introduced the original promissory note and the copy forged by the defendant as evidence, and then re-directed a question at Lynn's attorney. "Ms. Brandon, were Mr. and Mrs. Schockner disagreeing about the money to be shared?" she inquired.

"That's what divorce is all about," she replied.

• • • •

The final witness for that first day of the Schockner trial was Jason Curran, the enigmatic driver who drove the killer from Ventura County to Bixby Knolls three times in November 2004, including the day Lynn was killed. He told the court he knew Nick Harvey as a co-worker and friend, and shared duties as a bouncer at a nightclub in Oxnard.

"He told me he didn't like to drive and asked me to drive him down to Long Beach," Curran testified. "He had an address and directions, and we went down there three times." The witness recounted three separate trips: the first visit was early on the morning of November 2, 2004 when they parked in the back alley and "hung out" for about an hour. Two days later the pair returned to the same spot in the alley behind the Schockner house. The third was the day Lynn Schockner was killed.

"We met that morning at about 7 am at the Park & Ride (at Los Possas Road) in Camarillo," he said. "I left my car in the lot and drove Nick's car down to Long Beach. We went right back to that same alley where Nick got out of the car and I drove off around the corner to wait for his call. I had been waiting about ten or fifteen minutes when I noticed a lot of police vehicles in the neighborhood. I tried to call him three or four times, but didn't get an answer. I saw a bunch of cops there and didn't know what was going on, and I drove away."

He drove an hour north to the Park & Ride, left Harvey's car in the lot and motored home in his own car. He said he didn't learn about the murder until the following morning, informed by a friend who woke him with a call. Immediately after checking the news he called an officer he knew at the Oxnard Police Department and met him at the Park & Ride lot to identify Nick Harvey's car.

"The officer drove me to the (Oxnard) police station and I told him everything I knew," he said. Barnes didn't press him about these details and turned back toward her chair – she only needed to corroborate evidence collected from the car - but Perlo charged to the podium before the prosecutor reached her seat.

"You were never arrested for your role in this crime, were you?" he asked.

"No. I didn't see any weapons, the knife or the Taser, and I didn't know what he planned to do. Nick never told me. I saw the cops, got scared and left." Even at 6-foot-3 and well over 250 pounds, Curran looked soft and emaciated; like Schockner, Jaramillo and Harvey, his clothes hung loose on his large frame, and he spoke quietly, avoiding eye contact as he answered each question. Only one statement stood out from his testimony.

"It made me physically ill – I was sick," he admitted. "I've done everything I can to suppress what happened that day, but I'll never forget it. It was the worst thing that ever happened in my life."

I tried to grow angry with the only accomplice who escaped prosecution, but by the end of his statement I couldn't help but pity the man – yet another victim of the crime. As the prosecution progressed, we found more families irreparably ruined. Curran, still young by any standard, had the hunched, halting gait of an old man, someone absolutely unprepared for the bloody carnage in Bixby Knolls. Quick to help the police in their investigation, he dodged his day in court; but he was still marked by the murder he unwittingly abetted that November day. His life would never be the same, another unfortunate affected by Schockner's greed.

CHAPTER 20

Barnes rose with confidence as she resumed her case against Schockner on Friday morning by calling another LBPD veteran officer, Det. Brian Bishop, who seized Nick Harvey's car and inventoried the contents, including papers for the push dagger and stun gun. After a brief cross-examination, the state called LBPD Forensic Specialist Deborah Kruek, an eleven-year veteran at the crime lab.

"I've processed more than 10,000 crime scenes during my career," she stated after DDA Barnes inquired about her qualifications. Using her notes for reference, she relayed her report in concise terms: "Initially, I photographed the car, and then found a number of items inside the vehicle – a nylon pack, two walkie-talkies, a sheet of paper, two envelopes, a pouch containing three knives, a black knit cap, an empty box with a picture of a dagger, keys, a cigar, and a wallet. Inside the wallet, I found Manfred Schockner's business card with hand-written notes on the back of the card in the center console compartment. In the trunk, I located a black box and silver case containing hypodermic needles and medical vials labeled as steroid compounds."

Perlo declined cross, and then Det. Russell Moss, a member of LBPD's homicide team, testified about six search warrants for telephone records for Nick Harvey, Jason Curran, Frank Jaramillo and Manfred Schockner from May to November 2004. After recounting his tasks, Barnes inquired whether Moss ever found a single telephone call between Schockner and Harvey: "No," he testified. Perlo immediately objected, but Ferrari overruled him with a shrug.

When the prosecutor asked him to specify telephone records from October 20 to November 8, he cited sixty-seven calls between Jaramillo and Harvey, forty-three between Schockner and Jaramillo, and none between the killer and the estranged husband. He also identified November 2, 4 and 8 as days with "a large volume of telephone calls."

"On November 2 we traced eight phone calls between 7:13 and 9:48 am," he stated, identifying each call the first day Curran drove the killer to the Bixby Knolls home. The pair had returned two days later to carry out the contract, per Schockner's instructions, but Harvey backed off at the last minute and they drove back to Ventura County. The detective identified twenty-seven calls placed between 9 am and 2 pm that day, and then testified about sixteen calls on the day of the killing.

Defense counsel repeated his objection many times during Moss' testimony, reiterating his contention that the phone records revealed nothing relevant since none of the conversations were recorded. Ferrari admitted this condition and advised jurors to "please remember these are call between telephones, not people."

Perlo approached the podium with a list of notes regarding Moss's testimony. "The first call you identified between telephones owned by Manfred Schockner and Frank Jaramillo occurred on May 1, 2004, is that correct?" Moss agreed. "On May 5th, you identified seven calls between the two phones, is that correct?" Moss affirmed his testimony. "Over the time period between May 1st and November 8th of 2004, you have identified a record of 268 calls between telephones registered to Mr. Jaramillo and Mr. Schockner. Is that correct?" The detective agreed.

"Do you know the length of any of these calls, or if the call was ever answered?" Perlo asked. "No I don't," the detective replied.

"During this period of time, was Manfred Schockner involved in any business dealings with Frank Jaramillo?" Perlo continued. "I don't know," Moss answered. Consulting his list, the attorney picked out a number of dates identified in the police report and asked if that particular call was completed. Moss again said he didn't know.

"All you know is that someone with the Schockner telephone placed a call to the Jaramillo phone, isn't that right?" His question seemed rhetorical. The detective remained silent, and after an awkward pause Moss stood down.

Looking to wrap up the proceedings before lunch and clear the way for the long Labor Day weekend, the prosecutor called her final witness of the day: Timmi McShane, an investigator for Washington Mutual Bank, where Frank Jaramillo kept a joint checking account with his fiancée, Michelle Horowitz. Using an October 2004 account statement as a reference, she testified about two $25,000 transfers to a bank account on October 12 and October 26, with both drawn on a Wachovia joint checking account held by Manfred and Lynn Schockner.

"There is a note on the check dated October 26, 2004," Ms. McShane testified, consulting the photocopy of the draft. "*2005 BMW* is written on the memo line."

• • • •

Relieved for the lunch break from the tense courtroom drama we braced the upcoming weekend when our families would arrive for the second half of the trial. While glad to share the final stretch with our wives and children, we were still learning new details about the case against Schockner, and it was hard not to worry about Charlie's reaction to this sordid mess.

I recalled the conflicting emotions that followed me home after Harvey and Jaramillo were convicted and tried to explain them to my son: I couldn't rest until Schockner was convicted of the murder, even though that verdict wouldn't replace our loss. By then I only wanted revenge. The killer was a vicious thug who sealed his fate with his dagger, and the middleman tapped a wealthy old man for easy money. Both verdicts were edifying, but Schockner's crimes reached another malignant level entirely; there was the murder he commissioned, of course, but also the years of anguish he inflicted upon his wife and son. His trial would expose his depravity and, we hoped, deliver the same sentence as his counterparts. I was familiar with the tense moments court sessions invariably bring, but I couldn't imagine Charlie's pain; he was a sharp kid who knew how his father arranged his mother's killing, but his real test would come when he confronted the man who made his life a living hell all those years before Lynn's gruesome demise.

When my brother and I met the family on Monday at LAX, Libby and Susan were relieved to be off the plane but Charlie was excited to be back in California again. He always seemed to have pleasant memories from halcyon West Coast days with his mom, and returned gladly. I was pleased to see him happy in his old haunts, a young man comfortable in his own skin. We piled into the oversize SUV and cruised Charlie's old haunts, finally working our way to Beach Boulevard and the strip. He saw the California dream I still could not envision. This was one of the ways Charlie and I parted ways as father and son, but one of the few.

My memories of Long Beach bear Manfred's vicious stamp; every visit during their 25-year marriage ended with both my sister and mother in tears, manipulated into emotional corners by Schockner's hand. I had missed most of Charlie's early years simply because I refused to tolerate this miserable man, and now, Manfred was the only reason I ever returned to the coast. Each arrival at the LAX terminal was a sort of sentence: not a prison, by any means, but penance at the very least. But Charlie had to face his father, a watershed moment, and I hoped I had enough strength to share his pain. Together we found the solution that would forever bond us as father and son.

• • • •

PRESSTELEGRAM.COM — FRIDAY, AUGUST 31, 2007 — A3

Schockner accused of hiring hit man

Courts: Trial begins in murder of L.B. woman in 2004.

By Wendy Thomas Russell
Staff writer

LONG BEACH – A Bixby Knolls millionaire hired a hit man to kill his estranged wife two months after she filed for a legal separation and began the process of dividing their assets, a prosecutor told jurors Thursday at the start of the man's trial.

Manfred "Fred" Schockner, 67, could face life in prison if convicted of the murder of Lynn Schockner, 50, who was stabbed to death on the back porch of her pool home on Nov. 6, 2004, while the couple's 14-year-old son was away at school.

"The defendant is not the man who repeatedly plunged a knife into her body," Deputy District Attorney Cynthia Barnes said during her opening statement in Long Beach Superior Court. "But he did hire the killer."

The hit man and a middleman in the alleged conspiracy already have been tried and sentenced to life in prison for murder. Bodybuilder Nicholas Harvey was convicted of being the hit man, while a gym manager named Frankie Jaramillo was convicted of being the middleman.

Those men, both of whom tried in vain to minimize their own guilt by arguing that they had been pressured, implicated Schockner as the orchestrator of the murder plot during their testimony earlier this year.

Schockner, who wore a blue suit for his first day of trial, appeared significantly more frail than he had during his arrest two years ago. But he stayed engaged in the testimony Thursday, writing notes to his lawyers and often removing his glasses to view murder-scene diagrams as they were projected onto a screen in the courtroom.

As coroner's photos depicting his wife's body were shown on the screen, Schockner glanced at them only occasionally and, at one point, shook his head as he looked away.

Schockner's legal team, Stanley Perlo and Jack Stennett, are expected to argue that Schockner was betrayed by Jaramillo, who they say planned the murder without Schockner's knowledge and then pulled him into the fray.

Manfred Schockner, center, who is accused of plotting to have his estranged wife Lynn killed in November 2004, sits in the courtroom during the first day of his trial Thursday. Schockner faces a sentence of life in prison if he is convicted.

Scott Smeltzer / Press-Telegram

COURT TRACKER

TRACK LOCAL CASES ONLINE

Visit **presstelegram.com** and click on the Court Tracker logo to see a list of pending cases.

business" and the reasons Schockner gave Jaramillo the cash were not made clear.

Perlo also moved to undermine the prosecution's theory that Schockner wanted his wife dead because he stood to lose as much

ing Jaramillo conversing with Schockner about the murder.

"Not only did he implicate himself in the murder," Barnes told jurors of that taped conversation. "He blamed Nicholas Harvey for getting caught."

The morning's testimony was a virtual reenactment of testimony delivered during the trials for Harvey and Jaramillo.

L. Schockner

A crew of police officers were called to testify about how they had responded to the 1100 block of Andrews Drive at about 11 a.m. on Nov. 6, 2004, to investigate a prowler call in the neighborhood.

A neighbor had seen Harvey jump over a fence and into the Schockners' back yard and reported the suspicious activity to

Police found Lynn Schockner's lifeless body just outside her back door, the keys to the gate just a few inches from her left hand.

But the afternoon's testimony included that of two witnesses not called during the previous trials.

One was Lynn Schockner's divorce attorney, Lisa Emily Brandon, who said she was hired by the victim in August 2004 and later filed for a legal separation on behalf of her client.

She said Manfred Schockner had not hired an attorney, which she thought was "very unusual … particularly given the size of the estate" – an estimated $6 million.

She described Lynn Schockner as "afraid" – a word that invited a sustained objection from Perlo –

naive, not financially sophisticated at all, very reliant on Mr. Schockner for … about everything," Brandon said.

The last witness of the day was Jason Curran, a bouncer from Ventura County who agreed to drive Harvey to the crime scene in Long Beach on three occasions, on Nov. 2 and 4, 2004, and then on the day of the murder. On the first two days, he said, he and Harvey – both of whom had worked as bouncers at the same bar – sat in the car for about an hour and then returned to Ventura County.

Curran, who was never charged with a crime, indicated that he did not know he was being used as a getaway driver in a murder, and got scared when he heard all the police activity in the area during the last visit. He drove back to Ventura and eventually contacted

Family recalls a gentle soldier

State: Nathan, 21, was second Hubbard son to die in Iraq.

By Garance Burke
Associated Press

CLOVIS – A father who lost a second son last week in the Iraq war said Thursday the support his family has received has helped them sustain their belief in the United States' efforts to combat global terrorism.

"The nation's at war," said Jeff Hubbard, the soldier's father, a retired police officer. "We just want people to support the nation and what it's trying to get accomplished by making the world a better place."

Army Cpl. Nathan Hubbard, 21, died Aug. 22 in a helicopter crash. He enlisted at age 19 while still grieving for his older brother, Marine Lance Cpl. Jared Hubbard, who was killed by a roadside bomb in Ramadi in 2004.

A third brother, Army Spc. Jason Hubbard, 33, was part of the team that recovered Nathan's body from the crash site. After Nathan's death, Jason was sent home from his unit and was ordered not to redeploy to a hostile fire zone.

Both brothers were in the same platoon on a scouting mission observing a treacherous stretch of road south of Kirkuk, Iraq the day of the crash, the surviving son said. Jason's team left the area in a Black Hawk first; another soldier aboard that helicopter saw from the air the second aircraft had crashed.

"We kind of went into a holding pattern over this downed bird," Jason Hubbard told reporters, his voice steady. "It was at that point where I began to really fear that was the other helicopter that picked up our team."

His team was then assigned to return to the desert and secure the crash site, which meant removing weapons, equipment and the bodies of their comrades from the wreckage.

Our Labor Day weekend ended at 10:43 am on Tuesday, September 4 when LBPD Forensic Specialist Carmen Moncure took the stand. She testified that Nick Harvey's wallet, found in his car at the Park & Ride, revealed his own fingerprints. Barnes projected images corresponding to her testimony, specifically drawing her attention to Manfred Schockner's business card, also found in the killer's wallet, establishing their connection.

During his cross, attorney Perlo asked the CSI veteran why she kept referring to the business card "belonging to Manfred Schockner," asking if she didn't really mean the "card with [Schockner's] name on it?" She remained silent. He ended his examination by asking if she found any evidence bearing Manfred Schockner's fingerprint, which she denied.

Eight minutes later LBPD Det. Brian McMahon testified about wiretap warrants he prepared for phone numbers associated with the defendants: Jaramillo, Harvey, and other suspects - all his incoming and outgoing calls from November 13 through December 3, 2004. Barnes asked the detective to explain the way police distinguish the interaction between conspirators from non-criminal conversations. McMahon described a technique called "minimizing:" the officer is allowed to hear just enough of the conversation to determine whether a criminal conspiracy is being discussed; if not, surveillance is terminated for a full two minutes, after which the wiretap may resume. Investigators followed this procedure from 6 am until midnight for twenty-three days.

"I recognized his voice," McMahon said, referring to the defendant's whispered voice and familiar list of personal complaints. Barnes entered her next exhibit - a recorded phone call from Schockner to Det. Cardoza more than a week after the killing. During that call, McMahon's surveillance caught an incoming call from Frank Jaramillo. The audio illustrated how Schockner broke the connection with the detective, intercepted Jaramillo's call, and then calmly returned to answer the detective's questions. The episode portrayed Schockner's arrogance in uncertain terms.

In keeping with an oblique approach to Schockner's defense,

Perlo's initial questions were designed to catch McMahon off-guard: "You were not the lead detective in this investigation, were you?" he demanded. "You were given information that you investigated for other officers, did you not?"

McMahon agreed and then described his surveillance role in the wide LBPD investigation. Perlo then asked him to identify the "ten or eleven checks that passed between Schockner and Jaramillo." The detective again pled ignorance, but finally agreed other detectives had briefed him regarding the funds that passed between the conspirators.

"Was that money given or loaned?" Perlo asked.

"I don't know," McMahon admitted. Perlo retired to his table and the witness was excused. That set the stage for the state's lead witness: Det. Kris Nelson, the undercover operative who understood their plan and penetrated their conspiracy, the twenty-three year veteran who made the state's case.

'I've worked the Career Criminal Unit for the past seventeen years," he said. "We work pretty much exclusively with Class One felons – those people involved in major crimes – murder, armed robbery, violent assaults. After we were briefed by the homicide detectives running the Schockner case, we found a way to infiltrate the criminals who were involved in this crime. As it turned out, it wasn't very difficult.

"We knew Frank was the middleman who found Nick Harvey to do the job for Schockner, for five grand," Nelson said. "I played the role of 'Uncle John,' a family friend of Nick's. It was all a ruse, but Frankie didn't know that." After a few phone calls, he set up a meeting with Jaramillo at the Macy's in Thousand Oaks Mall. Driving down West Hillcrest Drive, Nelson was trying to collect money for Harvey, the balance owed him for killing Lynn. "Early on I knew we had to figure out a way to infiltrate the relationship between Frank and Manfred Schockner because I knew the murder was done for the old man."

Just before the lunch break, Perlo posed another objection, requesting Nelson's testimony of this witness be curtailed as it was "highly prejudicial hearsay testimony" based on his "personal opinions."

Barnes responded with a note of exasperation in her tone. "This is about the fifteenth time Mr. Perlo has objected to testimony even though I asked every witness very specific questions. He [Det. Nelson] is allowed to testify about his investigation, and that is not hearsay. Mr. Perlo's just being difficult."

The defense attorney reiterated his objection: "This officer can testify to anything he has been told or has heard, but his opinions and references to what other people told him give his testimony a patina of admissibility, Perlo insisted. "This is not right."

"Police officers are allowed to explain what they did during their investigation," Barnes countered. "They are allowed to include what they have been told. This testimony is absolutely admissible. I'm sure defense counsel doesn't like it and I know it doesn't help his case, but that's just too bad."

Judge Ferrari agreed, and Perlo retreated, crestfallen again as he shuffled back to his table. After lunch, the prosecutor carefully directed the undercover officer through his testimony, always specific in her questions. "After he was arrested, did Frank Jaramillo agree to cooperate with the police investigation?" she asked.

"Yes."

"Was the defendant given or promised any incentive to cooperate?"

"No," Nelson said. "I decided to have Frank meet Schockner while wearing the same wired jacket I wore during my meeting with him. That jacket is equipped with a video camera and audio microphone designed to record criminal evidence." Nelson explained the sequence of events. At the time of his arrest, Frank Jaramillo immediately agreed to call Schockner and set up the meeting the next day at the LV Seafood Restaurant in Long Beach. Jaramillo donned the jacket for their late afternoon meeting, but before the two arrived at 7 pm, Nelson and four other undercover officers took seats in the eatery, with another half dozen cops stationed outside the location.

"As soon as Frank sat down at the table, I watched Schockner write a note which he held up for Frank to read," Det. Nelson testified. "They argued for about twenty minutes. Then, Schockner seemed to be very stressed, and two or three times during their conversation he wrote out notes and held them up for Frank to read."

Barnes asked the detective to explain video and audio recordings of their conversation at the restaurant. Nelson admitted the camera did not work entirely as he had hoped, stipulating the grainy quality of the images. The prosecutor projected the pictures from the pinhole camera fixed to the jacket on a screen visible only to jurors and the court. Like us, everyone in the gallery listened raptly to the tape recording of their conversation, but we were left guessing as to the images on the screen.

Nelson was excused after the tape concluded. Det. Michael Dugan, a twenty-five year LBPD veteran, also posed as a restaurant patron for the meeting between Jaramillo and Schockner. He testified regarding the encounter.

"I saw Mr. Schockner hold up a small notepad for Frank Jaramillo to read, and I was also present the next day when Mr. Schockner was arrested at 6 am at his home in Bixby Knolls. We found a note in the trashcan in his kitchen, and the writing on that note showed the word 'sloppy' connected by an arrow to the name 'Nick.'"

Finally, Dennis Robbins, a fastidious, detail-oriented

homicide detective assigned to assist Barnes with all three capital prosecutions, presented the caseload of evidence prepared by the state. Perlo objected to the entire file, but Barnes argued defense had every opportunity to examine the evidence. "We provided them with accurate copies of every document and discovery," she said.

Barnes asked him to describe specific items collected from the Schockner residence, and the twenty-seven year veteran reported finding the defendant's personal identification, correspondence, checks, bank records, a 1996 copy of the couple's pre-nuptial agreement, and Schockner's bulging briefcase. The briefcase contained many documents as well as a small collection of photographs. When Barnes asked for their description, Robbins hesitated. "I would call them pornographic pictures of Mrs. Schockner," he reluctantly advised.

We winced at the odious image, thankful the prints remained obscured from view.

Robbins identified the notes Schockner passed to Jaramillo at the restaurant and said they had been scribbled from a pad found in the house, but his financial records proved most damning. Tracing the trail between the two conspirators, Robbins identified four checks totaling $12,000 Schockner wrote to the middleman in the three months before the killing, but account transaction records from February 5 to October 26, 2004 revealed that Schockner paid Jaramillo another $110,000 as well.

Perlo was strangely silent during his testimony – Robbins was the only state witness who didn't draw an objection. On cross, he posed a couple of oblique questions regarding computer records and their pre-nuptial agreement, and then retired. Barnes completed the state's case with a wiretapped telephone conversation between Schockner and Cardoza recorded two weeks before his arrest.

"That's all, your honor," she said before Judge Ferrari ended the session and advised all parties to return by 10 am the next day.

We kicked back at the Hilton for a couple of hours and hashed out the courtroom drama with our children and wives. Despite being hardened to the process, it was impossible to fully fathom what cut Charlie the deepest – the killing or his father's malignant side. Always guarded, my son seemed to retreat further into his shell as the trial progressed, but he relaxed after we hit the road. That evening we loaded the family into the rental to dine at one of Charlie's favorite restaurants, and tried to brace for the upcoming day, that started with a front page article in the *Press-Telegram*:.

Schockner Video Shows Meeting With Middleman

LONG BEACH – Grainy video footage from a hidden camera played Tuesday in Long Beach Superior Court provided some of the prosecution's most compelling evidence against a 67-year-old millionaire on trial for allegedly plotting murder of his estranged wife three years ago.

Cast on a large projection screen in the courtroom the 20-minute video captures the defendant, Manfred Schockner, talking to a co-defendant in the case just three weeks after his wife Lynn was found stabbed to death on the back porch of their Bixby Knolls pool home.

In the video, Schockner refers to the hit man as "sloppy" and despairingly grasps his head with his hands while talking about how the police investigation seems to be leading back to him.

"I'm a dead man – one way or the other," he says.

That evidence was presented on the last day of the prosecution's case – a court day attended, for the first time, by the Schockner's 16-year-old son, who now lives with an uncle in Georgia and stands behind the prosecution.

Schockner is accused of paying a middleman $50,000 to hire a hit man and kill his wife of 25 years, making it look like a botched robbery. His wife had filed for a legal separation at the time of her death, and he stood to gain an estimated $2.5 million in the pending divorce.

Schockner's own defense hinges on his contention that Jaramillo arranged the killing without his knowledge. His attorneys, Stanley Perlo and Jack Stennett, have said Schockner was bankrolling Jaramillo, a con artist, and that Jaramillo wanted the victim dead out of fear that divorce proceedings would tie up Schockner's finances.

It was Jaramillo who ultimately agreed to wear a police-issued "Jacket Cam" to a meeting with Schockner at the LV Chinese Seafood Restaurant on December 2, 2004. With five police officers stationed inside the restaurant and another six in the parking lot, the video is taken from the perspective of Jaramillo, as he sits in a round booth at the restaurant.

As Schockner approaches the table, Jaramillo greets him typically: "Hey old man," he says. "How are you feeling? You're skinny as hell now, man. How are you doing?"

"Absolutely shitty," Schockner responds, before writing a note asking Jaramillo if he's been "wired" by police.

"Oh no," Jaramillo says.

At first, Schockner seems hesitant to speak openly. When Jaramillo tells him that the two of them "would not be sitting here if you didn't want... Lynn killed," Schockner cuts him off.

"I don't know anything about that," he says. He tells Jaramillo their best course of action is refusing to talk to anyone. "There's nothing that's going to happen if we both maintain our cool."

But as Jaramillo becomes more agitated and aggressive in urging Schockner to take responsibility for what he's done, Schockner becomes increasingly more dejected.

"We have to settle this right here," Jaramillo says. "We would not be here if you didn't want Lynn killed. You know that."

"Look," Schockner retorts, getting angry. "You say that to me one more time, I'll just get up and leave and you can do what you want. It happened, OK?"

Finally, with nothing resolved and tensions still high between the two men, Schockner gets up and leaves the restaurant.

In addition, a wire-tapped conversation between Schockner and LBPD Det. Chris Cardoza was played for jurors. On the audiotape, Schockner can be heard providing information about checks he'd written to Jaramillo during the previous year for business they conducted and because Jaramillo, whom he had met at a local gym, needed the money.

"OK," Cardoza clarifies. "The other money was for your businesses and financial problems you said he had?"

"Yeah," Schockner answers. "And you got me

> thinking I've been a sucker."
>
> Schockner laughs heartily at times and sounds relatively upbeat, telling Cardoza that he's "not worried" because he's certain the police have caught the right man.
>
> "Happy fishing," he says at one point, apparently referring to the detective's probes into Jaramillo's involvement in the crime. He also appears to be telling Cardoza he wouldn't support seeking the death penalty against Harvey, saying "he probably doesn't know why he did what he did."

• • • •

I was grateful for the prominent headline which made me anxious to read the entire report, and Russell's story bolstered my confidence - her incredulous tone mirrored my skepticism – and I was more than happy to hope jurors viewed the proceedings in the same light. Even with this emotional lift, I remained apprehensive of the jury's take on the case, worried one or more would see the details in a different light. As the trial neared its end, I shunned every positive thought, superstitious that any confidence would vex the outcome. I was determined to be ready for the worst, and would deal with Schockner if he became a free man. If there was a mistrial, I would revisit Long Beach again and again. No matter the verdict, we would return home with our son, and that was all that really mattered.

Wednesday's session started with testimony from Wachovia Securities broker Richard Daniel, who explained his financial relationship with the Schockners. He provided a general description of the dozen or so accounts Schockner managed for his immediate family and the Schockner Family Trust. Barnes angled her cross-examination away from the $6 million estate by asking the broker to provide his personal impressions of his clients.

Working out of Pasadena, Daniel had only met the Schockners twice in person, when the accounts were created. He offered advice, though he said it was rarely taken. He brokered Manfred's buy and sell instructions for securities in each account, with little input from his wife. But he distinctly remembered a phone call from Lynn just few weeks before she was murdered, directing him to transfer funds to a new account she opened at a local bank.

The broker estimated the value of the Schockner Trust at $3.4 million, but identified another $1.3 million in trust for Manfred's parents: his now-deceased father, Herbert, and his institutionalized mother, Charlotte, who suffered from dementia. The prosecutor asked if Daniel's accounting revealed a questionable $500,000 loan or other curious financial transactions

"Wasn't that money coming and going all the time?" Barnes demanded. "Let me ask a specific question – there was a loan made to someone in Colorado sometime in November 2004 – did someone pay that money back?"

"I don't know," Daniel admitted. "There were so many financial transactions over the course of one to two years that it is hard to say. Manfred kept money coming and going from all of his accounts all of the time."

Perlo countered with plausible explanations for Schockner's financial dealings with Jaramillo by calling a witness who overheard a business conversation between the two, a man who claimed he overheard Jaramillo mention his "family's import-export business," and that Schockner wanted to invest in that enterprise.

Barnes objected. "Your honor, this client is not even on the witness list. As far as his testimony, I don't have a clue about relevance."

Judge Ferrari dismissed the complaint and then the witness, letting the statement stand; but before Schockner's scheduled appearance as a witness for himself, a Long Beach real estate agent appeared for the defense. The middle-aged man, a reluctant witness who was clearly uncomfortable with his dealings with the defendant, testified his client signed a purchase agreement on a Bixby Knolls home about three blocks from Lynn's house. "He opened an escrow account, signed the papers and gave me a check from the account of Mr. and Mrs. Schockner," he said.

"Was the check signed by Mrs. Schockner? Was the contract for the house signed by Lynn and Fred Schockner?" Perlo inquired. The witness affirmed their signatures, but added a confusing detail upon cross-examination by the prosecutor.

Barnes asked the real estate agent about the check. "Did you receive it more than once?"

"Yes. When we signed papers he gave me a check for the down payment. That check was dated Oct. 30, 2001." The realtor told jurors his client (Schockner) asked him to return this check so he could provide a replacement. He complied. "A few days later he gave me a check dated Oct. 30, 2004, but it was the same check. The date had been changed. It was forged."

• • • •

My last conversation with Lynn took place on Halloween Day 2004, less than two weeks before she was dead. Crying uncontrollably when she called that last day of October, unintelligible between sobs, it took many minutes for me to understand the latest catastrophy in her divorce. Coming on the heels of our very happy visit only two weeks earlier, I was stunned by Lynn's emotional collapse. She was a wreck.

A week earlier, she explained, Schockner emptied their joint account with a real estate transaction. The money wasn't that important to my sister, but his choice of new homes, only three blocks from her house, shattered her confidence. After learning Schockner could stalk her from his new residence and planned to share custody of their son, she was undone by his maneuvers, near another nervous breakdown. She believed she could never remove Manfred from her life and he would always be able to manipulate her with custody of their son. It was almost more than her fragile psyche could bear – this would be the first and only time I ever considered my sister suicidal, and I thought she might even surrender to her fears during our conversation. I considered breaking the connection to call 911, but she pulled herself back from the edge and explained her plight.

I never realized how her fears really ruled her life. Never one to be bullied or allow it to happen in my presence, I couldn't even appreciate her predicament – alone in Long Beach, with nowhere else to go. Violence never crossed my mind, despite my sister's forebodings. She was a broken woman. I hoped I could exhaust her tears, but logic had little bearing on her situation. I was reduced to platitudes, and encouraged her with greeting card advice, and reiterated Charlie's glowing attributes and promising future. Even as I interjected a steady stream of bright prospects into our conversation, she and I came to understand that as long as she lived in Long Beach, she lived within *his* reach. If nothing else, Schockner would remain a specter in her world, and he would never leave.

Nine days later she was dead.

CHAPTER 21

"I'm glad to finally be able to prove my innocence," Schockner replied to Perlo's first question: *Why did he want to testify, even though he wasn't required?*

His attorney continued with his next question: "Did you ever ask anyone to take your wife's life?

"I've been searching my mind for more than two years," Schockner testified in a hushed tone. "To the best of my knowledge I have not even come close to arranging Lynn's murder." Given the ease with which Schockner spoke falsely – he was always a terrific liar - it was bizarre that he never said the only words that mattered: *I didn't do it.*

After this half-hearted denial, Perlo led Schockner through different defenses: his cell phone placed many random calls to Jaramillo; his Cuban-American friend who attempted extortion; finally, he even tried to shift some of the responsibility to Lynn herself for wearing too much expensive jewelry, and drawing attention to her wealth. Instead of insisting on his outright innocence, he conjured up alternative explanations to create reasonable doubt.

His defense seemed erratic and off-center. There was no coherent narrative to his responses, and he never voiced outrage over the charges.

"Mr. Schockner, is it true you were involved in a divorce with your wife?" Perlo asked. Manfred agreed. "It is also true you were also involved in the purchase of a second home?"

"Yes. It was about a quarter mile from my home," he responded. "I used a $10,000 draft from our joint checking account, and Lynn signed the check. I stopped living with Lynn in May, but remained in communication with her, and she knew I wanted the second house to be close to my son."

Schockner told the court he and his wife began a division of their property, but even after receiving written notification from Lynn's lawyer he refused to hire legal counsel, despite the size of the estate.

"Why didn't you hire an attorney?" Perlo posed.

"First, I had verbal and written statements from Lynn that we would hold costs down to a minimum," he said. His statement sounded unreasonable for a couple going through a divorce. Less than a month before her murder, my baby sister uttered prophetic words: *He made me promise not to hire a lawyer – he said he'd kill me if I did.* Schockner planned to negotiate directly with his wife; when she hired Brandon he believed she had violated her oath. He would hold his son hostage to subdue his wife.

"The second reason was I was still interviewing attorneys and was having difficulty hiring the proper lawyer," Schockner insisted. Protests aside, we believed he used free legal advice from his friend, Neil Ivan, who was living with him in the Bixby Knolls home when he was arrested.

He testified as to copies of the validity of a pre-nuptial agreement found in his briefcase, indicating he needed those records to document expenses he had incurred on repairs to the house. He also cited the 1999 amendment to their will [also found in the briefcase] to his promise to share his assets with his wife if they divorced. His narrative recounted verbal and written agreements with his wife, as well as a current accounting of every asset in their household, and then his attorney turned to a different subject.

"Did you know Frank Jaramillo?" Perlo asked.

"Yes I did," Schockner admitted. "We met in 2002 at the LA Fitness Center he managed. Over the next few months, we struck up a friendship. He told me he had placed a $450,000 deposit on a car wash and owned a big share of the business, and he was looking for a partner. He did this in a very surreptitious way, suggesting his father backed him in the business venture, and another partner would be welcomed. After a while Frank quit the LA Fitness Center and told me he was working for his father."

"Did you ever lend him money?"

"Yes I did. In October or November 2003 our relationship became closer." This was a reference to undisclosed "loans" to his new friend and the car wash.

"Did you buy gifts from Frank Jaramillo?" Perlo asked.

"I bought a 60-inch Mitsubishi TV," he said.

Perlo let that stand and turned to the list of checks from Schockner to Jaramillo's account. He categorized some as investments and explained others as personal loans, totaling $121,000. Even though Jaramillo admitted to a $2,500 loan early in their relationship, none of the payouts were documented or collateralized, except for the initial loan, secured by a Rolex watch. That was so unlike Schockner's obsession with documented arrangements, signed and sealed, which we knew from our sister. We hoped his lies would be obvious to the jury.

He ended his statement with another incongruous statement: "Our business arrangement might have been a little bit looser than normal," he said, because he was always on the lookout for "a good business deal." Tellingly, not twenty minutes earlier he testified he had required a signed and notarized promissory note from his best friend during his divorce.

Stennett sat quietly in second chair while Perlo tried to refute one of the most damning pieces of evidence proffered by the state: Schockner's note with the words "sloppy" and "Nick" connected by an arrow. After Perlo handed him the note, Schockner examined the writing and stipulated that it "may" have been my handwriting. "I was with Neal at my home, and neither of us could remember the killer's name. We called him 'Sloppy Nick,' and I might have written this down to jog my memory," Schockner claimed.

Asked where he was when he learned of Lynn's murder, Schockner said he had been at his brother's home all day. (Even though he was contacted early that afternoon at his health club, Barnes didn't challenge his claim.). To another query, he explained circumstances involved with his conversation with Det. Cardoza recorded two weeks after Lynn was killed. "I was recovering from surgery and confused by the affects of pain killers and other medication when I spoke to the detective. I might have made a mistake."

As soon as Judge Ferrari called a two-hour lunch break I made a beeline for the restroom, all the way at the end of the hall. That was the moment Schockner chose to provoke an outburst from Charlie, who was still in his seat. I didn't know if he waited until I had left or just grabbed the moment, but before the bailiff could return him to his holding cell, Schockner turned to wave at Charlie, begging a moment with his eyes. He mouthed protests and yearning for the boy who was sitting quietly between our wives, Susan and Libby. The teenager shouted an angry reply heard by the judge, whose attention had been drawn to documents on his bench. Fortunately, the jury had retired, but Ferrari quickly reprimanded Charlie and insisted he refrain from further contact with the defendant. This was the measure of how far Schockner would go to derail the proceedings - he would seek sanctions against his own blood – his former son – to lay the groundwork for a mistrial or appeal. The incident was over long before I returned to the group, but during a quiet moment later that day I thanked the heavens I wasn't there. Bracing Charlie for even more courtroom gambits, we returned from lunch to hear Schockner resume his defense.

"I had been in a lot of pain that day," he recalled of his December 2 meeting with Frank Jaramillo at the LV Seafood Restaurant. He emphasized his discomfort from the hernia surgery three days earlier. "I was taking medication for the pain - extra strength vicodin – and sometimes I just didn't know what I was doing. The medication affected me that way.

"While I was driving to the restaurant, I was very confused and becoming scared at what was going on. I began to get the feeling that I was a suspect," he said, adding that he decided to attend the meeting despite objections from his brother and his attorney. "They did not want me to go to the restaurant, but I decided to go and remain very circumspect." Early in the meeting Schockner said he became "very concerned that Frank was trying to lead the conversation. He tried to force me to say certain things and I was scared. He was trying to lead me, push me into being responsible for Lynn's death."

When Perlo asked about the money Jaramillo owed him, Schockner admitted, "I was very concerned for my money. I learned Frank and Nick Harvey were very close when they worked together at LA Fitness gym, and I was worried I may be linked to what they'd done. I thought Frank was gong to demand more money and blackmail me." When his attorney asked if Jaramillo requested additional funds, he quickly agreed: "Yes he did – several times. In fact, he told me he needed anther $42,000."

"Did you give it to him?" Perlo inquired.

"No. I told him I could not give him any money because all my funds were frozen by the divorce," Schockner said.

"Did you ever indicate you wanted him to kill your wife?"

"No, not that I know of," Schockner said. "I was scared about the money trail between us, but I thought I had been swindled. I finally came to the conclusion Frank Jaramillo either killed or had my wife killed, and then planned to blackmail me."

That statement was all he ever said of Lynn's killing, incongruous because it sidestepped the main point: *why would they do that?*

Perlo kept his client on the stand for twenty-three minutes to allow him to explain his version of the events leading to his arrest, and Schockner finally sat tall and proclaimed his innocence, although he never said the words the jury wanted to hear: *I didn't kill my wife.* Barnes quickly abandoned her seat and moved in front of her table, eager to begin her interrogation; at the same time, Schockner hunched his shoulders and receded into the witness chair, avoiding eye contact with the prosecutor.

"Mr. Schockner, how much money do you control?" Schockner said his estate was valued at "five to six million dollars." The prosecutor asked how much his wife would have received in their divorce.

"That would be half of our community property which, including the house, came to about $3.4 million," he replied.

"Who would get the money if she died?" she pressed.

"Me."

She inquired about the dozens of phone calls between himself and Jaramillo, but Schockner blamed his phone. He explained how he would carry his cell phone in his front pocket, bumping it occasionally against furniture or a door. The device would automatically engage the call-back feature, and dial to the most recent number, time and time again. There were dozens of calls between the two in the less than three months.

"You're telling us the cell phone made calls by itself?" she asked with undisguised incredulity.

"I didn't know I had this problem until about four months later," he said.

"It took you four months to figure out your cell phone was making calls on its own?" she asked. "How could that be?" When he claimed he discovered the problem by examining his monthly bills, she cast a dubious glance in the direction of the jury. "So you had $9,000 to put in Jaramillo's account, yet you couldn't replace your phone or the leather pouch it came in? Do you expect the jury to believe that?"

"Absolutely," he answered. "It's the truth."

She didn't bother to hide her disbelief, but dropped the topic and asked about a note found at his home.

"When police searched your home after your arrest, they found a note with the name 'Nick' connected by an arrow to the word 'sloppy.' Do you remember that note?"

"Yes."

"Earlier in your testimony, did you tell the jury you could not remember the name of the man who killed your wife?"

"Yes. I had a mental block with his name," he replied. "I had to create a nickname."

Striding back to retrieve another exhibit, she obtained Ferrari's permission to approach the defendant. "Mr. Schockner, would you please tell the jury your occupation?" she inquired.

"I was a program control manager for Honeywell Corporation," he stated, briefly describing his duties at Garrett AirResearch, where he met Lynn. She worked there almost ten years as a service rep with military clients before retiring on disability, and a few years later he clashed with clients and superiors and was forced to resign, but not before he developed his own "disability" to ease him into retirement.

Looking to bolster this image of Schockner as an angry and abusive co-worker, Barnes brought forward two professional reprimands from other firms where Schockner had been employed, documents we found among Lynn's papers and passed to the police. Those notices warned Schockner about "any subsequent outbursts of temper, unprofessional conduct, or physical violence" that would result in his immediate termination; but they didn't clear Ferrari's "hearsay" threshold for admissibility and were excluded, to our chagrin. Both reported verbal and physical abuse in the workplace, but one letter was exceptional. Years after he left Honeywell, he joined a different boss for a round of golf. After a few clumsy holes, Schockner hit an errant drive, slammed the club to the ground, catching the crown of his boss' foot, crushing three or four bones. His employment ended that day, and it was only surprising the victim didn't press charges.

Barnes turned to another track. "Mr. Schockner, do you consider yourself a smart businessman?" He answered with a nod. Barnes requested he answer verbally for the record. "Yes," he snapped.

"Being a smart, shrewd businessman and a wealthy man, why would you enter a business relationship with Frank Jaramillo without documentation?" she asked.

"You have to understand," he replied, "this had the potential to be a very lucrative business. I researched the import/export business on the Internet, and I realized I could make a lot of money."

"Is it your practice to just lend out money without documentation?" she persisted, thrusting two additional exhibits into Schockner's hands. "Can you see that copy of a promissory note from Marty Chernoff dated April 10, 2002? The one describing a $500,000 loan to be repaid to Lynn Schockner?"

"Yes."

"Can you see the second copy of that note, dated Oct. 10, 2002?" she demanded. "Is this the same note forged to be paid to Manfred Schockner?"

He nodded and mumbled a reply, which she demanded he enunciate for the court. "Yes, I do." This had been Lynn's proof her husband was stealing assets from their divorce settlement, and didn't need an explanation. Barnes left that reply hanging in the tense air between them, hoping to lure Schockner in an angry outburst. He refused the bait. "So let me get this straight. You decided to get into the import/export business with Jaramillo, you lent him $102,000, and then you gave him $25,000 for a used BMW? Is that right – you gave him all that money?"

"Yes, I did," he said.

After he affirmed her assessment, the DDA continued to try to trip him with different questions about his actions and statements, as well as the unlikely coincidences of his alibi. Referring to Schockner's personal calendar found in his briefcase, Barnes asked why he broke his scheduled appointment with Lynn that morning, on November 8.

"This is a copy of your personal calendar, is it not?" Ms. Barnes asked, encroaching on his personal space while keeping a steady lock on his eyes.

"Yes."

"There is a notation here to meet Lynn at the Andrews Drive home on Monday, November 8 at 11 am. Is that correct?"

"Yes.".

"You didn't make that meeting, did you Mr. Schockner?" she demanded.

"No, I didn't," he replied. "I called her earlier that day and told her I had something come up and I couldn't make it."

"That was the exact time of the murder, wasn't it? That was the same time Lynn Schockner was killed, right?" she insisted. "Almost to the minute?"

"Yes."

She paused to let this coincidence register with the jury before proceeding to his other statements – both to the homicide investigators and to Jaramillo on tape. Barnes ended her cross examination by reiterating Schockner's lies, leaving the impression Schockner's testimony mattered much less than the admissions he made before he was arrested.

The defense called a final witness. Gilbert Sarmiento testified he overheard Jaramillo say his father owned an import/export business, ostensibly proving Schockner's claim he intended to capitalize on this lucrative overseas venture. Without a challenge from the DDA, the defense closed its case an hour earlier than Ferrari predicted as he gaveled the session closed. With an unrelated hearing slated for the following morning, he asked jurors to return at 1 pm, refrain from discussing the trial and avoid media coverage of the proceedings.

I left the court confident in the progress of the trial but confused by Schockner's testimony – despite the years between the murder and his court appearance, he failed to develop a believable alibi or even a coherent defense. Employing the same evasiveness he had used when we knew him as a loathsome brother-in-law, he used similar arguments in court, dissembling statements that didn't seem to pass muster with the jury, especially under Ms. Barnes's cross.

Hardly an unbiased observer, I was gratified but not surprised when Thursday's *Press-Telegram* reported a similar take on the trial. Even from the reporter's point of view, Schockner's answers sounded thin and his alibis contrived. With the entire morning to squander before the trial resumed that afternoon, I paced the Hilton courtyard, looking for signs in the obelisk or omens in the wind. Each trial was a draining process, but in this case, Charlie made the family protective of our nuclear core. He remained determined to see his father convicted, he invariably wore a polite demeanor like a mask. Harkening back to his days in drama and performance arts, I watched him retreat into character for the courtroom, only relaxing once we reached the hotel. He rarely showed any personal anxiety, and I marveled at his icy resolve, so different from my churning emotions. I sought simple vengeance and was grateful for whatever retribution I would find before Ferrari's bench, but my son eyed something closer to resolution and a ratification of his mother's love. It was hard watching him deal with his childhood demons, but he held up without a complaint, even in the comfortable but claustrophobic surroundings. We all looked forward to an end of these proceedings, and arrived for the afternoon session well before the jury began to trickle into court. None of us were prepared for Schockner's desperate last-minute delay.

Barnes approached our bench while we waited in the empty courtroom. She said Schockner had suffered a "panic attack" during the night and the trial would be delayed until he was cleared by a doctor. It was an ailment more than a few defendants experience as the end draws near, she allowed: a sudden loss of confidence, no doubt. Given Schockner's penchant for exaggerated or even feigned ailments, it was hardly a surprise. Ferrari informed the jury the trial would not happen that afternoon, simply indicating the defendant was unavailable. After the postponement, we chatted with the *Press-Telegram* reporter and explained Schockner's malingering ways Lynn had revealed during their marriage: her husband regularly manufactured maladies to justify his rude behavior, using this familiar ploy to earn another pass. We believe this was another transparent ploy to gain sympathy from the jury, and Russell's brief story on the delay ended with this paragraph:

> No further information on Schockner's condition was available Thursday, although he has long complained of a litany of physical and mental problems – including depression, heart palpitations, knee pain and irritable bowel syndrome – throughout his two-and-a-half years in jail.

• • • •

As we were leaving the courtroom, Ed Tynan, Schockner's self-described "half-brother" approached Det. Robbins and asked the detective if he could speak to me. His inquiry was oblique, speaking to the detective even though I stood within arm's length. I turned my back to allow him privacy and was surprised, even a little stunned, when he reiterated his request to "speak to Mr. Jacka," meaning me, butchering the pronunciation of my Czech surname, though clearly unintentional. The detective looked inquiringly at the man, and pointed at me: "He's right there."

I turned back to him in outrage, and when he offered his hand in consolation I just stared in stony silence. Ignoring my intentional slight, he made a quick admission: "I just wanted to tell you I now know Freddie did this thing," he said. "I can't tell you how badly I feel – especially about Charlie. I just didn't know until now. I'm sorry." His shoulders sagged as his voice trailed away.

I didn't bother with any pleasantries: "Anyone who knew Manfred Schockner would have known he killed my sister - anything else would be completely out of character for this piece of shit," I said. "You had your choice back when this happened, and you chose to believe that lying prick. Today you want me to tell Charlie you were wrong. Fuck you and fuck your apology. That's a decision you'll have to live with for the rest of your life."

He couldn't hold my gaze. I watched his eyes flood with tears. He appeared smaller, diminished by shame or regret.

"I know that now, I really do," he said with a catch in his voice. "The only thing I can say is that Manfred's father, Herbert, was a real son of a bitch, vicious and sadistic. He used a leather whip on Freddie until he bled. The kid lived in a pure hell." I was Manfred's friend, maybe his only friend, back when he was young. I had to keep that friendship until I knew, in my heart, he was wrong."

There was the affirmation of my most profound fear: Schockner's hatred and anger were legacies passed down from *his* father, a heritage that might overwhelm all our considerations for Charlie during the life that followed Lynn's murder. I never set out to be his father; my goal was to be an advisor and best friend, and I really hope I succeeded. Still, I worried those first fourteen years with his father would poison his outlook, and his problems would be more than a fumbling uncle like me could help him overcome. A few years later, I told Charlie I expected his complete emancipation after another fourteen years, when he was twenty-eight. In my mind, it would take that long to erase Schockner's presence from his life. I didn't have anything but a feeling on that, but figured it was a pretty good metric and still feel that way.

After Tynan, an elderly, unemployed medical assistant, followed me into the corridor, I told him I met Schockner's old man once, and found him a hateful octogenarian who never allowed a contradiction in his life. His need to explain Schockner's murderous greed was irrelevant to me, but as I turned to leave Tynan tugged at my shoulder and begged another moment. He confessed that Schockner still owed him $75,000, money he desperately needed for living expenses. He seemed to believe I would cover Schockner's debt, or act on his behalf. He was both pathetic and wrong. I wished him good luck and told him not to call. We parted company sharing the inevitable misfortune that came from knowing Manfred Schockner.

• • • •

We arrived well before court convened at 10:30 am on Friday, September 6, anxious to see the proceedings resume.

Having observed his contrived illnesses before, I figured he might be able to milk his act another day; but sixty minutes before the anointed hour, Judge Ferrari, who was well into his day with motion hearings and routine matters that kept his calendar full, announced the Schockner trial would re-convene when scheduled. It seemed Schockner's jailors were also all too familiar with his convenient conditions and no one gave much credence to his complaints.

Bailiff Edler ushered us into the front row facing the press table and the jury box, and after a few moments, the Schockner party entered. I motioned Tynan out into the hall on a private matter: conciliatory in my approach, I asked if he would care to join our family in the gallery. I admit it was less compassion than courtroom connivance; I hoped to let him assuage his conscience *and* distract the defense – it would be interesting to see Schockner's reaction to a defection from his thin ranks. He declined the invitation and decided to remain across the aisle with Schockner's brother and wife, but I made sure Charlie understood just where his priorities stood. "I know he just wants the money," Charlie said. "Too bad for him."

DDA Barnes rose ready from her chair, eager to argue points of law and allocutions by the defendant, anxious to close. Even her brassy hair managed to shimmer under the fluorescent fixtures as she stepped up to the podium. From our seats, we were able to watch her animated presentation with an eye on the entire court; a clear and unobstructed view of judge, court reporter, clerk and bailiff, those at the defense table, as well as the twelve Californians who would decide Shockner's fate. It was all there in front of us.

"The evidence clearly proves the defendant is guilty of killing Lynn Schockner," Barnes said, expounding upon elements of the law, including three thresholds required to find *aiding and abetting the commission of a crime*, a key element in the charges against Schockner. "The defendant must have knowledge of the unlawful purpose of the perpetrator, know this person's intent to commit the felony, and aid, promote or encourage the crime.

"Manfred Schockner master-minded this crime," she said. "He was the boss, the money behind the operation, the man who stood to benefit most from the death of Lynn Schockner. Frank Jaramillo was the middleman; Nick Harvey was the killer, and the crime was obviously not a random event." She ticked off different facts: sixty-seven phone calls between Harvey and Jaramillo in the twelve days preceding the murder, the $25,000 payment to Jaramillo coupled with his $75,000 debt to the man.

"Schockner put Jaramillo in a position where he could not pay him back," she said, contrasting this minor debt against an estate worth $3.5 million that Schockner stood to lose in the divorce. "But this was more than about money – it was about control. Schockner's wife was not going to give him his way, and he wouldn't stand for that. He had her killed."

To conclude, Barnes switched back to an analytical mode, identifying the differences between 1st and 2nd degree murder charges, reminding jurors of the legal ramifications of "willful, deliberate and premeditated intent." She said they should understand how the charge of "special circumstances" pertained to murder for financial gain. "They all stood to gain – Harvey, Jaramillo and Schockner," she said, "but Schockner stood to gain the most: more than three million in a divorce. Clearly Manfred Schockner is guilty of murder with special circumstances, and nothing less."

Perlo rose for the defense. He suggested a very different interpretation of the case, instructing jurors how the prosecution must have proved its case, beyond *any* reasonable doubt, suggesting Barnes had not. The attorney described justice as a remote concept in the course of the adversarial process, the evidence notwithstanding. In an obvious affront to our family, belied by his previous objections, he shifted the blackboard directly in front of our seats, blocking our view of the jury. His client was apparently concerned about our sympathetic impact on their deliberations, and Perlo's insult added yet another grievance. I was elated.

"When I heard of this case," Perlo began, "my first thought was 'oh my gosh,' this guy is going through a divorce and his wife is killed. When you look at it in this light, I would argue the prosecution jumped to the same conclusion." He questioned why Barnes only introduced two of Manfred Schockner's checks into evidence when so many more were found, and how this could be a relevant clue to their mishandling of the case. "We know Manfred Schockner gave Jaramillo two checks for $25,000, and even more," Perlo said. "But the prosecutor never told you that Manfred Schockner had given Frank Jaramillo a total of eleven checks. What about those other checks? What were those payments for?

"When you see this picture in total, it is not just about two checks written to substantiate the district attorney's foregone conclusion, but this was blackmail money that had already been paid," he claimed. "My client was being extorted by Jaramillo, and that's the reason for those payments."

Ticking evidentiary items off the state's list, the defense attorney insisted phone logs merely affirmed that "one telephone called another." Without recordings, they were meaningless, he claimed. "There is no evidence about the content of these calls. We don't know who talked. For all we know, Phone A dialed Phone B, and that's all that happened. Nothing more," he said. "The prosecution started with a conclusion and used evidence to support that conclusion, and that's why my client is sitting here today."

Perlo reiterated the "outrageous" hourly rate demanded by Lynn's divorce attorney and how Schockner refused to pay legal bills and relied on his own skills and knowledge in any sort of negotiation. "You have to understand – this was *his* money," he said. Shifting from subject to subject, he offered an alternate answer to each of the state's assertions and claimed police determined Schockner was a "mastermind" of the criminal conspiracy, and considered him guilty long before they completed their investigation or solved the crime. He admitted his client had "a business relationship" with Frank Jaramillo and became friends, but nothing more.

"Then there are two phone calls involving Detective Cardoza," Perlo mentioned. "During the first, the detective asks Manfred if Frank Jaramillo has contacted him. After he hangs up with the police officer, Frank Jaramillo calls my client to talk about the car. This is pretty good evidence Frank Jaramillo is looking for a car for Manfred Schockner."

Perlo tried to string these random events into a plausible explanation for his client's actions before and after his wife's murder, but they seemed more like anomalies than a coherent defense.

"The district attorney calls Frank Jaramillo the 'middleman' in this conspiracy, but he is the true mastermind of the crime," Perlo insisted. "He saw Fred as a 'cash cow,' and knowing he was in the middle of a separation from his wife, Frank Jaramillo figured if Lynn was out of the way, he would be able to get more of Manfred's money.

"Then consider Manfred's statements during his meeting with Frank at the restaurant – at no point in time does Schockner admit he wanted his wife killed," the attorney insisted. "I don't question his statements make Fred *look* guilty, but you have to remember that doesn't *make* him guilty. There are two dynamics going on in that conversation: first, Jaramillo is trying to get Schockner to admit his guilt; but second, Manfred Schockner is trying to find out what's happening."

"Do innocent men sometimes do things that make them look guilty?" he asked. "Yes, of course they do, and that is what happened here. The prosecution has given you the 'we know' case, but I'm here to tell you there may be another side to the story, or more than one other side.

"There is no direct evidence my client hired anyone to kill his wife," he said. "He was getting a divorce and he paid all the bills. The prosecution argues these points to their theory of the crime, but there is clear evidence that points to two or three or four other explanations, any of which is more than sufficient to find reasonable doubt. You do not all have to agree, but if anyone sees any part of this in both ways, you must acquit."

Just after Perlo began his closing arguments, Schockner staged a final attempt to derail the proceedings. Throughout the trial he had studiously avoided eye contact with me, even though I often stared with impunity or shot him hostile glances when he looked my way. As his attorney wrapped up his closing, Schockner turned his shoulders back in my direction and scowled with pure rage. Locking eyes in a silent struggle, neither he nor I blinked; but then he performed an unmistakably obscene gesture, raising his middle finger in my direction while he delicately stroked his long, hooked nose. He performed this insult for a couple of minutes, or so it seemed, gradually raising his finger more obviously while leering with a lascivious grin. He taunted my temper during these crucial final moments of the trial and almost got a rise; but then I broke the gaze and took a couple of deep breaths to ease the strain. I don't know if Schockner realized the entire jury could see his obscene performance, but nothing blocked their view.

• • • •

Using the prosecutor's prerogative, the state would have the last word. Barnes rose from her seat and began her closing with a back-handed swipe at her adversary across the aisle. "When I started my career as a prosecutor I used to get upset when a defense attorney would get up here and attack me," she admitted. "But then I realized they didn't have a choice. They couldn't rely on the evidence to clear their client, and so they tried to divert a jury's attention with personal insults and bogus claims. That is what has happened here."

Calling Schockner's testimony from the witness stand "a ridiculous series of lies," she proceeded to dissect his explanations and expose the implausibility of his claims. "Here was a businessman who worked for Honeywell for twenty years, and he was taken in by a gym manager? That doesn't make any sense. He was a conservative and frugal man – to say Frank Jaramillo duped him is preposterous.

"And then consider the so-called $25,000 payment for the BMW. Would you buy a car you have never seen, with no paperwork, title or documentation? Of course not. This was the story he created to excuse why he gave Jaramillo this money. Obviously, it was a cover-up."

She ridiculed his explanation of the "sloppy Nick" note found at his house, and then grew outraged with his suggestion his cell phone was responsible for forty-three calls from Schockner to Jaramillo during the twelve days preceding the murder.

"There are four ways to prove the defendant's guilt," she said. "First there's the money trail – Schockner gave $75,000 to Jaramillo in the year preceding the murder, and then two $25,000 checks in October 2004, one for a BMW that didn't exist and the other as a 'loan.' Then there was the Schockner divorce, and the millions of dollars he stood to lose to Lynn if she could get away from him.

"On top of that, there were forty-three calls between these two parties beginning the day Nick Harvey was hired," she reiterated. "The wiretapped recordings prove he Schockner is lying, and the only time he told the truth was when he said 'I'm not concerned about anything anymore.'

"Look at this man," she demanded, pointing out the defendant who raised a furtive glance at the jury before turning back to the table. "This is not the face of someone who's scared – it's the face of a man in control. And at the end of the day, that's all he cares about: himself and control of his money."

At 2:23 pm that afternoon, Judge Ferrari delivered his twenty-five minute instructions for the jury. After the panel filed into their chamber for deliberations, Perlo rose again to address the court regarding his client's medications – specifically his painkillers – prompting a rare outburst from Judge Ferrari.

"This is a court of law, Mr. Perlo," he snapped. "This is not an HMO, a PPO or any kind of health provider. This is a court of law. Enough of this, already!"

CHAPTER 22

We walked back to the hotel on tenterhooks, buoyed but subdued. Each person punctuated the five-minute stroll with personal observations on this long-awaited end of the trial, still keenly aware the only important part of the proceedings – the verdict – was anything but a slam dunk. Our emotions simmered near the surface. We polled each other on his or her take on the jury, but those ladies and gentlemen remained opaque to our questioning minds, strangers who held so much of our lives in their hands. It was easy to convince myself I saw outrage in their expressions, but in reality, I didn't have a clue. We were all pretty sure Schockner wouldn't be exonerated, but a single citizen could hang the jury, prompting a mistrial that would make subsequent trials much more problematic. That would also dictate many more trips to Southern California, a place intractably bound to this hideous crime. Despite a comprehensive and compelling presentation by the prosecutor and a sketchy defense vulnerable to serious scrutiny on many levels, I couldn't dodge a persistent pessimism about the outcome, and became incensed when my brother suggested a *guilty* verdict was assured.

"Its bad luck not being superstitious," I warned, "so shut up."

That first Friday in September in Long Beach was an unseasonably hot day, the mercury at or above 100-degres, more reminiscent of south Georgia weather than southern California. I soaked my short-sleeved cotton shirt on the three-block walk back to the hotel room and had just managed to shed my pants and shirt for a cold shower when Det. Robbins called: the verdict was "in." It was a stunning moment, one that seemed to bode well for our chances. I threw on my clothes, slicked back my hair and joined the family as we raced back down Long Beach Boulevard to the courthouse.

Little more than a forced march, this was a defining leg in our family journey, a moment none of us would ever forget. We sweated through the short dash to the courthouse, anticipation and dread pumping in equal measure. It seemed everyone awaited our arrival. Judge Ferrari, Bailiff Elder, both defense attorneys, DDA Barnes and Det. Robbins eyed our entrance, and everyone but Schockner looked our way. We ushered ourselves into the front row and sat on the hard wooden bench. It felt like the end of the world.

GUILTY
Jury convicts Bixby Knolls millionaire
Of hiring the hit man who killed his wife
By Wendy Thomas Russell

LONG BEACH – A jury deliberated for less than 40 minutes Friday before convicting a Bixby Knolls millionaire of murdering his estranged wife for financial gain three years ago.

Manfred "Fred" Schockner, 67, shook his head indignantly as the verdict was read before Long Beach Superior Court Judge Gary Ferrari. Despite a veritable mountain of evidence, Schockner had maintained that he never hired anyone to kill his wife, Lynn, who was stabbed to death on the back porch of their home on Nov. 8, 2004.

In the courtroom audience Friday was the couple's 17-year-old son, Charlie, who bucked back in his seat and said "Yes!" when the verdict was read. Alongside him – and equally emotional – were his mother's two brothers and their wives.

Later, the family tearfully thanked jurors as they walked out of court. While most nodded silently or smiled, one juror said, "You're welcome," as she passed.

Charlie and his uncles, Mark and Jon Jicha, were allowed to make what's commonly referred to as "victim's impact statements" directly after the verdict. "Manfred Schockner," Mark said, "my sister rests easier knowing you are a dead man walking."

Schockner turned to watch Charlie speak but showed no emotion himself. "I want you to know that I disclaim all relations to you," he said. "I will never be your son."

• • • •

The next twenty-four hours were a whirlwind.

After our initial euphoria, exuberant but reserved celebrations with Barnes, Robbins and the officers of the court, we went outside to conduct an impromptu interview with Ms. Russell of the *Press-Telegram*, where Charlie's joyous reaction was photographed for the front page article featured the next day.

As had become my habit, my first phone call went to Richard Birdsall. Next I contacted his former partner, Chris Cardoza, both outside the loop for these proceedings. These were followed by quick phone calls to extended families and close friends. Without more fanfare than a Hilton checkout and a rushed meal at the hotel restaurant, we were gone. Leaving Long Beach with an Old Testament verdict was an affirmation beyond our wildest dreams: my righteous indignation had been ratified, and

Press-Telegram

www.presstelegram.com

Long Beach, California — SATURDAY, SEPTEMBER 8, 2007 — 25¢ (plus tax)

GUILTY

Jury convicts Bixby Knolls millionaire of hiring the hit man who killed his wife

Manfred "Fred" Schockner reacts to the guilty verdict he received at Long Beach Superior Court Friday for the 2004 murder of his wife, Lynn. Below, Charlie Schockner, the couple's son, celebrates with his aunts Susan Shipman, left, and Elizabeth Jicha outside the courthouse.

Danfe Jay / Press-Telegram

By Wendy Thomas Russell
Staff writer

LONG BEACH – A jury deliberated for less than 40 minutes Friday before convicting a Bixby Knolls millionaire of murdering his estranged wife for financial gain three years ago.

Manfred "Fred" Schockner, 67, shook his head indignantly as the verdict was read before Long Beach Superior Court Judge Gary Ferrari. Despite a veritable mountain of evidence, Schockner had maintained that he never hired anyone to kill his wife, Lynn, who was stabbed to death on the back porch of their home on Nov. 8, 2004.

In the court audience Friday was the couple's 17-year-old son, Charlie, who bucked back in his seat and said "Yes!" when the verdict was read. Alongside him – and equally emotional – were his mother's two brothers and their wives.

Later, the family tearfully thanked jurors as they walked out of court. While most nodded silently or smiled, one juror said, "You're welcome," as she passed.

Charlie and his uncles, Mark and Jon Jicha,

PLEASE SEE **SCHOCKNER / A7**

BOOK CLOSED ON A BIZARRE CASE

Left, Stephen Carr / Press-Telegram; right, Diandra Jay / Press-Telegram

Frankie Jaramillo, 32, of Woodland Hills (left), and Nicholas Harvey, 25, of Port Hueneme (right), were both convicted of murder and given life sentences for their roles in Lynn Schockner's 2004 killing. Jaramillo was the middleman; Harvey stabbed Schockner to death.

Timeline of events in the Lynn Schockner murder case:

L. Schockner

- **Nov. 8, 2004:** Lynn Schockner, 50, is stabbed to death by an intruder on the back porch of her Bixby Knolls home.
- **December 2004:** Lynn Schockner's husband, Manfred Schockner, is arrested in her murder.
- **March 13, 2007:** Inexperienced hitman Nicholas Harvey is convicted of the murder of Lynn Schockner.
- **May 24, 2007:** Middleman Frankie Jaramillo is convicted of the murder of Lynn Schockner.
- **Sept. 7, 2007:** Manfred Schockner is convicted of the murder of his wife Lynn.

Boeing C-17 program gets new leader: Chamberlin

Aviation: 27-year company veteran will take helm of program in Oct.

By Samantha Gonzaga
Staff writer

LONG BEACH – Boeing on Friday announced the appointment of a new manager for its C-17 program.

The massive military cargo aircraft, manufactured at Boeing's plant on Lakewood Boulevard, will be headed by Jean Chamberlin, a program director for the Airborne Warning Systems – a system of airborne surveillance and "command and control" functions used for air defense.

Chamberlin

Chamberlin will become vice president and program manager. She succeeds Dave Bowman, who held the position for five years before being appointed in August to vice president and general manager of Boeing Mobility Systems.

"Jean brings the experience, leadership and vision

PLEASE SEE CHAMBERLIN / A7

Gas, oil prices going back up

Associated Press

NEW YORK – Oil and gasoline futures rose Friday, supported by concerns about tight supplies, while prices at the pump, which were falling just weeks ago, continued their recent spike.

The supply concerns were driven in part by Thursday's Energy Department inventory report, which said supplies of both crude oil and gasoline fell last week. Investors expect little relief from OPEC, which is widely expected to keep its output targets unchanged when oil ministers meet Tuesday in Vienna.

Light, sweet crude for October rose 40 cents to settle at $76.70 a barrel on the New York Mercantile Exchange.

At the pump, meanwhile, prices continued to rise. The average price of a gallon of self-serve regular gasoline rose in Los Angeles County 3.2 cents this week after dropping 15 of the previous 16 weeks, the Automobile Club of Southern California reported.

Unleaded regular in the Los Angeles area stood at $2.765 Friday morning. In Orange County, the average price rose 2.7 cents over the past week to $2.716, 76.3 The average national price of a gallon of gas rose 1.7 cents overnight to $2.824, according to AAA and the Oil Price Information Service.

For the cheapest local gas prices, see **Business / A13**.

TODAY ONLINE
PRESSTELEGRAM.COM

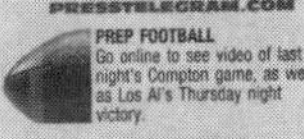

PREP FOOTBALL
Go online to see video of last night's Compton game, as well as Los Al's Thursday night victory.

TOP VIEWS

1. **News:** Burglary increase leads to task force
2. **News:** Heat suspected in death at L.B. retirement home
3. **News:** Local crime briefs

online POLL

Today's question: **Should college prep courses be required in high school?**

Yesterday's question: Do you think it's wrong to smoke in the presence of a child?

YES 86% — **NO** 14%

Charlie was on his way to becoming a free man.

The verdict also delivered a family forged stronger by crime, unified against this killer in our midst. We navigated a complicated course through California's legal system with the help of many able men and women, all looking to alleviate the wretched demands made upon victims, families and friends. Each must find their own way to survive, and anything is possible with a strong family at one's side. Never a religious sort, I've found my own gods and worship them in my own way. Some have claimed I would be a better man if I could forgive Lynn's killer, but even a life behind bars seems like a pass for what he had done to my baby sister.

• • • •

A week later I heard from one of the California detectives who played a crucial role in the criminal investigation. Even as we beat a hasty retreat from Long Beach, I hoped I could somehow repay the mountain of debt I had incurred along the way, and Kris Nelson gave me a chance.

The detective's daughter, now a young mother on the rebound from a bad divorce, hooked up with some sort of a self-proclaimed Christian man who had already graduated from verbal abuse to physical blows. Already at an impasse with his daughter, he asked me to share Lynn's revelations to me and the true nature of spousal abuse to the young woman. I did so in my September letter to his daughter.

> Dear KC
>
> I am writing to you as a friend of your father, a man I learned to respect and admire during the criminal investigation and conviction of three men involved in my sister's murder. Without your father's

insight, abilities and intelligence the case would not have been solved without his willingness to consort with criminals. He has skills and bravery I do not possess, and I will always be grateful to him.

I say all this by way of introduction, not only so you can appreciate my respect for your dad, but also to share a few of the thoughts about my sister's ultimate abuse. That brutal killing was simply the final mean-spirited act perpetrated during their 25-year marriage, not only on her, but also on their son.

Few people are capable of true change in their lives, none more than men and women involved in abusive relationships most of all. The abusive partner demands obedience and subjugates everyone to their will. They find ways to blame their victims for disagreements in the household or disputes with the world. Correct in every opinion, they seem to also gravitate toward religious beliefs that cherry-pick the scriptures and decide their "right thinking" not only permits corrective action, but also encourages "strict measures" to bring their "loved ones" in line.

They all fall back on the same lame excuse: "It's because I care for you so much," or failing that, "I love you so much."

Flowers, a card, and abject apologies usually follow in force. In my sister's case, it was jewelry - lots of jewelry - a carload of pretty trinkets that gradually increased in value over the years and severity of his malice. Lynn's abuse didn't stop until he finally had her killed.

I was saddened to learn you had been a victim of physical abuse, and hope you were not seriously injured. I don't know your family situation as a young lady, and it clearly is presumptuous on my part to offer opinions about your life. I only hope you avoid my sister's path, and consider not only your life, but that of your child. That may sound a bit melodramatic, but I also fear that might be true, as it was with Lynn.

Life is tough enough. No one, no matter how they profess love and affection, could possible lift a hand in anger to family or friend without showing their true colors.

Save yourself...save your child.

God bless you. MJ

• • • •

That was not the end, by any means; but it was the beginning of the end for Manfred Schockner. Jail turned into prison, and at his December 5, 2007 sentencing, Judge Ferrari leveled his verdict and his opinion on the man in that orange jumpsuit. Ms. Russell's final dispatch summed up the proceedings.

Schockner Gets Life
By Wendy Thomas Russell

LONG BEACH – The Bixby Knolls millionaire who ordered his wife's murder three years ago was called "insatiably greedy and a disgusting human being" on Thursday before being sentenced to life in prison without possibility of parole.

Long Beach Superior Court Judge Gary Ferrari delivered the sentence – and the biting remarks – to a frail-looking but defiant Manfred Schockner, convicted in September (2007) of planning the 2004 murder-for-hire of his estranged wife, Lynn.

Evidence during the trial showed that the defendant had feared losing half of his $7 million fortune in the couple's pending divorce.

"This case is all about you. It's all about your insatiable greed," Judge Ferrari said. "You could have walked away from this marriage a millionaire – you could have walked away from this marriage with more money than 95 percent of the people in this country will ever dream of seeing."

During his own opportunity to speak Thursday, Schockner denied his involvement in the murder, complained of a lack of medical attention in jail and blamed police officers for failing to protect his wife on the day of her death.

"Had they followed proper police procedures," Schockner said of the officers, "my wife would be alive today."

Judge Ferrari seized on the statement.

"The evidence given to me in this case – I'm not even sure the word 'overwhelming' describes it," Ferrari said. "And what you told us this morning was nothing more than sophistry."

Ferrari said he was particularly affected by the fact that Schockner seemed to carry out the crime without giving a second thought about the future of his 14-year-old son.

"It's absolutely disgusting," he said.

The sentencing brings an end to one of the most complicated Long Beach police investigations in recent history.

Three men were involved in the crime. Schockner masterminded the plot and then enlisted the help of Frankie Jaramillo, an acquaintance from a local gym. He paid $50,000 to Jaramillo, who then hired Nick

> Harvey, a steroid-addicted body-builder from Port Hueneme, to do the job for $5,000.
>
> All three men were found guilty after short jury deliberations and have been sentenced to life in prison without parole. While murder-for-hire is a death-penalty crime, the Los Angeles district attorney's office opted not to seek such a sentence in the Schockner case.
>
> No one from Lynn Schockner's family attended Thursday's hearing, though they did attend all three trials. They long have contended that Schockner was an abusive husband and father who loved nothing but money. The silver lining, they say, is that Charlie is now flourishing in school and safe from the oppression of his father.
>
> Before ordering a bailiff to escort Schockner out of the courtroom, Judge Ferrari issued one last rebuke.
>
> "All that money," he said. "Now, it's not going to do you a damn bit of good."

• • • •

Charlie was just fourteen when his mother was killed, but in many ways, he was mature for his years. A bright boy who built himself around a mother's love, he also learned to navigate Schockner's moods and demands, not to mention his blazing temper, with a deft touch and quick step. He was just able to keep his wits following his mother's brutal killing, even as the media threatened to make a circus of the entire proceedings. After that, he glimpsed the real possibility he would be left with this monster, the man who tried to steal every soul within reach, a father who arranged his mother's killing and would stop at nothing to get his way. Charlie remains the real hero of this adventure, not only able to emerge on the other side of the continent relatively intact, comforted by a family that offered support and unconditional love, but also adapting to distinctively Southern setting, and blooming in the strong Georgia sun.

. . . .

The newspaper's editorial board sided strongly with Judge Ferrari's verdict, and found the same lessons I tried to impart to my friend's daughter in their editorial that followed Schockner's sentencing.

Press-Telegram editorial
The Lessons of Denial
(December 9th, 2007)

The sad saga of Manfred Schockner, who hired a hit man to murder his wife, will come to an end today when he is sentenced to life in prison, without the possibility of parole. There are lessons to be learned from this tragedy, not the least of which are the worst outcome of domestic abuse, denial and utter stupidity of a man who thought he could get away with murdering a wife who was divorcing him.

Schockner hired a couple of two-bit crooks to do the job for peanuts, in order to save himself a costly divorce settlement. Whatever he saved, he more than spent on attorneys in a case in which it took a jury less than 40 minutes to convict him, so weak was his defense.

If there are tears to be shed, don't waste them on Manfred Schockner, a millionaire who abused his wife and young son for decades. Shed them instead for Lynn

Schockner and those like her who endure the endless roller coaster of an abusive mate. His son Charlie told P-T writer Wendy Thomas Russell that Manfred would beat his mother, deride her, then beg for forgiveness. That behavior is classic. Abusers are con artists of the first order.

Charlie, who was 14 years old when his mother was murdered at their Bixby Knolls home, also endured his father's abuse. He would stay late at school and go to his room to avoid his father. He suspected his father's hand in his mother's murder from the beginning. He now lives with relatives in a warm, nurturing environment.

The real tragedy is that there are many more Lynn Schockners living with tyrants like Manfred Schockner, women who spend years in denial. If you have the stomach for a classic portrait of domestic abuse, rent "Once Were Warriors," a 1994 movie set in New Zealand that tosses in alcoholism and racism for good measure. It's not a pretty picture.

If you recognize yourself in any of the roles in the movie you need to understand that you need help. If you're the abuser, you're probably in denial. If you're an abused spouse or child, run for your life to the nearest shelter. In Long Beach, call the Domestic Violence Hotline (562-437-4663) the very first time the love of your life uses you as a punching bag.

That's right – the first time. Don't give a batterer another chance to kill you. That's the real lesson of the sad saga of Manfred Schockner, who, despite overwhelming evidence against him, thought he could get away with murder, because he had gotten away with something close to it for so many years.

• • • •

The Press-Telegram's strong endorsement of Schockner's sentence ended our relationship with this fine newspaper, but not before I wrote the editorial board to thank all those who made this verdict possible. They published my lengthy "Letter to the Editor" that expressed our gratitude to the police, court connections and the criminal justice system, and affirmed our friendship with their fine reporter.

Lisa Brandon, who tried to help my sister make her own break from Manfred and represented me on Charlie's behalf, read the letter and replied with a gratifyingly appreciative note.

> *Hi Mark - Thank you for your acknowledgment by your letter to the Press Telegram. I must say, I watched over and over again the video of Manfred telling Judge Ferrari his wife would still be alive if the Long Beach Police Department had followed appropriate police procedure; and, despite his best efforts, he couldn't understand why he was being treated so badly.*
>
> *I was fascinated by Manfred's absolute disconnection from reality - he is such a raving sociopath, I believe he has convinced himself that either he can continue to try to persuade the world he is innocent, thanks to his superior intellect - or, he has convinced himself he really had nothing to do with Lynn's death. Either way, Manfred should not be free to roam this world and I am glad he will die in jail. I am only sorry Lynn stumbled into his life so long ago.*
>
> *Watching the video made me realize the ordeal is finally over. I believe I did what I could for Lynn - from reporting*

my suspicions about Manfred to the Long Beach Police Department, to meeting with the detectives and sharing my file, to testifying at the trial. I can't bring her back – I can't think about Charlie without worrying about how he will deal with his past over a lifetime. But I will never have any regrets about what I did for Lynn and each individual involved in this process can be equally proud. I cannot say enough how happy I am for Charlie that you and Susan stepped up to the parenting plate and have provided such a wonderful life for him. You probably saved Charlie's life – which in the end is the most important achievement of all. Manfred's soul has been rotten for decades. His body is following suit quickly enough. While his money will buy him certain comforts in prison, he will never be free and that is a great punishment for a man who obviously prides himself on living outside the "system." For whatever it's worth, Lynn likely did not suffer great pain before she died. Justice was achieved and now life will go on for all involved. Someday, maybe when Charlie graduates from college, we should all get together to celebrate. Lynn told me many times how important Charlie was to her. She chose to separate from Manfred because of the pain Charlie was enduring from his father. I know Lynn would agree protecting Charlie was her greatest goal and you, Susan, Jon, Eric, Al, the police detectives, Cindi and Judge Ferrari have guaranteed that goal will be realized

Best of luck to you Mark and to your family. I hope your holiday season is sweeter now that this nightmare is coming to an end. Please keep in touch and call should you need anything. – Sincerely, Lisa Brandon, Long Beach, CA

• • • •

Even Lisa was wrong in her assessment, giving my wife and I more credit than was due. It was Charlie who saved our lives, or at least my own. I had found my enemy and decided I would keep him close. Few nights passed when I didn't dream of killing him in horrible ways, and I never recoiled from that image the next morning. Self-defense aside, I had never imagined myself a cold-blooded killer, but that had changed. I hoped he would be shanked in his cell or suffer a terminal stroke in a helpless rage. In Schockner's case, I would still try to kill him if given the chance, using my bare hands if necessary. Charlie gave me the equilibrium I needed, pulling me back from the edge. In just a few months we were immersed in this wonderful young man's life, and helped each other over the rough spots that happened along the way. Charlie's love gave me the pass I needed to keep my promise to his old man.

For that, if nothing else, he will always be my son, the person who could matter more than vengeance and hatred, someone who measured more than my personal sense of retribution, a young man who made it all worthwhile. Charlie remains the hero in this venture, a young man who stood among men and women, both good and bad, and chose the right way to go. It was he who gave our life meaning, he who made success important, setting and achieving all sorts of goals in his young life. I had long since reached my zenith in life, so it was Charlie who made the future that much more imperative, especially breaking Schockner's legacy of manipulation, greed and abuse.

He made an honest man out of me, much the same way my wife did the same so many years ago. Charlie became more than a mission in life – he was just what the doctor ordered – a co-conspirator to bedevil our enemies and welcome our friends. Having survived my dad's sudden death when I was just a few years older than Charlie, and all but consumed with grief for so much of the decade after he was gone, I would try to level his days and become the man I always hoped I would be.

I'm still trying.

EPILOGUE

Publication of this book comes just after my 63rd birthday, more than ten years after this saga began. It is a celebration and a relief, a task completed and an obligation fulfilled. The book means to mark a journey not yet ended, but the completion of a promise to my wonderful son and his mother, my sister, now dead for a decade.

Almost in the same way Lynn had her fifteen minutes of fame back when she was killed in 2004, I marked the same passage of prominence with the Dateline NBC segment that will be broadcast this year. The pain has been more than worth the process: the embarrassing relief of tears on camera, the babbling idiocy of a man still hurt by the past. I could live with this self-immolation because it was cathartic, at the very least, and absolutely honest.

Their deadlines and due dates made me finish my work, completing the editing process that had become essentially endless. I was a journalist and publisher for more than 25 years, and yet when the perfect story came my way, I had to be pulled kicking and screaming to the task. The irony is inescapable, but the story still had legs.

I set out to tell my sister's full story, the highs and the lows, her journey though life that ended that fateful November day on her back porch in Bixby Knolls. That was where this tale began, and the trials and tribulations of the next decade would be

The author is pictured in three monitors in a San Diego studio while NBC Correspondent Keith Morrison, pictured in the monitor at right, conducts the Dateline NBC interview on January 2, 2015.

daunting. The events of that day proved transformational for our family, and in the mysterious ways of our lives on earth, Lynn's life ended as my elevation to fatherhood began. Childless after seventeen years of marriage, my wife and I suddenly had a son – Charlie. We hit a few bumps along that journey, but there were so many triumphs and wonderful turns that the difficulties were irrelevant in the end. Consider this: Schockner, an evil bastard I hated long before he commissioned a killer to avoid a costly divorce, gave me his only son without so much as a condition. This transformational passage opened exciting adventures, exceptional achievements and the promise of a future I would have never experienced. Talk about irony, this from a man who never gave away anything without conditions.

In another odd aspect to this saga, Schockner continued to try to steal money from Charlie's estate long after he was sentenced to life in prison, even though he still had over $3 million in personal accounts. In one effort he tried to claim my sister's pension from her career at Garrett AirResearch, a subsidiary of Honeywell Corp. After a protracted (and expensive) legal battle that brought us to U.S. District Court in New Jersey, we were able to secure a big portion of those funds in 2012. Perhaps the most unusual contact we had from Schockner came in the form of two letters – one to me and another to Charlie – he mailed in the same envelope from prison during that process. That would be the only time he contacted his son since he was arrested on Dec. 3, 2004. I could understand his reluctance to remain in contact with me, but Charlie had been his flesh and blood. He never called or attempted to communication with his former son, except for that one letter when he asked Charlie to abandon this lawsuit, claiming he needed the money while warning that further efforts to obtain Lynn's pension would jeopardize Charlie's status as "residual beneficiary" of his own estate.

I hoped Dateline NBC would interview the member of the trio, especially Lynn's husband, but California law prohibits televised inmate interviews. I heard Schockner had gone crazy, that he had attacked his own lawyer in private conference. I couldn't confirm that happened, but it seems to be totally within his character. All I could learn was this: Manfred Schockner is currently housed at Mule Creek Correctional Facility southeast of Sacramento; and both Nick Harvey and Frank Jaramillo are inmates at the California Correctional Institute in Tehachapi, CA, east of Bakersfield. Given their sentences, we don't expect to hear from any parole boards, but it's nice to know they're still where they belong.

Finally, I would hope Lynn's story would stand as a cautionary tale to anyone who finds themselves in an abusive relationship. Those folks should be aware of my sister's fate, because it could also be their own. Partners who must control all aspects of a relationship follow a predictable pattern. Mild complaints escalate into towering tirades; gentle rebukes become physical displays of dominance, inevitably ending in violence. After each instance, the abuser apologizes profusely and promises no more, often showering their victim with gifts. But the episodes always continue, and sooner or later the victim finds herself in the hospital or the morgue.

The first incident of violence is only a prelude. You should call the authorities and leave. Please remember my words to Kris Nelson's daughter: save yourself...and save your child.

Charlie and his beloved Labrador retriever, Kaylie, frollick on the lawn at Rollins College in Winter Park, FL. Kaylie was my gift to Charlie on his 22nd birthday, "the best present he ever received," he still says.

I built a cabin at Penholloway Swamp at McMillan Creek, a 100-acre wetland preserve in southeast Georgia. Charlie and I are shown planting bald cypress seedlings in 2006.

Our family shares a joyous moment at Charlie's graduation from Frederica Academy in 2009. Charlie thrived during his high school years at the school which offered a rigorous academic regimen and a full range of extracurricular activities. Below, Charlie celebrates with Jacob Barish after both graduated from Rollins College in Winter Park, FL in 2013.

MARK ALAN JICHA lives with his wife, Susan Shipman, on a small barrier island off the Georgia coast and frequents a cabin away on his 100-acre forest preserve in the Altamaha River swamp. His son, Charlie, returned to California in 2014, where he is a graduate student at the University of California at San Diego to prepare for a career in scenic design. Mark, an Ohio native who received his BA degree in American history at Kenyon College in 1974, moved to the "Inland Empire" to work as a surveyor in the US Forest Service in the Cour d' Alene National Forest and park ranger on Mt. Spokane State Park, as well as a fishing guide, professional fly-tier and logger. Relocating south in 1980 he was employed as a reporter or editor at a string of weeklies and dailies in South Carolina and Georgia, finally becoming editor and publisher of The Southeast Georgian before that newspaper was acquired by a competitor, now the Camden County Tribune & Georgian. Finally, he published is own humor magazine for ten years before retiring in 2007. Two years later he built an off-grid, solar-powered cabin at Penholloway Swamp at McMillan Creek, which he shares with family, friends and, of course, the dogs.